Trumpism, Mexican America, and the Struggle for Latinx Citizenship

School for Advanced Research
Advanced Seminar Series
Michael F. Brown
General Editor

Since 1970 the School for Advanced Research (formerly the School of American Research) and SAR Press have published over one hundred volumes in the Advanced Seminar series. These volumes arise from seminars held on SAR's Santa Fe campus that bring together small groups of experts to explore a single issue. Participants assess recent innovations in theory and methods, appraise ongoing research, and share data relevant to problems of significance in anthropology and related disciplines. The resulting volumes reflect SAR's commitment to the development of new ideas and to scholarship of the highest caliber. The complete Advanced Seminar series can be found at www.sarweb.org.

Also available in the School for Advanced Research Advanced Seminar Series:

For additional titles in the School for Advanced Research Advanced Seminar Series, please visit unmpress.com.

Trumpism, Mexican America, and the Struggle for Latinx Citizenship

*Edited by Phillip B. Gonzales,
Renato Rosaldo, and Mary Louise Pratt*

SCHOOL FOR ADVANCED RESEARCH PRESS • SANTA FE

UNIVERSITY OF NEW MEXICO PRESS • ALBUQUERQUE

Names: Gonzales, Felipe, 1946– editor. |
Rosaldo, Renato, editor. | Pratt, Mary Louise,
1948– editor.

Title: Trumpism, Mexican America, and
the struggle for Latinx citizenship / edited by
Phillip B. Gonzales, Renato Rosaldo, and
Mary Louise Pratt.

Other titles: School for Advanced Research
advanced seminar series.

Description: Santa Fe: School for Advanced
Research Press: Albuquerque: University of
New Mexico Press, 2021. | Series: School for
Advanced Research advanced seminar series
| The seminar from which this book resulted
was made possible by the generous support of
The Andrew W. Mellon Foundation. Support
for the book was provided by The UNM Center
for Regional Studies. | Includes bibliographical
references and index

Identifiers: LCCN 2021028020 (print)
LCCN 2021028021 (e-book)
ISBN 9780826362841 (paperback)
ISBN 9780826362858 (e-book)

Subjects: LCSH: Trump, Donald, 1946–
Influence. | Mexican Americans—Political
activity. | Hispanic Americans—Political
activity. | Political culture—United States—
21st century. | United States—Politics and
government—2017– | United States—
Race relations—History—21st century. |
United States—Social policy—1993–

Classification: LCC E184.M5 T785 2021 (print) |
LCC E184.M5 (e-book) | DDC973.046872—dc23

LC record available at https://lccn.loc.
gov/2021028020

LC e-book record available at https://lccn.loc.
gov/2021028021

Founded in 1889, the University of
New Mexico sits on the traditional homelands
of the Pueblo of Sandia. The original
peoples of New Mexico—Pueblo, Navajo,
and Apache—since time immemorial have
deep connections to the land and have made
significant contributions to the broader
community statewide. We honor the land
itself and those who remain stewards of this
land throughout the generations and also
acknowledge our committed relationship to
Indigenous peoples. We gratefully recognize
our history.

Cover illustration: Photograph of Eliana
Fernández and her family outside the US
Supreme Court on November 12, 2019.
Courtey of Eliana Fernández

Composed in Minion Pro and Gill Sans

Chapter Four. "Reckoning with the Gaze,"
© Michelle García

The seminar from which this book resulted
was made possible by the generous support
of The Andrew W. Mellon Foundation.
Support for the book was provided by
the UNM Center for Regional Studies.

To anyone with a spark of awareness, it was evident that Donald Trump's 2016 campaign for president promoted social divisiveness and posed threats to America's liberal value of inclusion. In the key effect, it promoted a return to a dominant-white-citizen nation. The general vulnerability of Latinxs appeared with considerable clarity as Trump racialized Mexican immigrants, pledged mass criminalization and deportation, damned amnesty, threatened DACA (Deferred Action for Childhood Arrivals), and in his first days as president, signed directives to build a wall along the Mexican border. Mexican American and Chicana and Chicano organizations and immigrant activists protested at the Trump inauguration and geared up for what looked like the sure need for continual resistance during his administration.

A week after confirmation of the results of the 2016 presidential election, the School for Advanced Research (SAR) in Santa Fe announced that it would be accepting proposals for its Advanced Seminar program. We had digested the dynamics of the presidential campaign, particularly as they touched on Mexican Americans, Mexican nationals, Central Americans, undocumented youth, asylum seekers, and Latinxs in general. Trump's threats, in particular those against people of Mexican extraction, prompted us to submit a proposal for an Advanced Seminar on the theme of the shifting terrains of citizenship among Mexican Americans and Latinx peoples in the United States. "Historically," we said, "Mexican Americans have been denied full and equal citizenship. Donald Trump's presidency may well emerge as the latest instance of citizenship restriction for them."

We planned our seminar, involving a set of scholars in Latinx studies with a range of disciplinary orientations to take place in Santa Fe about halfway through Trump's term in office. As we projected, by the time the seminar essays would be ready for publication, the Trump administration would be nearing the end of term of office that he would serve. One of our main intents was to develop analytical tools that would enable us to take stock of this historically unique presidency.

We envisioned the seminar taking on a number of questions. Some addressed the present. For example, to what extent would the Trump administration indeed make good on the anti-immigration, anti-immigrant, and anti-Latinx threats that candidate Trump made? What kinds of experiences would Mexicans, Mexican Americans, and Central Americans in particular have under a Trump presidency? What, if any, responses might they devise to an emerging era of repression? Another set of questions addressed the past. What strands of US history was Trumpism—the general practices and policies associated with Trump's leadership— mobilizing as sources of power? Who were Trump's ideological forbears, especially as regards Mexican and other Latinx people in America? What complexities did Trumpism overlook, at its peril?

Prior to our weeklong gathering in Santa Fe, each participant submitted a draft chapter for presentation. What each eventually produced for publication was shaped by responses from members of the group, the excitement of the highly energized interactions of the seminar itself, and specific events that subsequently took place over the course of Trump's presidential term.

We are grateful to SAR for providing us with the opportunity to meet, interactively explore, and address, within the scholarly specialties of our member scholars, themes of current political and civic importance. We owe our thanks to the following people: the members of SAR's proposal selection committee; President Michael Brown for his warm welcome to the wonderful SAR facility in Santa Fe; Maria Spray for her logistical and scheduling guidance during our stay; Sarah Soliz for the editorial assistance needed to get the volume out; and our two outside readers, whose input provided invaluable recommendations. With deep appreciation, we thank the indefatigable and attentive hosting team on the SAR grounds, whose provision of accommodations, meals, meeting spaces, and infrastructure made our gathering possible and deeply enjoyable. We are all the more grateful because, unbeknownst to us, that exciting face-to-face intellectual interaction was about to disappear from our lives, snatched away by the COVID-19 pandemic. Finally, we express our gratitude to the Center for Regional Studies at the University of New Mexico, under the leadership of Dr. Gabriel Meléndez and Dr. Lloyd Lee, for the support it provided toward production of the book.

Introduction

PHILLIP B. GONZALES, RENATO ROSALDO, AND MARY LOUISE PRATT

What does it mean to "belong" to a modern society and nation-state, or what is more properly called a territorial state? One of the major ways in which scholars have dealt with such a question is from the standpoint of citizenship. The concept of citizenship, traced to ancient Athens, is generally understood to embody two dimensions. First, it accords a legal status that grants individuals the rights, responsibilities, and liberties laid down by the formal charter of the territorial state, including participation in public institutions. Second, citizenship accords membership and belonging in a presumed, or perhaps "imagined" (Anderson 1983), national community. Citizenship involves both political and cultural dimensions. The European Enlightenment and the French Revolution are typically identified as sources of the modern ideals of universal citizenship, equality, and inclusivity.

These ideals have long held ideological sway as the foundation of membership in Western democracies. For T. H. Marshall (1987), one of the leading theorists of liberal citizenship, modern citizenship going into the twentieth century consisted of three elements: civil, political, and social. Civil citizenship involves "the rights necessary for individual freedom—liberty of the person, freedom of speech, thought and faith, the right to own property and to conclude valid contracts, and the right to justice." The political means "the right to participate in the exercise of political power, as a member of a body invested with political authority or as an elector of the members of such a body." Social citizenship is "the right to a modicum of economic welfare and security, to the right to share, to the full, in the social heritage and to live the life of a civilized being according to the standards prevailing in the society" (5).

Throughout their history in the United States, people of Mexican descent (our main point of focus in this volume, with one chapter on Central Americans) have been made to question their belonging to the American social fabric and polity. Throughout that history, the fact of the matter is that Marshall's model has rarely been adequately realized (Rocco 2014). Accordingly, the critique of liberal citizenship appears as the lens through which to consider Mexican America — that is, the very holistic experience of people of Mexican descent in US society.

The reason that the situation of Mexican America cannot be understood solely through European models of citizenship is that the territorial states in the Americas were founded on the basis of settler colonialism. The settlers, whether English, French, Spanish, or Portuguese, were regarded as the dominant ethnic nationals who were seen as superior to those of other ethnicities, whether enslaved people of African descent, or Native Americans, or Mexican Americans. As postcolonial theorists such as Partha Chatterjee and Americanists such as Maria Josefina Saldaña-Portillo, Greg Grandin, and Cristina Beltrán (this volume) demonstrate, any discussion of state and citizenship in the Americas must incorporate this foundational fact.

A major issue involves the relationship between citizenship, on one hand, and race or ethnicity, on the other. Anthony Smith describes the greater sociopolitical context: "Though most latter-day nations are, in fact, polyethnic, many have been formed in the first place around a dominant ethnie, which attracted or compelled other ethnies or ethnic fragments into the state to which it gave a name and cultural charter. The presumed boundaries of the nation are largely determined by the myths and memories of the dominant ethnie, which include the foundation charter, the myth of the golden age and the associated territorial claims, or ethnic title-deeds" (1991, 39). Stuart Hall and David Held framed the issue in relation to changing conditions in Europe: "Older European ideas of citizenship assumed a more culturally homogeneous population within the framework of a strong and unitary state. But social and cultural identities have become more diversified and 'pluralized' in modern society. The modern nation-state is increasingly composed of groups with very different ethnic and cultural identities" (1990, 187). The result, as Michal Hanchard observes, is that the "longstanding tendency in Western democracies" has been to envision citizenship "in ethno-racial terms" (quoted in Gooding-Williams 2019, 2).

These questions raised in the 1990s generated a critical rethinking of citizenship's liberal ideals. Critical theorists suggested that what drove principles of citizenship was not inclusion, but exclusion. Along with the category of citizen, they noted, Athenians themselves created categories of people excluded from citizenship: foreigners, slaves, and of course women (Gooding-Williams 2019). In modern liberal republics, theorists argued, structures of privilege and marginalization were not an unfortunate by-product, but seemingly the whole point. Creating a "hierarchy of political status," says Rocco, is "the real function of citizenship regimes" (2014, 22). Citizenship, in other words, does not simply establish a community of those who rightfully belong. It establishes a regime of power based on relations and policies of inclusion and exclusion, empowerment and disempowerment, privilege and subjugation (Telles and Ortiz 2008).

Within this theoretical development, Held and Hall (1990) wondered how concepts of national community would adapt to "pluralization" and heterogeneity? What kind of belonging could citizenship regimes offer to those arriving in large numbers from elsewhere, often uninvited and unauthorized? What kind of adaptation could they demand? How could the construct of legal citizenship cope with racial hierarchies designed to enforce inequality? How could citizenship be decolonized?

In reality, variations on this order of critical questions have been foundational for Mexican Americans and Mexican immigrants for a long time; in fact, they define the essential contours of Mexican American history. As historians have shown, the Mexican American struggle for full citizenship, recognition, and belonging in the United States has shaped the evolution of the American political landscape (see Montejano 1987; De León 1997; Foley 2014; Molina 2014). Themselves subject to racial discrimination, Mexican Americans and Native Americans fatally disrupted the United States' founding racial order: the Black/white binary. With Native Americans, the fact that they were subjugated and disenfranchised without having been enslaved created ambiguity and instability in the original white supremacist citizenship regime. With Mexican Americans, the ambiguity lay in their ability to participate in American democracy at the same time that they are subject to white America's racialized discriminations.

Mexican Americans were legally citizens at the outset of their US incorporation, but rarely members of the political community. Hence, it is no surprise that Mexican American and Latinx studies have had an extensive engagement with the study of citizenship. In the 1990s, an amplified concept of citizenship emerged in the work of the cultural citizenship project developed under the auspices of the Ford Foundation and organized around working groups at the Centers for Mexican American and Puerto Rican Studies in Los Angeles (Rosaldo 1997), New York (Flores and Benmayor 1997), Austin (Flores 1997), and Stanford (Rosaldo and Flores 1997). Rosaldo and Flores, who headed the project, defined cultural citizenship as "the right to be different (in terms of race, ethnicity, or native language) with respect to the norms of the dominant national community, without compromising one's right to belong, in the sense of participating in the nation-state's democratic processes" (1997, 57; see also Rosaldo 1997). It is important to add that this project generated a discussion of women remaking citizenship (e.g., Coll 2010), building on major feminist theorizations of gender, sexuality, and difference (e.g., Rich 1986; Lorde 2003; Anzaldúa 1999). For other discussions of citizenship see Ong (1996), Sassen (2002), and Song (2018).

Structural inequality, dispossession, and marginalized citizenship are thus an old story for Mexican Americans, and a foundational one. It began the moment Manifest Destiny policies set their sights on the American West. The tenth US president, John Tyler, got the ball rolling with Manifest Destiny policies that ended up creating the population category of "Mexican American" in the 1840s. In December of 1844, he finally succeeded in getting Congress to carry out his goal of making Texas a state of the American Union. The annexation of Texas finished off the decades-long process of tearing that province away from Mexican ownership, bringing eleven thousand longtime Tejanos, who were concentrated in south Texas, into the United States (Jordan 1968, 85, 95–102).

President James K. Polk furthered the process of incorporating Mexicans via territorial annexation. A year after Texas became a state, and on a pretext of a Mexican threat to US border security, Polk coaxed Congress into ratifying his call for a war declaration against the Mexican Republic. Polk followed his Democratic party's policy of expanding US borders westward, eyeing California and Oregon in particular (Henderson 2007, 139). As Polk (1846) clearly understood, taking over Mexican territory meant adopting Mexican people into the American fold.

When the US invasion of Mexico spent itself out, the Treaty of Guadalupe Hidalgo gave the United States ownership of California and a large area comprising New Mexico and parts of Nevada and Utah. Mexicans in those regions could relocate across the new border with Mexico, remain while retaining the character of Mexican citizens, or remain and acquire bona fide US citizenship. The greater majority elected to embark on the new nationality. Another seventy thousand to one hundred thousand Mexicans living in New Mexico and California became permanent residents of the American Union (for best estimates, see Martínez 1975).

Polk and Senator Thomas Hart Benton, partners in instigating the Mexican conflict, may have truly thought they were absorbing Mexicans into a land of democracy, equality, and opportunity. Indeed, for four decades the Mexicans of New Mexico enjoyed full political citizenship in Marshall's terms, for example, controlling the position of territorial delegate to Congress as well as the territorial legislature. Ultimately, however, *nuevomexicanos* lost this unique form of power sharing. In a second stage of American colonization, Euro-Americans took political control of New Mexico as the territory entered the modern industrial age (Gonzales 2016). Indeed, the greater experience of internal/settler colonialism for Mexicans who were native to the Southwest resulted in the denial of Marshall's three-fold citizenship through forces of land displacement, vigilante violence, and classic Southern-style residential segregation. In canonical Mexican American history, Mexicans were rendered "foreigners in their native land" (Weber 1973), placed in a perennial "crucible of struggle" (Vargas 2017).

With the dawn of the twentieth century, immigration became the principal channel for Mexicans to enter the United States, joining those already here. The key studies find that between 1900 and 1930, 1 million–1.5 million Mexicans settled in the United States (Romo 1977, 194; Hernández Álvarez 1966). The many relevant studies document Mexicans forming a key labor segment during this major period of US development, enabling the industrial and agribusiness expansion of the Southwest and West, and contributing to urban industrialization in the Midwest (see for example, Weber 2015; Calderón 2000; Ruíz 1987; Vargas 2017; Garcilazo 2012).

Here again, however, Mexican workers were denied any practical chance of political, civic, and social citizenship, primarily by their super exploitation and class marginalization. Dual wage systems, subpar housing, and white-only unions kept them in impoverished and segregated living environments with poor schooling for their children (Zamora 1993, 20; Smith 1980, 41; Garcilazo 2012). As a result, mainstream Americans tended to view Mexicans as "perpetual foreigners" (Rocco 2014, 21), foreign not just in terms of national origin, but foreign to America culturally, racially and linguistically. It helped set the stage for what came next.

The stock market crash of 1929 blew in a foul anti-Mexican hysteria. In such a climate, President Herbert Hoover's 1930 State of the Union address called for a revision of US immigration laws "upon a more limited and more selective basis." Looking to deny visas to immigrant applicants who might become direct or indirect public charges, and calling for an "exhaustive reconsideration" of the visa provisions, Hoover pointed explicitly to Mexico and mentioned no other country of origin. Hoover followed this message up with a call to deport those who had entered the United States illegally, for, as he put it, the "very method of their entry indicates their objectionable character, and our law-abiding foreign-born residents suffer in consequence" (Hoover 1930).

Hoover's message kicked off a national program of formal deportation of Mexican immigrants. Secretary of Labor William Doak saw the Mexican problem going beyond welfare dependency. Utilizing the slogan "American jobs for real Americans," the program led to such policies as local laws barring anyone of Mexican descent, including permanent residents and US citizens, from being hired for a government job. Ford, U.S. Steel, and the Southern Pacific Railroad laid off thousands of Mexicans. Congressional, state, and new local measures enabled the forced repatriation of Mexicans, without legal proceedings. Most egregiously, Mexicans were rounded up in the public spaces of Los Angeles, San Antonio, and other cities, and put on buses or trains for transport to the Mexican border (Balderrama and Rodríguez 2006).

According to one study, 33,674 Mexicans were deported during the three remaining Hoover presidential years (Gratton and Merchant 2018, 955). For the decade 1929–1939, one authoritative estimate finds about half a million Mexicans repatriated to Mexico (Hoffman 1974). Los Angeles lost a third of its Mexican residents (Sánchez 1993, 12). Because of the power of this scapegoating dynamic, no discussion could be had concerning the possibility of undocumented workers acquiring citizenship, or belonging by right of their contributions to the material well-being of America.

Decades later, Mexicans figured in Barack Obama's political awareness, beginning with his days as a community organizer in Chicago, which has a huge Mexican community (Obama 2006, 262–63). In his 2004 run for the Illinois Democratic Party nomination for the United States Senate, Obama adopted ¡Sí, se puede! (Yes, we can!), the motto that Dolores Huerta had famously coined on the United Farm Workers' drive for union contracts (Shepherd 2017). Suggesting at least a commitment to the interests of Latinx people, Obama used the phrase again during his 2008 presidential campaign. Speaking before the National Council of La Raza in that campaign, Obama vowed to reject deportation as a solution to the status of undocumented immigrants and promised a pathway to citizenship (Obama 2008).

While president, Obama responded to the pressure of the immigrant rights community by devising DACA (Deferred Action for Childhood Arrivals), which shielded from deportation hundreds of thousands of Mexicans and others brought as children by their undocumented parents (DeParle 2019). However, deep disappointment settled in as Obama continued the Bush-era practice of deploying ICE (Immigration and Customs Enforcement) to round up undocumented immigrants. Those with criminal records faced formal deportations involving legal proceedings, as opposed to simply being returned to the border. Obama inherited a formidable immigration enforcement machinery launched in the aftermath of 9/11. The year before Obama took office, this enforcement system led to a record 360,000 formal removals, 234,000 of which occurred far from the Mexican border. Bipartisan congressional appropriations for increased border enforcement fueled the momentum: the rates of noncitizen removals under Obama went beyond those of Bush and Clinton, even though illegal border crossings were clearly diminishing (Chishti, Pierce, Bolter 2017).

Perhaps Obama found it impossible to blunt, or slow down, the powerful machinery of deportation. That he looked the other way as it ground on may have reflected his own ambivalence over unauthorized immigration. In his best-selling *The Audacity of Hope*, he expressed belief in strong border protection. Commenting on the ease with which Mexicans could cross into the United States, he lamented that immigration no longer occurred "on America's terms" (2006, 264). Obama subsequently earned the title "deporter in chief." In one assessment, widespread disgruntlement over deportations led Latinx voters to support Bernie Sanders in the 2020 presidential primaries over Obama's former vice president, Joe Biden (Ulloa 2020).

Mexicans under Trump

As happened with Polk, Hoover, and Obama, people of Mexican descent came into the political crosshairs of Donald Trump both before he ran for president and during his 2017–2020 term. In fact, they figured so prominently in Trump's political vision that it called for examination as it happened. In the infamous "escalator speech," in which Trump (2015) announced his candidacy for president, he swore: "When Mexico sends its people, they're not sending their best. They're sending people that have lots of problems, and they're bringing those problems with us [*sic*]. They're bringing drugs, they're bringing crime, they're rapists. And some, I assume, are good people." Due to its shock value, the verbiage has been quoted a thousand times and is destined to survive in public memory. It marked the beginning of a new phase of experience and struggle for Mexicans and Mexican Americans.

Conventional conservative Victor Davis Hanson generally supported Trump, yet even he recognized the stream-of-consciousness escalator performance as "the strangest presidential candidate's announcement speech in memory." Reporters "were stunned but also mesmerized by his lowbrow, sometimes crude tone and its content" (2019, 14). Anti-Mexican and anti-immigrant sentiment were among the chief forces that hoisted Donald Trump into the presidency. He tapped into deep and widespread discontent over this issue, driven by xenophobia and racism, and by the downward mobility of working-class Americans, whose earning power had diminished steadily since 1980. Immigrants were blamed for stagnant and declining wages, and immigration was to become one of the issues about which Trump's supporters would say that "he did what he said he would do."

For Latinx people living in the United States, Trumpism represented a new phase in the old struggle to achieve a sense of belonging and full citizenship. This book seeks to elucidate this new phase, especially as experienced by people of Mexican and Central American descent. At the same time, our volume situates this new phase of presidential politics in relation to what went before, and looks past this phase toward the futures that lie before us, asking what new political possibilities emerge from this dramatic chapter in our history. In the next section, we examine the Trump presidency (2017–2020). We then situate it within the historic Mexican American, Central American, and overall Latinx struggle to achieve full citizenship, recognition, and belonging in the United States in the face of exclusion and racial animus.

TRUMPISM/TRUMPWORLD

To Marxist sociologist John Bellamy Foster (2017), Trumpism pointed to an emerging neofascist politics, a popular movement led by a head of state to advance the hegemony of a capitalist system in crisis, in line with other such efforts in Britain, France, Italy, the Netherlands, and Sweden. To US-based Russian scholar Masha Gessen (2020), Trumpism represented an attempt to establish autocracy in the United States, parallel to Vladimir Putin's takeover of Russia. To presidential scholar Michael Nelson (2018), however, Trumpism meant nothing more than President Trump extensively utilizing the executive order to effect his policies, rather than having to horse-trade with congressional leaders of either major party.

Trumpism definitely established a distinctive style of politics. Politically inexperienced, Trump came on the scene "untethered from any particular ideology" (Davis and Shear 2019). He was known as a ruthless and combative businessman. There were political and economic practices he had long believed in, such as the tariff as a tool for serving American economic interests. However, Trumpism never came wrapped as a preexisting program or set of principles, certainly not one designed to give the Republican Party its rebirth. Rather, Trumpism exploded as "a reaction, *not* a catalyst" (Hanson 2019, 47).

Trumpism spun into a kind of alternate universe anchored in the persona of Donald Trump and sustained by a dense web of media apparatuses including Facebook, Twitter, and Fox News. Beyond institutions, masses of white Americans cleaved to Trump's towering figure. Referred to as "the base," this mass of supporters defined itself during the election campaign, mobilized by Trump's insurgent war drum. Energized at mass rallies, their steadfast loyalty was driven less by a clearly defined set of principles than by Trump's unique personality and charisma, and his insurgent rejection of the "status quo."

In Trumpworld, the popular base was assigned the role of shock troops charged with enforcing his revivalist, white nationalist meanings and messages. Membership in Trumpworld involved action, including participation in interactions and civil rituals in and around the presidency, notably demonstrations and mass rallies. In Trumpworld, a vast political community was energized by experiences of solidarity, liberation, empowerment, resentment, catharsis, and humor.

TRUMPISM'S PLAYBOOK

As the authors in this book repeatedly show, far from propounding new ideas, Trumpism greatly reenergized attitudes and ideas with long histories in US politics. Indeed, Make America Great Again (MAGA) presented itself as a revival of "beautiful" (one of Trump's favorite words) American virtue lost to globalism and political correctness. What was new and original in American politics, however, was the Trumpism playbook, Trump's "way of doing business" as president. This playbook, adopted by his supporters and subordinates, defined Trumpism's most distinctive features. As Applebaum (2018), Gessen (2020), and others show, it very much resembled the practices of illiberal one-party autocratic states first developed by Lenin in Russia, and now found in many countries the world over. The substitution of loyalty regimes for meritocracy, Applebaum (2020b) observes, is a recurring trait of autocratic regimes.

Five elements of the Trumpian administrative style stand out. They are (1) the exercise of power through conflict and the will to dominate; (2) the overthrow of civility and decorum in public behavior and speech; (3) the suspension of truth as authority over fiction; (4) the cultivation of showmanship and theatricality;

and (5) the "pocketing" of ideological blocs without ascribing to their ideology. We speak briefly to each.

First, the will to dominate and win drove Trumpism's operations. Problem solving and deal making did not center on the search for common ground or compromise, but rather on combat with the aim of Trump winning out. Displays of strength and acts of domination prevailed. Attack and scorn in public became everyday modalities, routinizing threats and savage reprisals against those who merely disagreed with the president. This warlike exercise of executive power required a constant supply of adversaries to be challenged and dominated, figures of weakness against which to appear strong. It also involved escalation, a tactic Trump claims to have learned from his mentor, McCarthyite Roy Cohn. One way to win a fight is to take it to a level of nastiness the opponent declines to occupy.

One lexical study (Dictionary.com, n.d.) found that in addition to "winning" and "tough," Trump's twenty most frequently used terms included the insults "stupid," "weak," "loser," "bad," as well as the more specialized insults "fake news," "the swamp," and "political correctness." Repeated over and again, such terminology became the lexicon of Trumpism. Classic examples include "Free trade can be wonderful if you have smart people. But we have stupid people"; "I am strong, politicians are weak"; "Political correctness is killing our country." As Genovese put it, "Every insult, instead of disqualifying Trump, made him *more* popular with Republican voters" (2017, 12), a testament to the level of degradation to which common norms of civility and decency had sunk among broad swaths of the American public.

Second, not only did Trump gain attention by calling for a travel ban for people from a list of several Muslim countries, but he publicly insulted a pair of Muslim gold-star parents (the Kahns) who had lost their son in the line of duty for the American military. He trashed the likes of an American war hero (John McCain), made a series of misogynist remarks, and mocked a disabled reporter (Genovese 2017, 8). The gleeful violation of norms of civility and decency pumped the president's display of strength and entertainment. Causing pain for some provided pleasure for others (for more on this tactic, see Beltrán, this volume). The excitement and chaos kept the public in a constant state of agitation.

Trumpists were licensed not just to condemn the social norms of civility but to violate them openly in word, deed, and displays of armed aggression. Their tough assaults on news reporters and dissenters, authorized by Trump at his rallies, exemplified their shock-troop role. Even school children had their fun hurling Trump's inflammatory insults in order to bully classmates, especially Mexicans (Zoellner 2020; Gessen 2020).

Third, suspending the distinction between fact and fiction was a particularly powerful Trump tactic for disabling democracy, creating parallel universes built on fantasy and prevarication. As Applebaum (2018) recalls, "Trump entered American politics on the back of birtherism." He used the lie that Barack Obama had not been born in the United States not to persuade people these claims were true, but to create a political space in which he could undermine and humiliate President Obama without having to care about truth. The strategy required media support to magnify false claims in the ideational echo chamber, and Trump's personal service, Fox News, provided it. So did centrist and liberal media, by repeating the false claims in order to condemn them.

Nearly every day of his presidency, Trump used deliberate falsehood to deprive truth and evidence of the power to settle disputes—and under his control, practically everything that did not work to praise and support him became a dispute. Expert knowledge became the equivalent of any other invented account. Disputes were to be won by strength, measured in one's ability to control the story or hold the stage. There were facts and alternative facts, true stories and stories that might as well be true. The term "fake" came to mean something like its opposite, a hallmark of the Orwellian universe. If truth threatened to prevail, as it eventually did in the birther controversy, disputes could be nevertheless be perpetuated indefinitely simply by continuing to adhere to the disproven story. Throughout his presidency, Trump upheld the claim that the crowd at his inauguration was larger than that of his predecessor. He could ask his followers to hold to this belief even though they knew it was not true. As Applebaum (2020a) observes, the aim was not to get people to believe a falsehood, but to display the power "to promulgate a falsehood."

Fourth, Donald Trump is certainly the most performative, theatrical president ever elected in the United States. In tweets, speeches, interviews, press conferences, and mass rallies, Trump was the star in a theatrics of his own making, honed in the laboratories of reality television and celebrity culture. Though his presidency was unique in this respect, Trump's theatricality drew on a long-standing American tradition of populist demagoguery, often associated with religious, not political, revivalism. "Eighteenth-century American evangelists," says historian Brenda Wineapple, "held their audiences spellbound with invective, histrionics, bellicosity and divisiveness—the same techniques employed by one demagogue after another" (2020, 26). In language to presage Trumpism, one critic described the speech of the famed evangelist George Whitefield in the 1740s as "a medley of truth and falsehood, sense and nonsense, served up with pride and virulence, and other like-saucy ingredients" (Dickey 2019).

Though Trump is not an evangelical preacher, the MAGA movement not coincidentally counted Whitefield's heirs—evangelical Christians—among its most ardent followers. As the opening chapters of this volume make clear, when we speak of Trumpism we are referring to a political program that conjoins white nationalist counterculture with business-friendly governance and conservative social doctrine, all enduring threads in American politics. But we also speak of a repertory of demagogic communicative practices—histrionic drama; bellicosity; an insurgent, anti-institutional posture; demotic language; and populist show-manship. The combination won him the enduring support of some 40 percent of the American electorate, and changed the lives of the millions of people identified as his adversaries and targets.

Finally, Trump showed an extraordinary ability to draw new parties into the fold, including former adversaries. Despite the rancorous primaries, within months of his election, the Republican Party and its elected representatives had, en masse, taken up residence in Trumpworld. We borrow the term "pocketing" (from Wolff 2018) to refer to Trump's ability to gain the loyalty of ideologically driven constituencies without fully ascribing to their ideologies. The Trump team "pocketed" such constituencies by incorporating one or two of their key priorities into their legislative program, and fighting for them as his own. For evangelicals, it was the Supreme Court and reproductive rights; for corporations, it was tax cuts and deregulation; for farmers, it was subsidies; for workers, it was tariffs and repatriation of jobs; for white nationalists, it was immigration. The Trumpist strategy made each group a winner on at least one of its own key issues. The fact that the different priorities might be incompatible with each other is irrelevant if what counts is winning. Pragmatism ruled. In her study of autoc-racy, Gessen notes that autocrats do not consolidate their power by claiming a higher moral ground, but rather by "dragging everyone down with them" into an amoral sphere where there are no ideals (2020, x).

For Trump supporters, no inspiring ideals or coherent program were ex-pected. What Trump really believed remained irrelevant; he delivered the goods. Make America Great Again was a collage of not necessarily related causes, each of which enfolded a particular constituency into Trumpworld's pocket. Just as Trumpworld absorbed the whole Republican Party, despite its upstart status, so too it was able to win over the full spectrum of the Republican money machine, from right-wing radicals like Sheldon Adelson to the moderate heirs of Rockefeller Republicanism. "How did America's country-club Republicans . . . learn to love Donald Trump?" asks Evan Osnos (2020), writing about his hometown of Greenwich, Connecticut. Many affluent Trump voters, Osnos found, supported him quietly. Many silently agreed with illiberal positions on social welfare, immigration, and wealth. Understanding Trumpism's takeover of the party, Osnos argues, requires grasping "not only what he promised Americans at the bottom, but also what he provides Americans at the top." Here too, Trump's rise was the culmination of a steady shift in the party's values that had been trending since the 1980s.

TRUMPISM: DEGRADING LATINX PEOPLE

Such was the overall climate of presidential rage that targeted Mexicans, Mexican Americans, Central American migrants, Puerto Ricans, and asylum seekers. Immigration, legal and otherwise, became one of Trumpism's most galvanizing obsessions. Throughout the Trump presidency, in ways legal and not, the executive branch endlessly sought ways to prevent people from emigrating to the United States. He banned travel from Muslim countries, barred whole categories of foreign workers, refused refugees and asylum seekers, denied green cards to legal candidates who might need government services, and attempted to deport international students during the COVID-19 pandemic. Trump assailed mainstream attempts to enact comprehensive immigration reform that might include a path to citizenship. He scowled at previous administrations for their alleged lack of border enforcement. Trump enacted one measure after another to prevent entry, legal or otherwise, and to expel anyone who could be expelled.

Trump came out against unauthorized immigration two years before announcing his run for president, in remarks delivered at the 2013 annual Conservative Political Action Conference (CPAC). He declared, "We have to make America strong again and make America great again. Now this is a hard one, because when it comes to immigration. . . . the 11 million illegals, even if given the right to vote . . . every one of those 11 million people will be voting Democratic." Republicans were on a "suicide mission," Trump argued, should they support immigration reform. His candidacy was already in the making, and CPAC donors would fund it. A different reproach would come out of the Trump presidency, less concerned with votes, more absorbed with the impact of undocumented people on American jobs and American life.

It should be noted that Trump did not always scorn undocumented immigrants. As Joshua Green notes, only four months prior to the 2013 CPAC, Trump decried Mitt Romney's "mean-spirited" charges against immigrants and deemed immigration a good resource for business (2018a, 109). Indeed, for over two decades, his business and property enterprises across several states—golf resorts, a vineyard, hotels, private residences—gave employment preference to Mexican and Central American immigrants, many of them undocumented. Trump said he did not know if undocumented workers were under the employ of his enterprises. "But," he followed up, "I would say this. Probably every [golf] club in the United States has that, because it seems to me, from what I understand, a way that people did business" [*sic*] (Partlow and Fahrenthold 2019). And it was.

The business of getting elected president sent Trump down a different but equally well-worn path, a pandering to nativist and racialized anti-immigrant attitudes. The effectiveness of this strategy had to do in part with the fact that by the early twenty-first century, Mexican and Latin American immigrants had fanned out across the United States, in part fleeing crackdowns in places like California and Arizona in the 1990s (Montejano, this volume). By 2016 nearly every community in the United States, big and small, had Mexican or Central American immigrant residents. Their presence gave Trump a broad stage on which to promote hateful attacks on one of his favorite targets, Barack Obama.

From the escalator speech on, Latinx people were among the favorites of Trump's invective, theatrics, and efforts to punish. Trump invited his supporters to do the same, and they did, often identifying themselves as acting in the name of Trumpism and its MAGA mythology. All over the United States after the 2016 election, everyday aggression and cruelty spread to public spaces across the land, white people attacking Brown people, immigrants, and other people of color in public places, including schools, often condemning them for speaking Spanish (see Gonzales, this volume, for more on this trend). Trump defiantly praised such aggressors at rallies and in tweets as they engaged in the project of making sure that Latinx people would not belong in their society.

The theatrics went far beyond Trump's personal performances, especially when it came to Mexico and Central America. Using all the forces at his command, Trump made the two-thousand-mile Mexico-US border into a theater of domination and cruelty, a giant stage for spectacles of mass subjugation, dehumanization, and expulsion. He commanded territory, built detention camps, sent troops to hang razor wire, used ICE and the Border Patrol to separate families, and caged immigrant children. Then of course, there was "The Wall" (see Montejano, this volume).

The border was an ideal theater for Trumpism not only because the anti-immigrant, anti-Mexican message played such a prominent role in his program, but also because the president had almost total power over the people arriving there. The tens of thousands of Central American asylum seeker who, with their children, surged toward the border in 2018–2019 were perfect foils for theatrical displays of strength and domination. The Trumpian play was to intensify their abjection.

There was also the business of "white nationalism" casting its shadow over Mexican America. The twenty-first-century resurgence of white nationalism in the United States, out of the ashes of the Ku Klux Klan, was driven by demographic anxiety. White people made up a declining proportion of the US population and the US citizenry, and according to the United States Census Bureau, were on track to become a minority by 2045. These anxieties were codified in a classic work of xenophobia, Samuel P. Huntington's 2004 manifesto, *Who Are We? The Challenges to America's National Identity* discussed by two authors in this volume (Montejano and Rosaldo). Huntington, a British-born political scientist at Harvard, feared that due to demographic shifts, the United States was in the process of losing key principles of the American creed—liberty, equality, individualism, representative government, and private property. Rather than see these as civic principles, Huntington ethnicized and essentialized them as inherently Anglo-Saxon and of British derivation. Moreover, as Montejano and Rosaldo discuss, he linked them with Protestantism, the Protestant work ethic, the legacy of the Reformation, and the English language.

Huntington explicitly singled out Hispanics as the main threat to the United States' Anglo-Saxon character and traditions. Mexicans, quite particularly, challenged America's ethnic nationality, Huntington argued, bringing poverty, Spanish, Catholicism, authoritarianism, and a whole set of civilizational norms antithetical to the Anglo-Saxon model on which the nation had supposedly been founded. In a way that was not visible in 2004, Huntington's book portended the resurgence of white nationalist sentiment and militancy that was to come, especially following the 2008 economic collapse and the election of Barack Obama. Huntington, among others, set the white nationalist table at which Trumpism would sit.

Much ink has been spilled debating whether Trump himself is a white nationalist. "Make America Great Again" catered to a variety of nationalisms. Economic nationalists could cleave to its demands for better trade deals, revived manufacturing, and the return of jobs. Geopolitical nationalists could applaud withdrawals from global organizations and agreements, foreign wars, and foreign aid. The brand of nationalism that Trumpists most conspicuously cultivated was ethnic: the white nationalist movement that, in various forms, had resurged in the United States after 9/11, especially in the Obama years. In our view, the relevant question is not what Trump was or is, but what Trumpism did. How did Trumpism use white nationalism for its own ends? How did Trumpism gain the loyalty of white nationalists? Gonzales in this volume lays out some of the specifics that swayed Trumpism in the direction of white nationalism.

Here, it can be noted that Trump never deployed Huntington's Anglo-Saxon Protestantist vocabulary, nor that of nativist Stephen Bannon, for whom America's ethnic core was expressed as a European-style "peasant wisdom and peasant loyalty" (Wolff 2019, 275). Yet Bannon was a key agent in the construction of Trumpism, joining the campaign when it was declining in the polls and reenergizing it with his vision of a "party of peasants" as the vanguard of a revolution against the regulatory state (Wolff 2019, 275, 262). If Trump's brand rested partly on economic nationalism, it originated in one of Bannon's chief aims—to protect the American working-class base from the ravages of globalization. The language of peasant revolution never crossed Trump's lips. Over and again, however, he signaled to racist movements that they had his recognition and stamp of approval, e.g., pointing to "fine people on both sides" after the white supremacist rally and counterprotests in Charlottesville (see Gonzales, this volume).

More important, he shared the main targets of their hatred: immigrants, prospective immigrants, refugees, asylum seekers, and Mexicans, US-born or not. By failing to disown race hatred when it flared, Trump signaled his preferred nation (Shephard 2018; Elfrink 2019). He went out of his way to make white supremacists feel at home in the Trumpist tent. By attacking immigrants and Mexicans, Trumpism "pocketed" white supremacists without targeting the real foundational object of their hatred, African Americans. Trumpism paid lip service to post–civil rights taboos against racist anti-Black speech, but here too, he sent messages by failing to denounce anti-Black violence, by defending police who murdered Black men, by offering no policy initiatives directed at reducing racial inequality.

Some scholars see Trump's endorsement of white nationalism as a step in the direction of fascism and authoritarianism. In *Surviving Autocracy*, Masha

Gessen suggests a move toward autocracy, a type of regime that seeks to do away with politics and "demands a narrowing of 'us,' in opposition to an ever greater and more frightening 'them'" (2020, 171). Autocracy moves to narrow down the range of people entitled to full recognition as citizens as a way of concentrating power in fewer and fewer hands, placing more and more people in exploitable states of precarity and vulnerability. In Gessen's two case studies, Russia under Putin and the United States under Trump, religious discrimination is one such mechanism, and stigmatizing all forms of nonbinary sexuality is another. In the literature on citizenship and belonging, the case for ethnic equality and inclusion has been developed alongside the case for inclusion across heterogeneous forms of gender and sexuality.

The narrowing of the American "us" against the reality of ethnic pluralism was demonstrated clearly in the Trump presidency by its disparaging treatment of Puerto Ricans. Hurricane Maria did $94 billion in infrastructural damage in Puerto Rico, and caused three thousand deaths. A month prior to Maria, Hurricane Harvey, a Category 4 storm, slammed into the Gulf Coast of Texas and into the Houston area, with damages assessed at $125 billion. Harvey displaced 30,000 residents while home destruction in Puerto Rico proved inestimable, plunging "all of its 3.4 million residents into humanitarian crisis" (Schwartz 2018). Yet the double standard in the federal relief response in the two cases pushed Puerto Rico's catastrophe into a cataclysm.

Investigation revealed that the Trump administration, "and the president himself," responded far more aggressively to the recovery of Texas, with faster and greater support from key institutions, including the military, the Federal Emergency Management Agency, and others (Vinik 2018; Parker 2017). Houston was on its feet and on its way to recovery in four months. For Puerto Rico, by contrast, financial and other forms of recovery remained elusive eleven months after Maria, including the basic matter of full restoration of electrical power (Levin and Cruz 2018; Campisi and White 2018).

The president had fiduciary responsibility for the safety and essential well-being of the citizens of Puerto Rico. Facilitating Trump's neglect was Puerto Rico's status as a federal territory, an actual colony without a voting member in Congress, its governor appointed by the president. Trump also knew that residents of the island could not vote for a US presidential candidate while Texas, a red state, had two US senators who, in the aftermath of Harvey, "loudly" demanded "proper resources for their state" (Vinik 2018).

Expressing amazement at Harvey as a "once in 500 year flood," Trump blamed the victims in Puerto Rico for their catastrophe, tweeting that they wanted "everything to be done for them and it should be a community effort" (quoted in Vinik 2018). Trump's focus on issues other than Maria during its peak impact sent a "subtle yet important signal to the federal bureaucracy" to take it easy on the island's recovery effort (Vinik 2018). In one opinion, the administration "is due a serious reckoning. That's because for millions of fellow Americans in the Caribbean this is serious, if not deadly, business" (Parker 2017). Claiming that the death toll in the case of Maria was sixteen, Trump told Puerto Ricans they should be relieved that were spared "a real catastrophe like Katrina" (Schwartz 2017).

Puerto Rican officials were left feeling like colonized underlings. Illinois Democratic congressman Rep. Luís Gutiérrez had hoped for "some sort of apology" from the administration. However, as he said, "If you look at how the president has treated Puerto Rico, you have to conclude that he just doesn't care and probably thinks of Puerto Rico as just another shithole country," referring to a term Trump had used to describe African countries (Chávez 2018). Annette Martínez Orabona, director of the Caribbean Institute for Human Rights, made a heartfelt statement after a Trump speech about the spate of hurricanes that had hit the United States: "We have a problem in Puerto Rico, and it's one of discrimination. It's about discrimination that stems from our colonial relationship because we haven't been given the opportunity to practice our right to self-determine, and that should remain clear" (Funes 2017). Even the governor of Puerto Rico, Ricardo Rosselló, who had been a friend of the Trump administration, got fed up with the lack of administration response. "There is no doubt that Puerto Rico gets treated differently to a state," he conceded. "And there is no doubt that it has been true for the disaster response as well." Rosselló declared that the objective of his administration was to "eradicate this notion of second-class citizenship in the United States, so that whenever a disaster hits—whether it's Texas, Florida, New York or Puerto Rico—the federal government responds equally in all cases" (Vinik 2018).

In his whole treatment of Puerto Rico, Trump showed that he could disregard civic citizenship as a basis for belonging to the American polity, devaluing some citizens while valuing the rights and needs of others.

For Suzanne Oboler, the complexity and dynamism of the evolving Latinx presence places it at the center of both the politics and the study of citizenship in the United States. As she puts it, "to the extent that Latino/as continue to be the one population that, whether formally citizens or not, is consistently considered 'alien' in their own land, they will continue to be an essential component of discussions on the changing meanings of citizenship in the U.S. context, while also remaining central to U.S. immigration policy and hemispheric power dynamics" (2006, 10).

The Chapters

This book contributes to several threads in the scholarly investigation of the regimes of citizenship that struggle for dominance in the United States, and of the struggles of Latinx people with and within those regimes. That ongoing scholarly conversation now faces the challenge of understanding Trumpism, white nationalism, and the resurgence of white supremacy and exploring their implications for Latinx struggles around citizenship and belonging.

A major theme in several of the chapters is the finding that Trump drew into his camp elements of racism and nativism that remained very much alive in white America. Several explore the complicated positioning of Latinxs in relation to these ideologies. A second key subject are Latinx responses to these forces and their struggles to achieve full recognition as citizens, to expand rights in areas like language and education, and to secure legal status and rights—whether documented or undocumented—all in the face of anti-Mexican and anti-immigrant attitudes that wax and wane in their ferocity.

In chapter 1, sociologist Phillip B. Gonzales examines Trumpism's discursive or meta-violence, linking the dramatic public events that characterized Trump's policy of attacking Mexicans and Mexican Americans, both rhetorically and physically, to a clear and consistent history of white nationalism and anti-Mexican politics. At the conclusion of his chapter, Gonzales gives a partial account of the collective resistance Mexicans offered to the onslaught of Trumpism, with important implications for the incorporation of undocumented youth into the field of American citizenship and community. In chapter 2, political theorist Cristina Beltrán diagnoses Trumpism and white nationalism through the paradigm of Herrenvolk democracy, a theory originating with ex–settler colonial states like South Africa that are founded on racial hierarchies that liberalism is unable to level. In Herrenvolk democracies, ideals of freedom, equality, and liberty exist among a dominant, usually white, group and are defined by that group's ability to subjugate and terrorize a subordinated group to whom full citizenship is denied, usually slaves or their descendants. Beltrán reviews the history of the United States and Mexican America through this lens, then applies its analytical powers to the Trump era. Beltrán argues that much of American white supremacy has sought to enact this form of political inequality, with Mexican Americans playing a singular and highly consequential role in shaping and inhibiting it. In chapter 3, historical sociologist Davíd Montejano defines Trumpism as a movement based in Anglo-Saxon populism and looks back across the twentieth century to remind us that violence, dehumanization, and hatred toward Mexicans has a long legacy in US history. Montejano examines the right wing's policies toward immigration, then traces their antecedents in California in the 1990s and back to the deportation regime of the 1930s. In chapter 4, critical journalist and border scholar Michelle García reviews this history from the Texas borderlands through the lens of contemporary theories of power, exploring the alienation and experiential dissonance experienced by Mexican Americans in Texas, as subjects in their own eyes and objects of the Anglo gaze. She diagnoses this imposed state of simultaneous belonging and unbelonging as a long-term existential predicament. In chapter 5, following Beltrán's lead, anthropologist Renato Rosaldo explores the dynamics and implications of Herrenvolk democracy in two contrasting texts, Helena María Viramontes's novel *Their Dogs Came with Them* (2007) and Samuel Huntington's ideological manifesto *Who Are We?* (2004). Looking back from Trumpism, Rosaldo sees Huntington's book as a primer for what was to come, and Viramontes's novel as prophetic fiction, a warning of what could possibly happen to Latinx communities under an implied Herrenvolk condition. The existential aspects of Latinx struggles are also a focus of chapter 6, in which cultural anthropologist Alyshia Galvez focuses on the contemporary context. Gálvez describes undocumented youth activists devastated by the series of defeats that thwarted the Dream Act, placed DACA in peril, and stymied progress on an agenda for which they had labored hard and risked everything in the Obama years. Her findings illustrate the altered forms of activism arising from these devastating circumstances, including a reconsideration of the power of storytelling and the power of silence. The work leads her to rethink the ethical foundations of ethnographic engagement in this context.

Chapter 7 turns to the all-important question of Central American migration and the Central American experience in the United States. Central American studies scholar Arely Zimmerman shows how, across the twentieth and twenty-first centuries, Central Americans have been separated out from policies aimed at Mexican migrants and subjected to administrative regimes that reflect their different historical experiences and possibilities. Under Trump, Central American asylum seekers flooded toward the border in huge numbers, replacing

Mexicans as the most numerous group in the migrant pipeline. While Mexican migration declined to practically zero, hundreds of thousands of Guatemalans, Hondurans, and Salvadorans arrived at the border by caravan to apply for asylum. As Zimmerman shows, these migrants were read mainly through what Leo Chávez (2013) called "the Latino threat narrative," invoking invading hordes bringing danger, criminality, and violence. The threat narrative, Zimmerman shows, was used to mark a line between "good" and "bad" immigrants, and to justify border cruelty.

The book's final two chapters return to questions of cultural citizenship, identity, and belonging. In chapter 8, sociologist Tomás Jiménez explores Mexican American culture and identity across generations and the prospects for both in the twenty-first century. Having researched these issues comprehensively prior to the 2016 election, he asks how Trumpist border-closing and deportation policies will impact Mexican American communities that for a century have been continuously replenished by new arrivals. Comparing communities in Kansas and California, Jiménez anticipates what the end of replenishment will mean for Mexican Americans.

In the final chapter, education scholar and activist Ángela Valenzuela reviews political and legal struggles around ethnic studies curricula in the framework of decolonization and decolonial practice. Valenzuela argues for the continued importance of ethnic studies in enabling democratic challenges to Trumpism and post-Trump futures. Not surprisingly, Trump weaponized the conflicts around the study of ethnicity and race in his failed 2020 reelection campaign, arguing that, along with anti-racism training, such educational projects should be outlawed because they taught students to "hate their country." Critical race theory has become the new educational target in Texas and other conservatively governed states.

Conclusion

Trumpism is far from over. The work of grasping how it came to be, how it operated, its impact, and the future of democracy in the US will go on for a long time. The essays in this volume suggest directions for this conversation from the perspective of Mexican America and Latinx people whose presence and actions continue to shape US history.

CHAPTER ONE

Meta-violence, Expulsive Nationalism, and Trumpism's Crackdown on Mexican America

PHILLIP B. GONZALES

Donald Trump's rise to power was nothing if not a politics of conflict and divisiveness. Trump made the generation of social conflict a mainstay of his run for president and the taproot of his governing (such as it could be called). Aggression and rancor, not American unification, guided Trump's political game. They reshaped the practice of politics in the United States, perhaps for good.

A remarkable amount of expert popular and academic analysis addressed this aspect of the Trump phenomenon as it manifested itself. Samira Saramo defined Trumpism as a political movement best examined through the conceptual lens of "meta-violence." In meta-violence, the use of language relies on "emotional evocations of violence—fear, threats, aggression, hatred, and division" (2017, 2). As core Trumpism, meta-violence grew omnipresent in a process of "slow violence," Rob Nixon's phrase denoting a long period of conflicts turning aggression into normal politics, affecting the way "social afflictions" are perceived and addressed (quoted in Saramo 2017, 3).

Strikingly for a presidential creed, Trumpism marked out "enemies of America" from among the people of America itself. In Saramo's frame, Trumpian meta-violence was expressed in three political modes: "populism," "strongman politics," and "identitarianism." Trumpist populism came out of a prior state of mass resentment of the political establishment. Members of this camp hailed their candidate for being a nonpolitician, rebelling against the Republican Party, being a (falsely assumed) self-made/shrewd businessman, and not afraid to speak for them as common folks even as he boasted of his billions. As strategy, this populism exploited the anxiety and frustration felt by Americans who lived in the "long shadow of the Great Recession," particularly "largely white, male, non-college-educated, and rural supporters" (Saramo 2017, 9), although the volume of women devoted to Trumpism is yet to be quantified.

Trump's strongman persona stemmed in part from the mentoring of Roy Cohn, the ruthless, corrupt, "right-wing dirty trickster" who served as Senator Joseph McCarthy's chief counsel, conducted anti-Communist witch-hunts in the 1950s, and served as consigliere to New York's mafia families. Cohn taught Trump to never compromise, always declare victory, and deflect criticism without answering to it (Goldberg 2018). Trump as president (and presidential candidate in 2020) identified with the leadership styles of dictators who commonly resorted to illegal violence against the enemies of their rule. Trump as strongman "marshalled a sense of 'we'" to protect himself politically along "racial and nativist lines," starting with his "birther" campaign of 2011 to discredit President Barack Obama, including the accusation that Obama was a Muslim terrorist. The nucleus of a populist constituency emerged here, Trump calling his birther supporters, "great American people . . . unbelievable salt of the earth people" (Saramo 2017, 11–12).

The self-labeled identitarian movement, with roots in European Islamophobic populism, consisted of underground alt-right white supremacy organizations. Trump's meta-violence stimulated them to come out publicly and they responded with "tremendous" support for Trump. Identitarians prioritized white identity, promoted misogyny, heterosexuality, and Christianity. The likes of the American Nazi Party came to regard Trump as a kind of demigod. According to Richard Spencer, president of a white supremacist think tank who shouted "Hail Trump" at the results of the 2016 presidential election, identitarianism posited "identity as the center—and the central question—of a spiritual, intellectual, and (meta) political movement. . . . And Identity is not just the call of blood, though it is that" (quoted in Saramo 2017, 13).

People of Mexican extraction counted among the many whom Trumpism targeted as "enemies of the people." This chapter describes some of the major ways that Trumpian meta-violence operated to blot out the principle that Mexicans and Mexican Americans belong to the social fabric and political community of the United States. In addition to populism, strongman tactics, and identitarianism, this chapter shows, Mexicans were targeted through the medium of white nationalism, which congealed not only in the president, but as thoughts and behaviors across ordinary citizens, elected officials, and policy wonks. I conclude by highlighting some of the ways Mexican America sought to fight off the Trumpian assault, suggesting that Mexicans are indeed integral parts of the American "community."

White Nationalism in Base Assailment

One day in early 2019, Dulce Nereyda, her daughter, and her mother browsed the aisles of a Walmart in Phoenix when out of nowhere, according to the online account, "an unnamed bearded man began yelling at them for speaking Spanish." As Nereyda posted on Facebook, "This man starts yelling, 'I can't wait until Trump does away with you all!'" Pointing to the fear in the eyes of her daughter, Nereyda exclaims, "Excuse me?" The accoster, who in Nereyda's phone-recording video looms as a large white man, shouts, "Leave, just leave. YOU DON'T BELONG HERE!" Walking straight at him, Nereyda fires back, "So, do you want to tell me to get out again? Because this is my country, too." The man reiterates his support for Trump, warning of the coming "wall" (quoted in Simón 2019).

If in his strongman persona Donald Trump operated as "a big bully," his meta-violence clearly enabled what one commentator called "many little bullies" (Heer 2016). As Saramo notes, meta-violence is "closely bound to emotion" (2017, 3). The man who accosted Nereyda, whom I shall call Burly White Guy (BWG) for ease of identification, did so in a heat of anger. However, far from a singular outburst, it represented a general behavior pattern. Under Trumpism, "base assailment" despoiled everyday life. Members of Trump's "belligerent faction" (Krugman 2020) openly harassed individuals of certain color, Asians, Asian Americans, Arabs, Arab Americans, people mistaken for Muslims, as well as Jews.

Enacted by BWG, base assailment would seem masculinist, perhaps misogynistic. However, a YouTube video (ABC7 2020) enables the witnessing of a middle-aged white woman, walking through Wilson Park in Los Angeles, becoming irritated at a young Asian American woman as she worked out on concrete steps that the lady is about descend. In the course of a tense exchange, Wilson Park White Lady (WPWL) lets fly: "Go back to whatever f*****g Asian country you came from. This is not your home." In the backdrop, President Trump had just racialized the COVID-19 pandemic, calling it the "Kung Flu" and the "Chinese virus." On the macho meter, WPWL outdid BWG, hounding her mark with "my whole family is going to f**k you up." All too soon, the base lashing of Asians and Asian Americans spiked in Facebook and Twitter hashtags (Alba 2021), upticking to a record-breaking volume of hate crimes, including the physical beating of elderly persons on the street, the grotesque "you don't belong here" profaning the legacy of the 2020 presidential election (Hong et al. 2021).

Sara Ahmed argues that white hate works to "secure collectives" (2014, 41). It promotes the fantasy of the "ordinary white subject . . . a fantasy that comes into being through the mobilization of hate as a passionate attachment closely tied to love" (of one's whiteness). In a state of rage, the ordinary white person self-defines as the "real victim" (43). The politics of meta-violence becomes the means of realizing the passion.

Both WPWL and BGW told their targets to "get out," Nereyda to Mexico presumably, and the young woman in the park "to whatever . . . Asian country you came from." Logically, the phrases were meta-violent expressions of nationalism in the sense of wanting to keep certain elements out of the bordered territorial state. More specifically, they reflected Trumpism as white nationalism, the banishing of people of color in particular. How, one can well ask, did white nationalism in the Trump administration evolve?

In the presidential campaign of 2015–2016, observers suspected that what Donald Trump meant by "Make America Great Again" was some unseemly sense of nationalism. In a speech at a Houston rally, Trump defiantly pronounced that he *was* a nationalist, and he exhorted the members of his excited crowd to make nationalism their identity as well (Cummings 2018).

When the chief executive of a territorial state (the so-called "nation-state") invokes nationalism, theorists call it "dominant nationalism" (as opposed to the nationalism of, say, a regional minority). When the expression of nationalism includes the most advantaged group in the state system, it reflects dominant ethnoracial nationalism. Especially in the context of a multicultural state, dominant nationalism is generally called upon to affirm what grouping it is that constitutes its privileged "nation" or "sovereign body" (Wimmer 2002, 1–2).

In a speech delivered at the 2016 Republican National Convention, Trump seemed to herald delimited nation. Sounding much like a modern liberal, he exclaimed, "Every day I wake up determined to deliver for the people I have met all across this nation that have been neglected, ignored, and abandoned." The candidate meant what a sociologist calls "reformed liberalism" (Haltinner 2018, 450), the Tea Party view of working people victimized into inequality by the liberal state. "I have visited the laid-off factory workers, and the communities crushed by our horrible and unfair trade deals," Trump (2016) put it. "These are the forgotten men and women of our country, and they are forgotten, but they're not going to be forgotten long. These are people who work hard but no longer have a voice. I AM YOUR VOICE."

Stephen K. Bannon, the former executive chair of the far-right Breitbart News, who came on as chief adviser late in Trump's campaign for president, reinforced Trumpism as a working-class movement. Bannon, stylizing himself a rough-hewn intellectual light of US populism, saw such a politics as part of the rising populist movements in Europe (Green 2018a, 109). Trump came off in such a scenario as a champion of conservative, religious, small-town America. If the self-appointed Braveheart promised safekeeping for the legatees of economic restructuring (1980s decline of industrialization and family farms) or current downfalls in extractive industries (Potts 2019), he signaled what Benedict Anderson (1983) would have called "nation-ness," in this case, an imagined electoral nation. Wolff called it Trump's pocketed "35 percent" (2018, 179). The 35 percent put Trump over in the battleground states of Pennsylvania, Iowa, Wisconsin, and Michigan (Cohn and Palapiano 2018).

In theory, the 35 percent might have spelled a European-style populist administration, a form of government that would have suited Bannon. However, "working class" was not the only code for Trump's base of support. A racial undercurrent shimmied through. Ethnographic observations suggested an enmeshment of race and class. Many white rural Americans lived in isolated, low-income hamlets and towns, defining government as primarily concerned with giving immigrants and minorities welfare preferment (Potts 2019). Those in former smokestack suburban communities burned with particular resentment toward African Americans but also Latinx immigrants (Cherlin 2019).

Nevertheless, 35 percent would not have been enough nationally. Overall white non-Hispanic voters went for Trump by 21 percentage points, 58 percent for Trump versus 37 percent for Clinton (Tyson and Maniam 2016). Trump also won among white college graduates, 49 percent versus 45 percent for Clinton, women going surprisingly strong for him (Smarsh 2018). Emphasis on white economic anxiety hid a greater "racial anxiety" (Ali 2018). "Just plain whiteness" seemed to be at stake (Smarsh 2018). Leonard Pitts (2018) put it in dominant nationalistic terms: Trump, Republicans, and 64 million voters "sold out America on a promise of white primacy."

With such a showing, Trump might have gone on to develop an "insidious" nationalism based on a policy of ethnic majority rule akin to dominant Hindu nationalism in India (Nehru [1953] 2018). Indeed, Indian prime minister Narendra Modi resembled Trump, thriving on a policy of social divisiveness (Shear

2019). One problem, however, involved the profit-obsessed, "ultra-rich finan-
ciers" and hedge-fund moguls, a kind of "one-percenter" nation that Trump
favored with massive tax cuts and deregulation (Tankersley 2016; Hohman 2018).
For them, an explicit ethnoracial nationalism would not have worked.

Yet Trump saw where his obsessive base lay. As alt-right innovator Richard
Spencer put it during the Trump presidency, "On a gut level, [Trump] kind of
senses that this is about demographics, ultimately. We're moving into a new
America" (quoted in LeTourneau 2019). Spencer here evoked the white supremacist fear of "demography as destiny" (Judis and Teixeira 2002), the theory of the
"great replacement" of whites by migrants from the Global South, as this fear
had disseminated to the United States from conservative populism in Europe.
Bannon believed in the race-threat philosophy popularized in the writings of the
French traditional extremists Jean Raspail and Renaud Camus (Peltier 2020). In
the United States, the fear of alien races leaving whites out in the cold sounded in
the slogan "Diversity equals white genocide" (ADL n.d.). To Spencer, Trump had
"an unconscious vision that white people have, that their grandchildren might
be a hated minority in their own country. I think that scares us. They probably
aren't able to articulate it. I think it's there. I think that, to a great degree, explains
the Trump phenomenon" (quoted in LeTourneau 2019).

As the 2020 presidential election neared and his poll numbers dipped below
those of Joe Biden, Trump blew the white-nationalist dog whistle, retweeting a
video of a supporter sporting "Trump 2020" and "America First" signs on his
golf cart while shouting "white power!" to Trump opponents (Shear 2020). The
president even sounded the theme of replacement in a Fourth of July speech
affirming, "We will never allow an angry mob to tear down our statues, erase
our history, indoctrinate our children. And we will defend, protect and preserve
(the) American way of life, which began in 1492 when Columbus discovered
America" (Berry and Madhani 2020). Never mind that Columbus never set foot
on the land that became the United States.

Expulsive Ethno-nationalism

When dominant nationalists perceive elements threatening their sovereignty,
they automatically seek those elements' exclusion "from the privileged seats in
the theatre of society by virtue of their ethnic background" (Wimmer 2002, 4;
see also Gellner 1964, 168). "Exclusion" commonly refers to marginalization in
relation to mainstream institutions. However, as Rubén Rumbaut (2017) noted,

Trumpism's random and purposed exclusionary actions often included a policy of outright national expulsion. The emotive force of Trumpism's meta-violence evoked what can be called a meta-violence of "expulsive nationalism." Trump treated people of color with expulsive disdain. For example, he pushed to have undocumented individuals not counted in the 2020 census in spite of the US Constitution's stipulation that all "inhabitants" be recorded. If it had passed, the policy would have spelled a meta-violent hurt put on the individual states of the Union as much as the undocumented (Turner 2020).

Back at the Phoenix Walmart, Burly White Guy made a grandstand for American nativism. His verbal violence demanded literal expulsion for the violation of speaking Spanish in an American national framework, evidenced as he roared to Nereyda, "Leave, just leave. YOU DON'T BELONG HERE!" As the online report affirmed, across the United States speaking Spanish—or any other non-English language—could subject one to "offensive and racist comments" and mistreatment (Simón 2019). Trump had cued up the issue during the presidential campaign, taunting rival Jeb Bush for speaking Spanish on the stump. "This is a country where we speak English, not Spanish," Trump jabbed. The Trump campaign did not reach out to Spanish-speaking voters with Spanish-language ads, relying totally on white support (Goldmacher 2016).

It is important to note that, through the lens of nativism, the objection to speaking Spanish is not the same as biological race prejudice. Nineteenth-century nativism hailed Anglo-Saxon values, customs, and practices as the fundament of American culture during the era of Manifest Destiny (Higham 2002). In the new millennium, nativism revitalized in the face of powerful forces of globalization. More immediate roots to Trumpism lay in the conservative hysteria over the rise of undocumented migration starting in the 1970s (Massey, Durand, and Pren 2016). In this decade, Congressman Tom Tancredo (Colorado) and Steve King (Iowa) embarked on a campaign to pass English-only and anti–bilingual education laws in their respective states. Tellingly for white nationalism, Tancredo later founded his campaign for the 2008 presidential election on one principle: "Massive uncontrolled illegal immigration threatens our survival as a nation" (OnTheIssues n.d.; Gabriel 2019a).

The speaking of Spanish has a long, unbroken history in the United States, since the forcible annexation of Mexico's northern territories in the mid-nineteenth century (Lozano 2018). Dulce Nereyda educated BWG that English was not the sole language of the country. Yet Tancredo tried making it so in a proposed amendment to the US Constitution to designate English as the official

US language (US Congress, 2007). Stoking fear of replacement, King pledged to fight alleged threats of foreign cultural influence on "Western culture" and "Western civilization" (Gabriel 2019b). Twenty-seven Republican-controlled states advanced Anglo-Saxon nationalism by defining English as their official language in the 1980s–1990s, including Arizona.

Had they been honest enough, they would have realized that Spanish posed no threat to the dominance of English. Statistical research found that Latinx immigrants were picking up English successfully through family generations (Krogstad, Stepler, and López 2015). But of course, the point was to push "white"-inflected nationalism. As such, it is highly likely that Trump was keyed to attack Bush on the language issue by Stephen Miller, his chief speech-writer during the campaign, whose own right-wing perspective included a bitter opposition to Spanish speaking as an expression of disloyalty to American patriotism (Guerrero 2020, 56–57, 61, 71).

Alien Crime as a Threat to American Civilization

The English-only movement would serve as a springboard for King and Tancredo to chum it up with Trump, going on to dance around another pet white nationalist pairing: immigration and crime. Trump stamped his presidential calling with immigration reform, shrouding the issue in a kind of anti-Mexican nationalism (Varela 2019).

Prior to running for president, Trump was "the furthest thing from a racial innocent," with his racist tendency showing not only in his "birther" attack on Obama. In 1989, he spent $85,000 for full-page ads in New York newspapers to condemn five Black teenagers accused of raping a white female jogger in Central Park, failing to apologize when they were later exonerated of the crime (Green 2018a, 1001). Yet, for purposes of a presidency, Trump needed to learn how to be a more effective racializer, the better for pandering to white prejudice. To beef up this side of his political portfolio, he appropriated the material of racism that circulated through extremists and the media. Journalist Charlie Warzel (2019) described the mechanism of the "circular flow chart": Outlandish white nationalist race theories came to "burble up from the depths and [got] laundered up through increasingly mainstream channels until they reach[ed] the president. Once amplified by Mr. Trump, the idea [was] lent more credence and [was] cited more frequently in right-wing media, which ultimately [led] Mr. Trump to amplify it more aggressively."

The circular flow chart operated during Trump's presidential campaign. Indeed, it pumped strongly in Trump's escalator performance. In the infamous, meta-violent announcement that he would run for president, it was Mexicans whom Trump associated with the problems of drugs, crime, and rape. In her book *¡Adios, America! The Left's Plan to Turn Our Country into a Third World Hellhole*, the far-right personality Ann Coulter included extreme stereotypes, referring to the "Latin American rape culture," describing "the gusto for gang rape, incest and child rape of our main immigrant groups," and claiming that "the rape of little girls isn't even considered a crime in Latino culture." (quoted in Beinart 2016). Shortly before his run for president, Trump called *¡Adios, America!* a "great read" (quoted in Beinart 2016; see also Montejano, this volume). After the speech, Tancredo (2015a) praised Trump in a Breitbart News commentary for forcing the other Republican presidential candidates to address the social costs of illegal Mexican entry.

In another flow chart example, presidential candidate Trump tweeted as authoritative certain crime statistics that were previously posted by a neo-Nazi website depicting Black people as the largest group of murderers of white people (Thompson 2015). In this regard, Trump may have amplified "fake" news to a gross art, but he did not invent lying as a political modality. Instead, he picked up the practice from a prior generation of Republican Party nationalism.

For decades, Tom Tancredo and Steve King had been projecting incredible links between immigrants and hypercrime. One such example was Tancredo (2015b) dog whistling the case of Kate Steinle. With the news that Steinle was shot and killed by an undocumented immigrant, he snapped that it was "the tip of a massive iceberg [of] illegal alien crime." Among the fantastical statistics he cited was one that said between 2008 and 2014, 40 percent of all murder convictions in Florida were committed by criminal aliens; in New York, 34 percent; and in Arizona, 17.8 percent. As Tancredo (2015b) claimed, "criminal aliens accounted for 38% of all murder convictions in the five states of California, Texas, Arizona, Florida and New York, while illegal aliens constitute only 5.6% of the total population in those states." Feeling the power of statistics, Tancredo called for increasing deportations (McMahon 2006).

The slashing meta-violence of outright lies continued in the voice of right-wing radio firebrand Michael Savage, who called Steinle's death and other cases of violence committed by "illegals" the result of Obama's policy of "importing crime" (2015, 201, 169–72). Obama's administration actually exerted a great deal of energy to sweep up undocumented people and deport them. Sophisticated research proved the irrationality of it all: crime rates among undocumented immigrants fell far lower than those of the general population (González-Barrera and Krogstad 2018; Guerrero 2020, 117).

Alas, "the myth of the criminal migrant" won out in 2016 (Varela 2019). No sooner than he was elected, Trump flashed the images of undocumented immigration from the Tancredo-King-Savage propaganda crew. After a jury acquitted José Ines García Zarate of the second-degree murder of Kate Steinle, recognizing the accidental nature of the tragedy, Trump called the verdict "a complete travesty of justice." The killer had come back and forth over the weakly protected "Obama" border, he exhorted, "always committing crimes and being violent, and yet this info was not used in court" (Valverde 2017). In one fell swoop, the president took a punch at a hated Democratic president who was Black, skewered a presumptively liberal jury, promoted what fact-checking proved to be false biographical information on García—the charge that he had a violent record—and essentialized undocumented immigrants as inveterate criminals.

Shortly after his election, Trump appeared on *60 Minutes*, exercising his felt right of expulsion. He would "immediately" deport two million, "it could even be three million. We are getting them out of our country or we are going to incarcerate" (quoted in Hellmann 2016). In his patented authoritarianism, he suggested suspending due process for detained individuals at the border (Hellmann 2016), a policy that he would indeed put in place.

Invasion: A Meta-violent Trope

As sociologists have emphasized, social and political movements generate their characteristic expressions and language in order to coherently isolate and frame their issues (Ryan and Gamson 2006). Distinctive words feed in to stigmatize, valorize, divide, unite, and inspire political actors to what Sidney Tarrow calls "the construction of contentious language" (2013, 13). In the political dialect fostered by Trumpism, "invasion" became a favored notion to stoke white nationalist fears (Chávez 2008, 13; Zimmerman this volume). It originated in a late nineteenth-century concern for Italian, Jewish, and Polish arrivals. The momentous panic over Chinese immigration was enshrined in the Supreme Court's expulsive rulings beginning in 1889 (*Chae Chan Ping v. U.S.*, 130 U.S. 581). Jennifer Wingard pinpointed the visceral power of invasion, the idea of "somebody coming in and taking what is ours," presupposing a "centralized

American identity that's under siege. . . . Typically that centralized identity is kind of Anglo, European; it's white" (quoted in Greenberg and Prignano 2019).

Fear of "Mexican invasion" sprung five years after World War II, in reaction to the unauthorized settlement of would-be contract workers (braceros) migrating for work opportunities. An immigration official described the mass migration of Mexicans as "perhaps the greatest peacetime invasion ever complacently suffered by any country under open, flagrant, contemptuous violation of its laws" (quoted in Foley 2014, 124). Invasion alarm expanded in the 1970s. Immigration and Naturalization Service (INS) commissioner Leonard Chapman publicly warned of the "silent invasion of illegal aliens" threatening the United States. Without restrictive immigration measures and massive increases of funds to the INS, Chapman (1976) argued, it would be impossible for the United States to halt the "robbing" of jobs from Americans and the illegal accessing of social services (see also Massey, Durand, and Pren 2016). In 1977, the *U.S. News & World Report* cover announced the "Time Bomb in Mexico: Why They'll Be No End to the Invasion by 'Illegals,'" warning of the fertility rate of Mexican women in the United States compared to bare growth rate among white women. The magazine followed up in 1983 with a story titled "Invasion from Mexico: It Just Keeps Growing" (Chávez 2017, 8).

"Invasion" ramped up among pundits under Trump. The conservative American Immigration Control Foundation equated immigration to a "'military conquest'" with the effect of "substantially replacing the native population" (quoted in Kulish and McIntire 2019). Pat Buchanan declared on Fox News that migration across the border involved "a peacetime invasion of the United States," that illegal migration formed part of an "Aztlan plot" hatched by Mexican elites to recapture lands lost in the 1848 Mexican-American War. "If we do not get control of our borders and stop this greatest invasion in history," he pronounced, "I see the dissolution of the U.S. and the loss of the American southwest" (quoted in Massey, Durand, and Pren 2016, 1562). According to conservative radio host Todd Starnes, the invasion involved a voter-registration drive for the Democratic National Committee (Peters et al. 2019).

By the time he assumed the presidency, Trump held fast to the view that the United States was "being taken advantage of by hostile foreigners" (Green 2018a, 109), "really an invasion without the guns" (Greenberg and Prignano 2019). It was as if, in the dominant nationalist's worst fear, Latinx aliens conspired to literally take over the country (Wimmer 2019). Here lies rhetorical violence, the dehumanizing, expulsive mischaracterization of the motivations of the great majority of normal, decent Mexicans who move to the United States with hopes of nothing more than obtaining life-sustaining jobs to support their families.

Nationalism and Disease

If it were not enough that they stole jobs, relied on welfare, and threatened national security, the perception that Mexicans needed ousting to stem the "invasion" of disease also inflated to gross proportion. This idea was historically ingrained as well. Through the twentieth century, foreigners were consistently associated with germs and contagion. As research has found, "Anti-immigrant rhetoric and policy have often been framed by an explicitly medical language, one in which the line between perceived and actual threat is slippery and prone to hysteria and hyperbole." Through immigration increases and decreases, retrenchment, and exclusion, the social perception of the infected immigrant threat was "far greater than the actual danger. Indeed, the number of 'diseased' immigrants has always been infinitesimal when compared with the number of newcomers admitted to this country." Americans viewed illness among immigrants already settled in the United States as an imported scourge. Policymakers employed "strikingly protean medical labels of exclusion" as a pretext for demanding immigration restriction (Markel and Stern 2002, 757).

In a prelude to Trump, Fox News anchor Lou Dobbs constructed a gargantuan myth of the diseased foreigner, his meaning Mexicans. In 2005, Dobbs cited a report that documented seven thousand cases of leprosy appearing around the country in the previous three years. "The invasion of illegal aliens is threatening the health of many Americans," he warned (quoted in Leonhardt 2017). Health authorities confirmed the seven thousand cases of leprosy in the United States, but over the previous thirty years! Dobbs admitted privately that he erred, yet never conceded it on air (Starkman 2007), as doing so would have deflated his campaign to smash undocumented immigration. In 2008, Michelle Bachmann stated in her campaign for reelection to the US Congress that unauthorized immigrants were "bringing in diseases" along with drugs and violence (quoted in Doyle 2008; see also DeParle 2019).

According to Steve Bannon, himself a believer of the "invasion" threat by "low-life" elements (Peletier 2020), Trump watched Dobbs for thirty years, "the only show he watched from beginning to end" (Wolff 2019, 159). Michael Savage, who interviewed Trump in 2011 (Peters 2019), later broadcast the absurd charge of the Democratic Party "importing disease" as a matter of policy (Savage 2015, 172–78). Echoing Savage, candidate Trump declared that Mexicans were bringing "tremendous infectious diseases," part of Mexico's policy of "forcing their most unwanted people into the United States" (Neate and Tuckman 2015).

Dobbs visited newly elected President Trump regularly (Zengerle 2019), undoubtedly advising him on health and immigration. Indeed, Stephen Miller, the president's chief adviser on immigration, tried repeatedly to use an obscure law "designed to protect the nation from diseases overseas as a way to tighten the borders." Miller, likely with more hope than suspicion, scrutinized an outbreak of mumps in immigration detention facilities and a flu outbreak in Border Patrol stations in an attempt to track down diseases among a caravan of migrants at the border, and requested updates on American communities that received migrants about new diseases and their spread (Dickerson and Shear 2020).

As Lucas Guttentag, a counselor at the Department of Homeland Security, and Stefano Bertozzi, a dean emeritus of the School of Public Health at the University of California confirmed, the Border Patrol carried out the "expulsion" (their term) of anyone arriving at US land borders without valid documents or who crossed the border illegally. It was "not because they are contagious or sick but because they come from Mexico or Canada, regardless of their country of origin." The directive to deport that the White House laid on the Centers for Disease Control violated the legal right to apply for asylum. Invoking an "arcane" provision of a quarantine law from 1893 (amended in 1944), Miller skirted laws for processing asylum applicants, expressly calling it "expulsion." Unaccompanied minors found themselves expelled at the Mexican border without any testing or finding of disease or contagion (Guttentag and Bertozzi 2020).

Immigration officials sent some 43,000 migrants back to Mexico and their home countries in the last half of the Trump presidency without due process, with more than 20,500 deported in May 2020 alone. In addition to the claimed fear of virus contagion, White House officials claimed that these steps helped conserve jobs for Americans in the ravaged economy (Kanno-Youngs and Haberman 2020). Not only did this go against data showing that immigrants were strengthening the American economy; it also portended a major squeeze on meatpacking and poultry plants that relied on immigrant labor at a time when they badly needed it (Wester 2020). Of course, the urgency of deportation intensified as the COVID-19 pandemic surged.

One citizen recognized the meta-violence behind the disease trope, in a local newspaper op-ed. The cynical use of disease for purposes of a people's expulsion followed a script long used in cases of Western nationalism. As it went: "Wherever ____ turn up, they carry . . . diseases and plagues such as cholera, dysentery, leprosy, and typhoid fever . . . just as ____ do among mankind.'" It explains that "the missing words are 'rats' and 'Jews,' and the source is the film 'The Eternal Jew,' produced in 1940 in Germany." As the citizen noted, "It is widely considered the most successful propaganda film of all time. This kind of rhetoric is bound to repeat itself. The interesting thing to observe is against whom it is delivered, and by whom it is delivered" (Phillips 2019).

Also occluded in Trumpism's rhetoric was the fact that Europeans brought disease that wiped out so much of Indigenous America, and colonizers distributed infected blankets in the name of genocide. The modern construction of the disease threat seems like a psychosocial fantasy perverting history, keeping official America from facing its historical violence.

Identitarian Whisperer

Speaking of Stephen Miller, this fellow rose to become a veritable bombardier in the political attack on the Latinx "invasion." As President Trump's chief policy adviser, Miller carved out a substantial record of repressive immigration policies and enactments, some of them already suggested above (for a full list, see Hildreth 2018). Moreover, Miller was the key driver of Trump's expulsive approach to Latinx people generally. A major takeaway from *Race Monger*, Jean Guerrero's recent biography of Miller (2020), is that he carved his white ethnic nationalism precisely out of his direct, real-life, face-to-face encounters with Mexican Americans.

Miller grew up amid California's climate of hate against undocumented Mexicans and the attempts of Republican governor Pete Wilson to deny them public services and even public education (see Montejano, this volume). On top of that, Miller became a child of the hard-core reactionary movement as it started to boil in the 1990s. With this influence, Miller became something of a right-wing prodigy.

While in high school, Miller got turned on to the ideological radio radicalism of Rush Limbaugh and the writings of National Rifle Association executive vice president Wayne LaPierre. More personally, he came to know Larry Elder, the Los Angeles conservative radio talk host who gave Miller airtime to express the reactionary views he was developing in high school. More fatefully, Miller was taken under the wing of David Horowitz, owner of the white nationalist David

Horowitz Freedom Center. A prominent enemy of liberal academia, Horowitz, in the name of freedom of speech, once defended a white fraternity charged by its university with racism, sexism, and homophobia for propagating a lurid portrayal of a Mexican preteen girl (Guerrero 2020, 6, 12).

Miller attended Santa Monica High School, which had a large ethnic-Mexican student body. As his conservative consciousness expanded, he came to the point of having what one former classmate called an "intense hatred toward Mexicans in particular," not least because he perceived them not assimilating yet "getting extra help" from the government (Guerrero 2020, 71). Miller taunted Spanish-speaking classmates, telling them that they should go back to their country. He opposed bilingual education, as an example of multiculturalism and therefore anti-American. He cut his confrontational teeth by attacking the prominent civil rights activities of students, including the Chicana and Chicano organization Movimiento Estudiantil Chicano de Aztlán, mislabeling the youth empowerment organization as a "radical national Hispanic group that believes in racial superiority" (Osnos 2018; Guerrero 2020, 56–57).

Miller argued with Mexican American students on whether or not racism existed. He engaged with the school's Mexican American counselor over the question of institutional racism and the causes of Chicano gangs, criticizing sociological explanations while claiming that their members had bad character, and lacked personal responsibility. The deadly serious student challenged the school district for funding bilingual education. To justify his grievances, he waved a racist flier that was sent anonymously to students from the Santa Monica High Association for the Advancement of Conservative White Americans. Miller brought Elder and Horowitz in to speak at the school. Elder lectured students to pull themselves up by their bootstraps and not rely on their racial identity to succeed in society, and Horowitz instructed students not to believe their high school education, especially the lie that America was racist (Guerrero 2020, 58–63, 75–76, 93; Osnos 2018; Montejano, this volume).

Miller intensified his politics at Duke University, attacking in his school paper column the institution's multicultural programs as so much "racial animus" that divisively extolled non-American cultures while ignoring the "culture we all hold in common" (Guerrero 2020, 97–98). It was at Duke that Miller turned on to immigration as politically key for conservatism. Here, he and neo-Nazi, alt-right nationalist Richard Spencer sponsored an immigration conference. Miller was greatly influenced by one participant, Peter Brimelow, whose book *Alien Nation* (1995) laid out a defense of restrictions on legal immigration, argued that undocumented immigration had negative effects on the US economy, and criticized the poem on the Statue of Liberty that called for the humanitarian inclusion of the downtrodden of the earth. Brimelow's VDARE.com promoted the idea of a white ethnic core in the United States being threatened by immigration from Third World countries. Miller would later use much of the argumentation in *Alien Nation* to advise President Trump on immigration (Guerrero 2020, 101–3, 104–5).

After college, Horowitz got Miller a job in the office of Republican Minnesota congresswoman Michelle Bachmann. As Bachmann's press secretary, Miller jumped at the opportunity to exploit the case of an undocumented Guatemalan woman who ran a stop sign, hitting a school bus and killing four white kids. Prompted by Miller, Bachmann decried the anarchy of undocumented migration and its challenge to the rule of law (Guerrero 2020, 117; DeParle 2019; Doyle 2008).

Based on Horowitz's glowing recommendation, Miller was hired in 2009 as press secretary for Alabama senator Jeff Sessions, himself a stiff foe of cross-border migration. Miller urged Sessions to oppose the appointment of Sonia Sotomayor to the US Supreme Court based on the claim that "her position as a Latina woman created conflicts of interest because she would rule with a racial bias." In addition to bashing migrants as criminals, he argued that they were bad for the economy, which Sessions applied to undermine immigration reform. Miller alerted Sessions of the need to attack President Obama's Deferred Action for Childhood Arrivals (DACA) as "back door amnesty," demanding that Obama do more to deport people to Latin American countries (Guerrero 2020, 118, 120, 123, 125–26).

While still in Sessions's office, Miller hooked up with Steve Bannon, who remembered Miller's high school activism. In 2015, Bannon made Miller part of the team at Breitbart News, a far-right media blog (Guerrero 2020, 120). This association ended up revealing Miller's white identitarian self. In news reports exposing Miller's ideological ties (including over nine hundred leaked emails), he was identified as a "de facto assignment editor" for Breitbart (Rogers 2019b), said to exude a "single-minded focus on nonwhite immigration and his immersion in an online ecosystem of virulent, unapologetic racism" (Bouie 2019). Miller had Breitbart link up with white nationalist propaganda media and figures, including Brimelow's VDARE; white supremacy theorist James Simpson (Rose 2019); and *The Camp of the Saints*, Jean Raspail's French xenophobic novel

(Peletier 2020). Miller also encouraged Breitbart to download the work of Jared Taylor's *American Renaissance* magazine, with its theories of innate Black and Brown criminality (Guerrero 2020, 121).

Eventually leaked to the public, this work to shape Breitbart coverage bared Miller as a white culture supremacist (Bouie 2019), as opposed to a white race supremacist (which he denied being) (Guerrero 2020, 274). Running with the invasion trope, Miller had Breitbart headline refugee resettlement as a plan to erase American sovereignty and culture (Rogers 2019a; 2019; King 2019). In a replacement theme, he pushed an argument by the conservative RealClear Politics that the importation of millions of low-skilled immigrants from Latin America had stalled US social mobility (Jason Wilson 2019).

Miller had already forged ties with the Federation for American Immigration Reform (FAIR) while working for Sessions. FAIR was founded by avowed white nationalist John Tanton (Kulish and McIntire 2019; Rosaldo, this volume), who criminalized Mexicans in academic publications (e.g., Tanton and Lutton 1993). FAIR embedded itself in the anti-immigration network funded by Cordelia Sciafe May, the heiress who saw southern border migrants "as a nameless, repulsive horde en route to destroy a white society" (Guerrero 2020, 127–28). A eugenicist who supported population control, May suited Miller's ethnic perspective by promoting closing off the border to stem the Mexican "invasion," their breeding "like hamsters" (Kulish and McIntire 2019). Tanton joined the meta-violent chorus, decrying the "Latin onslaught," expressing preference for "a European-American majority" (DeParle 2019).

Under Sessions, Miller laid siege on a bipartisan immigration reform bill that included a path to citizenship for unauthorized immigrants (DeParle 2019). Miller's 2013 white paper, which included large amounts of data and obscure immigration policies, argued that the bill would "decimate" the country and "cost trillions in welfare." Sessions used the report to lobby the House of Representatives. As right-wing media pressured House Republicans, Tea Party members shot the bill down. Donald Trump praised the result in an interview with Breitbart News, claiming, "Our country, our whole country is rotting, like a Third World country," and Miller later emailed friends expressing his wish that Trump would run for president (quoted and noted in Guerrero 2020, 132–36).

Miller talked his way into becoming a part of the Trump campaign for president based on his comprehensive immigration plan to make America great again. Putting forth such ideas as "Mexico's leaders have been taking advantage of the United States by using illegal immigration to export the crime and poverty in their own country," and other drastic positions to revamp immigration policy, Miller made himself at one with Trump's mindset. He helped convince Sessions to endorse Trump, which proved important for Trump's chances in the primary (Guerrero 2020, 147–48, 150–52).

Upon Trump's victory, Miller moved into the most powerful office in the land, empowered to launch a meta-violent agenda of expulsion upon the Latinx "invasion." Within days of his administration, Trump signed Enhancing Public Safety in the Interior of the United States, the executive order aimed at aliens engaging in criminal conduct, who overstayed or otherwise violated the terms of their visas, or posed "a significant threat to national security and public safety" (Trump 2017a; Orr and Restuccia 2019). Intending the order as a game changer in the war on migrant invasion, Miller asked the White House Press Office to publish a "comprehensive list" of crimes committed by migrants, which advisers warned could lead to violence against people of color (Guerrero 2020, 184). Miller continually pushed a zero-tolerance policy for unauthorized border crossings, from Sessions's authority through to the end of Trump's term, which led the number of deportees under Trump to surpass those of the two-term Obama administration (Kulish 2019; Fredericks 2018).

Section 8 of the order empowered state and local law enforcement agencies to perform the functions of an immigration officer under certain circumstances. Joe Arpaio, sheriff of Maricopa County, Arizona, exemplified the policy in action. Under Section 287(g) of the Immigration and Nationality Act, he made the apprehension of undocumented Mexicans his highest law enforcement priority. He negotiated with Immigration and Customs Enforcement (ICE) to have 160 of his deputies cross-designated by completing the ICE apprehension course. As a measure of his self-declared success by 2008, he boasted that out of 5,650 inmates, he found "an astounding 3,388 illegals among them" (Arpaio and Sherman 2008, 30–32).

A judge convicted Arpaio for ignoring the order to stop using his office for racially profiling detainees. Trump disrespected Mexicans in the presidential race by bringing him on stage, and he wanted then attorney general Jeff Sessions to drop the charges against Arpaio. Remarkably, Sessions refused to weaponize his office for Trumpian meta-violence, the start of a permanent rupture in their relationship. Shortly after Arpaio's conviction, Miller processed Trump's presidential pardon of the former sheriff (Rucker and Nakashima 2017; Bertrand 2018).

According to Guerrero (2020, 161), Trump drew from Miller's "playbook" in the way he dealt with the lawsuit against Trump University on charges of defrauding students. The judge in that case was a Mexican American, Gonzalo Curiel. Raging against Curiel's rulings for plaintiffs, Trump argued that it was Curiel's "heritage" (not his race, be it noted) that determined his judicial decisions (Epstein 2016; Ford 2016), turning him into a "Donald Trump hater" (Liptak 2016). Curiel, it should be noted, was born in Indiana. As Trump told the *Wall Street Journal*, "I'm building a wall." Curiel's involvement in the case, Trump maintained, "is an inherent conflict of interest" (both quoted in Sullivan 2016). Trump expulsively demanded an investigation of Curiel and his removal from the case. Trump alarmed legal experts with his authoritarian contempt for the First Amendment and failure to respect the separation of powers and the rule of law (Liptak 2016).

On another matter, Miller waged on in the attempt to take down Obama's DACA once and for all. DACA had been popular, with eight out of ten citizens being in support (DeParle 2019). An enlightened administration would have recognized and acknowledged that, in terms of culture and identity, DACA recipients were essentially Mexican Americans, hardly the "invaders" of conservative agitation. For these Americans, the rescission represented effective meta-violence, the prospect of banishment to a country they knew nothing about, many of them non-Spanish-speakers.

Miller doomed compromise on a bipartisan congressional bill to give Dreamers permanent protection, packing it with anti-immigrant demands that Democrats and moderate Republicans could not support (Mueller 2019; Wolff 2019, 195). Based on Miller's hard-line position, Trump signed the order terminating the program even though he privately had sympathy for the impacted youth (Guerrero 2020, 202). While federal injunctions kept DACA alive, Miller advanced social cruelty by proposing the deportation of unauthorized parents who had lived in the United States for decades, even if they had children who were US citizens and they had not committed any crimes (AV Press Releases 2018). In June 2020, the Supreme Court rejected Trump's DACA rescission, 5–4. In violent imagery, Trump called it "shotgun blasts into the face of people that are proud to call themselves Republicans or Conservatives" (tweet quoted in Williams and Edelman 2020).

Nationalistic Violence

Trump rendered the line between meta-violence and overt physical violence practically nonexistent. Letting his disaffected fans know that real violence was now legitimate politics, he intoned that perhaps "Second Amendment people" might be the ones to do something about gun-control advocate Hillary Clinton. He wished aloud that he could "punch" a heckler in the face, and he asked supporters to "knock the crap" out of protesters, promising to pay their legal fees if charged with assault (quoted in Saramo 2017, 1, 8). In chanting "U.S.A., U.S.A." at clashes with opponents, Trump supporters equated violence with "Americanness," drawing a line between those who belonged in the American nation and those who did not (Saramo 2017, 7).

Far-right domestic terrorists killed eighty-seven people in the first three years of the Trump presidency, compared to forty-six in the final three years of the Obama administration. Many of the right-wing killers supported, defended, and enabled Trump and his political agenda (Neiwart 2020). The FBI's *Hate Crime Statistics* report showed the soaring number of Latinx victims in 2018: 671 compared to 552 in 2017, an increase of over 21 percent (Brooks 2019).

Trump himself helped to set Mexicans up for political violence. When he asked a Florida crowd for ideas on how to stop migrants coming across the border, someone came back with "Shoot them!" With his sly little laugh, Trump replied, "That's only in the Panhandle you can get away with that stuff . . . only in the Panhandle" (quoted in Baker and Sheer 2019).

But not only there. On August 3, 2019, a white supremacist from Allen, Texas, walked into a Walmart in El Paso, holding a modified AK-47 at the ready, and commenced to scatter-fire across the store. Twenty-one-year-old Patrick Crusius told police on his arrest that he wanted to kill "as many Mexicans as possible" (quoted in Choiniere 2019). Twenty women, children, and men lay dead at the scene, three dying later. All but one were Mexican, five of them citizens of Mexico. In his manifesto, remarkably posted on a white supremacist site right before the attack, Crusius (2019) indicated that he was doing a favor to the white people he loved but were too stubborn and neglectful to do the things needed for their own preservation.

Did the president share in the culpability of the El Paso massacre? Beto O'Rourke, Democratic presidential candidate who represented El Paso's Sixteenth Congressional District in the House of Representatives, did not doubt it: "I'm saying that President Trump has a lot to do with what happened in El Paso yesterday. [He] sows the kind of fear, the kind of reaction that we saw in El Paso" (quoted in Baker and Shear 2019).

Among the doubters of Trump's influence, one columnist noted a "vast gap" between human slaughter and building a wall via legislative or administrative action (Lowry 2019). As possible evidence, Crusius stated in his manifesto that his ideology pre-dated Trump, forecasting that people would wrongfully blame Trump and his rhetoric for what he did. Moreover, he affirmed that his inspiration to go after the "Hispanic community" came from *The Great Replacement*, a conspiracy theory treatise penned by French racist Jean Camus (admired by Steve Bannon and Stephen Miller, who had one degree of separation from the president). The book claimed that a global elite conspired to have Western whites replaced in their countries (Cruisius 2019; see also Peletier 2020).

Trump should not be blamed, some commentators said, because he and Crusius belonged in different "moral universes" (Lowry 2019). This position seemed to be backed by what Trump tweeted after the attack (2019a):

> I know that I stand with everyone in this Country to condemn today's hateful act. There are no reasons or excuses that will ever justify killing innocent people. Today's shooting in El Paso, Texas was not only tragic, it was an act of cowardice. I know that I stand with everyone in this Country to condemn today's hateful act. There are no reasons or excuses that will ever justify killing innocent people.

Cowardice indeed. Yet it is legitimate to argue that such a cowardly act occurred at this particular moment within the field of the movement known as Trumpism. In relation to this massacre and others that took place during the administration, Jean Guerrero observes that Trump and Stephen Miller "packaged the hate that fuel[ed] white terrorism and sold it like cotton candy at an amusement park" (2020, 5).

The evidence is strong that Crusius acted in party to the "moral universe" of Trumpism. His manifesto exclaimed that "America is rotting from the inside out," just as Trump had said in an interview that Miller liked and shared, "Our whole country is rotting" (Crusius 2019; Guerrero 2020, 272). In a clearer connection, Miller in 2017 tweeted and retweeted pro-Trump photos and memes. He liked a tweet by a user showing a photo of rifles positioned to spell out "Trump." As the tweet read, "I'm extremely proud to call Trump my President! He's doing a wonderful job and is truly going to #MAGA!" Similarly, Crusius retweeted from alt-right nationalist Scott Presler, "Build that wall, Trump. Build it tall, Trump . . . #ThankYouTrump" (quoted in Choiniere 2019). This is what participation in a political movement means—accepting the leader and their word.

While much of Trump's meta-violent speech bordered on incitement, the First Amendment protected his right of freedom of expression and political speech (Saramo 2017, 20). Yet the justification seems dubious when it is remembered that the president served as leader of a vernacular movement, a meta-violent one that at moments "erupted into physical displays of aggression" (Saramo 2017, 1).

Within the parameters of a sociopolitical movement, consonance of language matters. It is thus difficult to ignore the conjunction of Trumpism's meta-violence and Crusius's violent rhetoric. Just as Crusius affirmed that his attack on El Pasoans was his "response to the Hispanic invasion of Texas" (Crusius 2019), so it happened that in the months prior to El Paso, Trump had "significantly ramped up his use of the word 'invasion'" (Greenberg and Prignano 2019). Indeed, as Carl Cameron observed, the El Paso shooting followed on Trump's "obsession with the Mexican border" (quoted in Peters et al. 2019), which prompted him to dramatically appear at security and military stations on the border and remove his secretary of Homeland Security for not being "tough enough" in the treatment of refugees (Varela 2019).

Fox News followed the leader in lockstep—and often scouted in front with ideas, stories, terminology, and Twitter food. Right up to the El Paso tragedy, celebratory anchors and guests fetishized violence in the name of nationalistic loyalty. At least eighteen talking heads boomed the fantasy banalities of invasion, replacement, "crimmigration," and drugs. In the social movement contract between Trumpism and this corner of the media, Fox laid a wreath on Trump for his "great accomplishment" of exposing an insecure border and an invasion (Peters et al. 2019).

In this zone of conservative punditry, the rhetorical venom of Ann Coulter glittered. In the month prior to the El Paso tragedy, Coulter put out what Peters et al. (2019) called "a dispassionately violent suggestion about what could be done to stem the flow of migrants"—that is, she suggested, "You can shoot invaders."

Crusius's expulsion of Mexicans from life itself appeared in the overlap of Trumpism and alt-right nationalism. His position embodied white nationalist victimism. "They [Mexicans] are the instigators, not me," he claimed. "I am simply defending my country from cultural and ethnic replacement brought on by an invasion" (Crusius 2019). Trump's protestations that hate had no place in the country and his pledge to "take care of it" (quoted in Baker and Shear 2019) rang speciously inauthentic. To some, it just made sense that the El Paso massacre followed as a "natural progression" to Trump's "unrelenting campaign to Make America White Again" (Navarrette 2019a), his meta-violence embodied.

Still, the tragedy gnawed at the sensibility of columnist Rubén Navarrete (2019b). "What do you call it," he asked, "when Mexican Americans are hunted like animals for supposedly launching an 'invasion' of a city on the U.S.-Mexico border that has a Spanish name, whose population is 80 percent Latino, mainly Mexican and Mexican American, and which used to be part of Mexico?"

The media, customarily, called it a "hate crime," but this failed to capture the political essence of the crime. This dimension of crime is explored in the HBO feature series *Our Boys*, in which the battered and burnt body of a kidnapped sixteen-year-old Palestinian is discovered; three murdered Jewish youths had turned up earlier. Mass tensions between Jews and Palestinians boiled to the brink of war. For the investigating police, the key question is whether the murder of the Palestinian constituted a (nonpolitical) "criminal killing" or a "nationalistic killing," i.e., an act of retaliation on behalf of Jews, which would have applied as well to the Palestinian killing of Jewish civilians.

Of course, Mexican/white relations on the border and the historical tensions between Jews and Palestinians in Jerusalem do not equate. Yet Crusius's unequivocally political manifesto supports the proposition that the El Paso incident constituted a "white nationalistic killing." It is worth noting in this regard that in 2019 the Department of Homeland Security finally categorized white supremacist terrorism as a primary security threat (Kanno-Youngs 2019).

Anti-Trumpism

Back at the Phoenix Walmart, Dulce Nereyda pushed back. Educating BWG in the plainest of English, she exclaimed that the United States was her country too. In the El Paso case, Trump's denunciation of the massacre sounded like so much public relations, his "false . . . fear-stoking" leaving him "ill equipped to provide the kind of unifying, healing force that other presidents projected in times of national tragedy" (Baker and Shear 2019). Wounded survivors refused to receive the president in the hospital. Cassandra Hernandez, an El Paso City Council member who represented the neighborhood where the shooting occurred, spoke for the surviving families: "Don't come here President Trump," she demanded. "You are not welcome" (quoted in Fritze and Jackson 2019).

Nereyda and the El Paso families enjoined the spirit of anti-Trumpism, the massive opposition to the president's outrageous and dangerous presidency. Trumpism's combative approach required continuous opposition from which to mobilize. Anti-Trumpism—what Cornell West defined as the "Prophetic Fightback" (quoted in Naughton 2017)—cut across a broad domain. It ranged from Democratic Party members in Congress and political institutions to highly influential news columns, social media, nonprofit organizations, donor circles, left-wing organizations, academic organizations, reform-oriented churches, classrooms, and spontaneous protesters. It even included conservative Never Trumpers, such as the Lincoln Project, with its mission to defeat Trump and protect the Constitution, and the Republicans for the Rule of Law initiative. Prophetic Fightback captured fundamental American political/civic values.

Having heard Trump "declaring a war" on their community, Latinx people joined the thousands who protested at his inauguration. One complaint focused on the exclusion of a Latinx voice in the president-elect's cabinet, a "historic setback," it was called (Gamboa 2017). Congressman Joaquín Castro, chair of the Congressional Hispanic Caucus, collaborated with then senator Kamala Harris to introduce a resolution calling for Stephen Miller to resign for his hateful, cruel, and white nationalist shaping of the presidency (Wermund 2019). Electorally, Mexican Americans counted among a stream of progressive Democrats, most notably women dedicated to combatting Trump, winning primary elections up and down the 2020 ballot. The case of Teresa Leger Fernandez particularly stood out. This win spelled an all-woman and all-person-of-color congressional delegation for New Mexico, two Latinxs and one Native American (Epstein, Medina, Corasaniti 2020). The Congressional Hispanic Caucus also challenged Trump's orders to deploy ICE and other border protection agencies to help the Secret Service and other federal and local law enforcement detain suspected unauthorized immigrants during the George Floyd protests in Washington, DC (Congressional Hispanic Caucus 2020; Acevedo 2020).

Mexican American law enforcement officials were not afraid to challenge. Art Acevedo, Houston's chief of police, registered objection to Trump's law-and-order edict to governors to deploy the National Guard during the Floyd protests, and his threats to send in US military "to solve the problem for them." Acevedo informed a correspondent that the nation's police chiefs were not in favor of "domination," Trump's meta-violent code for wholesale clampdown on protestors. Addressing the president, Acevedo said, "if you don't have something constructive to say, keep your mouth shut because you're putting men and women in their early 20s at risk" (quoted in Barker 2020).

Undocumented students formed a major force of resistance. Raymond Rocco's (2014) theory of "associative citizenship" argues that national belonging occurs when immigrants and nonimmigrants unite to engage the conditions of their marginalization. In his key example, it was in 2006 that 3.7 to 5 million people "filled the streets in over a hundred and sixty cities in forty-two states. In every region of the United States, immigrants and their allies contested the harsh anti-immigrant policies and practices that had gone on for nearly 20 years, and that culminated with the House of Representatives passing HR 4437 in December 2005." As Rocco states, it was not simply a challenge to the issue of the regularization of the status of undocumented people. It was "a declaration of the demand for full membership . . . an indication that the protesters were advancing a new concept of what it means to be 'an American.' It was in fact about the need to expand the notion of 'belonging' and citizenship to include those who have for so long been perceived and treated as lying outside the boundaries of the normative public imaginary of who is an American" (209).

Reenacting associative citizenship two months after Trump's inauguration, thousands of undocumented high school students throughout the country staged school walkouts in protest of the president's pledge to deport millions of immigrants. Students at hundreds of universities and colleges followed suit. Professors and other allies joined students in classroom walkouts, sit-ins, freeway blockages, and informational gatherings (Cosecha 2017).

The impact of this mobilization had added significance for "belonging." Sarah Song elaborates on the proposition that in a democracy, membership in the polity among noncitizen immigrants should be predicated not on legal status or ethnicity/race, but on collective action that affects shared institutions. While the provision of basic rights and other substantive goods "is a necessary condition of legitimate political authority," Song writes, "it is not sufficient. People have an interest not just in receiving goods but also in shaping the institutions under which they live." It is part of the meaning of "collective self-determination" for "a people" covered by a democratic polity (2018, 55).

Undocumented anti-Trumpers fulfilled this realization. The student group Cosecha led the launch of the #SanctuaryCampus campaign, in which students challenged universities and other institutions to provide protection, respect, and dignity for undocumented students, particularly around the potential of ICE raids on campus (Cosecha 2017). Significant for belonging through engagement, the national council of the American Association of University Professors backed the call (AAUP 2016). Faculty members across the country enlisted in the campaign. Hundreds of colleges and universities publicly announced that they would support their undocumented students either by the use of the #SanctuaryCampus hashtag or through a similar designation such as "safe harbor campus" (Flannery 2017).

The wave spread far and wide. By 2020, over 171 municipalities and/or counties and 11 states declared sanctuary status (Griffith and Vaughan 2020). Trump threatened to withhold millions of dollars of federal funds to sanctuary jurisdictions for limiting cooperation with federal immigration enforcement. The United States Court of Appeals for the Seventh Circuit upheld two lower-court rulings that blocked the administration from placing immigration-related conditions on law enforcement grants (Hesson 2020).

Through such anti-Trumpism, Latinx communities demonstrated the strength of their commitment to belonging within the American political fold. Significantly, staff at American institutions agreed. Student civic engagement, performance, and direct confrontation with Trump's anti-immigration policies gave the lie to white nationalism and the suggestion that only whites belonged to the privileged circle of people in the United States. Anti-Trumpism was seen as well in the celebratory mobilization that erupted among Latinx and undocumented forces to the news that the Supreme Court had denied Trump's attempt to call off DACA, illustrated profoundly by an elated undocumented family holding up a sign that read, "Here to Stay" (de Vogue, Cole, and Ehrlich 2020).

By such action, undocumented participants established their belonging to "the people" of the United States, not by cultural criteria, but in their assertive resort "in efforts that aim at collective self-governance" (Song 2018, 57). Through such voluntary acts of political agency, reshaping public institutions, and, quite significantly, working with non-Mexicans, undocumented youth challenged the American state to meet its humanitarian obligation to "protect the human rights of all territorially present persons" (188).

If such a recognition of participation and belongingness were to find itself institutionalized policy-wise, normatively, and legally—starting with the Biden administration—Mexican immigrants, and Mexican Americans by extension, would gain the respect of self-actuated members of the American polity. Mexicans and other groups of color would, as members of true standing in American "peoplehood" (Song 2018), be shielded from the indignities of the base assailment, metapolitical violence, and nationalistic homicide that occurred during Donald Trump's presidency, 2017–2020.

CHAPTER TWO

To Wield and Exceed the Law

Mexicans, Migration, and the Dream
of Herrenvolk Democracy

CRISTINA BELTRÁN

Introduction: Immigration and the Politics of the White Racial Imaginary

That Donald Trump exploited and encouraged anti-immigrant sentiment to win the American presidency in 2016 is a political fact as obvious as it is incontrovertible. One of the rare points of consistency in Trump's politics has been his unwavering commitment to stoking nativist animosity, from his pledge to build a wall at the southern border, to his call for a "deportation force" to round up unauthorized immigrants, to his proposals to deport Dreamers and defund sanctuary cities, to his "zero tolerance" policy that put children in cages, to deploying US military troops to "defend" the US-Mexico border.[1] More recently, in confronting the global pandemic of COVID-19, Trump began referring to the disease as "the Chinese virus" while exploiting public health law to deny refugees the ability to apply for asylum. Faced with an unprecedented public health crisis, Trump's response was to revert to his earlier practice of characterizing migrants as agents of contamination.[2]

Yet long before the election of Donald Trump, vitriolic and dehumanizing rhetoric against migrants was already part of our national political conversation.[3] Anti-immigrant hostility was already visible in a stream of xenophobic and racially charged statements, proposals, and policies coming from a variety of organizations and individuals (Ibe 2019). In 2010, Tennessee lawmaker Curry Todd likened undocumented immigrants to "rats [who] multiply," while in 2011, Kansas state representative Virgil Peck suggested that illegal migrants be shot "like feral hogs" (quoted in Wing 2010; quoted in Murphy 2011). In 2006, Congressman Steve King of Iowa, one of the most well-known anti-immigrant members of Congress who has a long history of denigrating migrants and people of color, suggested that the United States build an electrified fence to keep out migrants. Six years later, King gave a speech comparing immigrants to dogs.[4]

The ugly rhetoric of Todd, Peck, King, and others shows how immigration has become an increasingly partisan issue, dividing conservatives from liberals. At the same time, anti-immigrant sentiment has grown so intense that it is also fracturing the American Right. This divide—between conservatives who favor neoliberal forms of free trade that depend on immigrant labor and the more nativist wing of the party—was on spectacular display at the 2018 Conservative Political Action Conference (CPAC), the annual political conference attended by conservative activists and elected officials from across the United States and, increasingly, Europe.[5] At the only panel dedicated to the topic of immigration at the 2018 gathering, audience members "drown[ed] out panelists' presentation of the data about the benefits of immigration" with boos and jeers:

> During a heated question and answer session during the immigration panel, a man from Four Corners, Virginia, went on an extended diatribe about a Latino man who once crashed his car in front of his house. "I had to go down to court to testify, and I was the only white face in the crowd other than the lawyers being paid to translate for these people," he said. "You can go down to Four Corners Park and see obvious illegal immigrants defecating in the woods, fornicating in the woods, and on and on and on. These people are not the immigrants of the '20s and '30s. They will *never* be able to get good jobs here and be good citizens. Is *that* in your study?" (Ollstein 2018)

As David Bier, a policy analyst with the libertarian Cato Institute funded by the Charles Koch Foundation, attempted to lay out research proving that immigrants actually have lower crime rates than native-born Americans, contribute significantly to the economy, and are assimilating just as well or better than past generations of immigrations, his fellow panelists derided his statements as "nutty," and angry audience members shouted him down. As Bier cited research to counter incorrect claims from his fellow panelists and the audience that recent immigrants were disproportionately criminal, an economic drain on government, or took several generations to learn English, he experienced vocal hostility (Ollstein 2018). Insisting that today's immigrants are demographically and racially threatening ("I was the only white face"), disproportionately criminal, "obviously" illegal, impossible to assimilate, and spectacularly bestial ("defecating in the woods, fornicating in the woods"), it became clear why CPAC organizers had decided to hold only *one* panel on the issue of immigration: additional events would have made the deep divide among conservatives even more conspicuous. Yet even at this one event, the split was as unmistakable as it was ontological. Both attendees and panelists at CPAC refused to accept not only the accuracy but also the very *reality* of the facts and data presented by the Cato Institute. For a specific segment of politicians, pundits, activists, and voters, immigrants—particularly those from Mexico and other parts of Latin America—serve as a kind of affective trigger, touching off paroxysms of rage and frustration regarding what they see as an existential threat to the United States, its economic future, sovereign integrity, and its racial and cultural identity.

This chapter seeks to answer a fundamental question: Why has immigration—particularly from Mexico and Latin America—become such a potent and emotionally galvanizing issue for the American Right? What is driving this upsurge in anti-Latinx nativism at this particular historical moment? And why are Latinxs (particularly migrants, but native-born Latinxs as well) such an affectively charged population for political conservatives—most of whom identify with the Republican Party?

The intensity of nativist sentiment on the Right—their conviction that the United States is facing an ever-worsening immigration crisis that must be confronted with violence and increasingly draconian measures—is made all the more striking by the fact that unauthorized immigration has been falling for more than a decade. In 2007, for example, there were 6.9 million unauthorized Mexicans living in the United States. A decade later in 2017, the number was down by 2 million. Mexicans now make up less than half of all unauthorized immigrants living in the United States (González-Barrera and Krogstad 2019; Passel and Cohn 2018), and since 2015, Mexican migration to the United States has been net negative (González-Barrera 2015). As Tomás Jiménez discusses in this volume, even before the economic downturn of 2008, the incentives for Mexicans to go north had sharply declined. Indeed, today, the steady size of the Mexican-origin population in the United States "is maintained entirely by the birth of *US-born individuals*, creating a Mexican-origin population that is now more demographically dominated by the US population than at any point in the last three decades" (emphasis added). Shifting economic opportunities in Mexico and the United States and changing fertility patterns—not "tough, zero-tolerance" policies—are what have reshaped patterns of migration. And while migrants are still coming from violence-plagued Guatemala, Honduras, and El Salvador to seek *legal* asylum, those three countries *combined* contain "about one-quarter as many people as Mexico" (Beinart 2018).

Alongside these demographic realities, polls also show that immigration is becoming a far less divisive issue for the majority of the US population. The share of Americans calling for lower levels of immigration has fallen from a high of 65 percent in the mid-1990s to just 35 percent today, a record low. Today, the percentage of Americans saying immigrants "mostly help the economy" is at its highest point since Gallup began asking the question in 1993 (Jones 2019). A Pew Research Center (2017) poll asking if immigrants "strengthen [the] country with their hard work and talents" found affirmative responses at an all-time high. Yet for nativist voters, the United States remains a nation besieged. A study of the 2016 presidential election by Diana Mutz at the National Academy of Sciences found that Trump voters in 2016 were motivated less by economic anxiety and more by fears of cultural displacement and the waning power and status of whiteness. For example, whites who said discrimination against white peoples is "a serious problem" were much more likely to favor Trump. Even more significantly, white voters who favored deporting immigrants living in the country illegally were 3.3 times more likely to express a preference for Trump than those who did not (Mutz 2018).

Of course, anti-immigrant policies that make life more violent and precarious for immigrants have long been bipartisan, including at the executive level. Before Trump, Ronald Reagan, George H. W. Bush, Bill Clinton, George W. Bush, and Barack Obama all supported laws and policies that made migration a more punitive and perilous process.[6] Yet despite this long history of both parties criminalizing migration, a growing share of Republican politicians and voters seek something beyond enforcement. They also desire visible displays of cruelty and suffering aimed at migrants. Increasingly indignant over what they perceive as government tolerance for "illegal" immigrants, nativists take satisfaction in the violent targeting of those they feel have broken laws with impunity.

Numerous studies show that support for punitive immigration policies is central to why certain voters support Republicans more generally (and Donald Trump in particular), yet there is little in-depth analysis as to *why* this support is so central. For example, political scientists Abrajano and Hajnal provide outstanding data analysis showing that anti-immigrant (and often anti-Latinx) policy preferences play a significant role in the large-scale defection of whites from the Democratic to the Republican Party, yet they acknowledge, "One question we have not answered is why so many white Americans feel threatened by immigration in the first place" (2015, 49). Ultimately, like a number of scholars whose research measures anti-immigrant sentiment, Abrajano and Hajnal simply note, "There is something significant about immigration itself that matters to white Americans when they make basic political decisions" (51).

This chapter, which is part of a larger book project, seeks to identify that "something significant" and explore questions about long-standing nativism.[7] Namely, what constitutes the nativist imaginary? What becomes politically possible in the worlds that nativists envision? Finally, while recognizing that anger, resentment, and fear are central to nativist sentiment, how should we understand the various pleasures that come with describing and enacting antimigrant practices and policies? Why do certain forms of performative cruelty resonate with so many Republican voters? What sorts of civic satisfaction and meaning are made possible through anti-immigrant speech and action? Moreover, what is the historical and political context for such delightful horrors?

As I explore these questions, I seek to make sense of contemporary antimigrant sentiment by confronting the violent and emotionally fraught history that political theorist Joel Olson (2004) refers to as the "democratic problem of the white citizen" and that W. E. B. Du Bois (1915) described as "democratic despotism." Moving beyond studies that treat *whiteness* as a "neutral physical description of certain persons," this chapter approaches whiteness as a *political project* — "a social relation that is both dynamic and historical" (Olson 2004, xix, 9–10). Turning to works of political theory, history, and cultural and critical race studies, this essay examines how whiteness functions as an ideology invested in the unequal distribution of wealth, power, and privilege — a form of racial hierarchy in which "the standing of one section of the population is premised on the debasement of another" (Alcoff 2005, 15; see also Olson 2004, xv).[8] As Olson notes, racial oppression "makes full democracy impossible, but it has also made American democracy possible" (2004, xv). According to Olson, the United States can best be understood as "a white democracy, a polity ruled in the interests of a white citizenry and characterized by simultaneous relations of equality and privilege: equality among whites, who are privileged in relation to those who are not white" (xv). Indeed, for the majority of its history and until the passage of the Civil Rights Act of 1964, whiteness operated as a form of racialized *standing*, a status that "granted all whites a superior social status to all those who were not white, particularly African Americans" (Olson 2008, 704). Scholars have sometimes referred to the form of white democracy and whiteness-as-standing as Herrenvolk democracy, a regime that is "democratic for the master race but tyrannical for the subordinate groups" (van den Berghe 1967, 18).[9] Feeling victimized by the rich and powerful while also feeling under assault from those "below" (often people of color), white citizens in this form of racialized republicanism were reassured that "one might lose everything but not whiteness," despite the system's failure to produce greater social and political equality overall (Roedigger 2007, 60).

Following this vein, this chapter explores how white racial standing offered American citizens the material, psychological, and political satisfaction of being white subjects protected by individual rights and the rule of law while simultaneously allowing them the freedom and power to deny those same protections to those deemed nonwhite. Most significant here, under Herrenvolk democracy, whiteness as standing was *legally* sanctioned. Indian removal, chattel slavery, the Chinese Exclusion Act, inferior Mexican schools, all-white police forces, racially exclusive housing covenants, Japanese internment, all-white juries, segregated facilities under Jim Crow in the South and Juan Crow in the Southwest—all these examples demonstrate that for the majority of US history, white supremacy was not simply culturally acceptable but also *legally* authorized; racial discrimination not simply de facto, but often de jure. White citizens had the legal right to deny equal rights to nonwhite citizens. Democratic for whites, but tyrannical for subordinate groups, Herrenvolk democracy meant white citizens had access to the key components of constitutional liberalism defined by the rule of law and characterized by civil and political rights and civil liberties. Yet this form of liberalism was situated within a symbiotic relationship with white supremacy, in which the value of liberal citizenship was made manifest through the denial of equal rights and legal equality to nonwhite populations.

Of course, it is important to recognize that the political meaning of whiteness emerged through a series of choices that could have gone differently. In his seminal work regarding England's first and most important continental colony, historian Edmund Morgan (1975) chronicles the devolution of racial politics in colonial Virginia and how cross-racial association among Virginia's lower classes was transformed over time into a political system based on race hatred, enslavement, and contempt.

In Virginia, the labor needed for the cultivation and export of tobacco was met initially by use of indentured servants.[10] Subject to beatings, abuse, and overwork, servants were sometimes sold without their consent up to the expiration of the indenture. Many did not survive the terms of servitude. However, those who survived and gained their freedom could then work to become planters in their own right. Alongside indentured servitude and free wage labor, chattel slavery was also established in the colonies, with Portuguese ships supplying the Spanish and Portuguese settlements in America with African slaves. The first Africans arrived in Jamestown, Virginia, in 1619, and as historian Winthrop Jordan has observed, while very little is known about their precise status during the next twenty years, we do know that slaves formed only a small part of the Virginia labor force until the 1680s (1968, 44).

While indentureship was never as dehumanizing as lifetime, hereditary slavery, in their shared exposure to servitude, at least some servants and slaves initially saw each other as experiencing a similar predicament. As Morgan demonstrates, Black and white servants laboring on the plantation and bound to the same master "worked, ate, and slept together" and shared in "escapades, escapes, and punishments" (1975, 155). It was not was uncommon for servants and slaves "to run away together, steal hogs together, get drunk together" (327). Indeed, during Bacon's Rebellion in 1676, "one of the last groups to surrender was a racially mixed band of eighty Negroes and twenty English servants" (327).

Bacon's Rebellion revealed the possibilities of an alliance between white and Black servants and slaves against the policies of the ruling class. At the same time, the rebellion highlighted how race hatred (in this case, against Indigenous populations) could unite subjects across their differences. For the colony's elite, the lesson of the rebellion was that "resentment of an alien race might be more powerful than resentment of an upper class" (Morgan, 269–70). The gradual substitution of African and Indian slaves for white servants after 1680 helped resolve Virginia's labor problems, enhancing the experience of freedom and equality among whites through the increased degradation of Blacks. Laws made it illegal for whites to be employed by Blacks, and prohibited Blacks, regardless of status, from owning firearms. Poll taxes were drastically reduced, making it easier for free white men to vote while free Blacks were being stripped of the right to vote, testify in court, or serve on juries (Olson 2004, 37). Over time, Virginia's white small farmers began to perceive a common identity with the large farmers, because "neither was a slave. And both were equal in not being slaves" (Morgan, 381). In sum, the story of colonial Virginia helps us see how racism became an "essential if unacknowledged" aspect of America's attachment to the values of equality and republicanism.

Premised on colonial dispossession and settlement and enriched through the stolen labor of human beings held as property, the story of colonial Virginia demonstrates how white democracy both precedes and undergirds the very existence of the American nation-state. White citizens came to see themselves and their communities as defenders and beneficiaries of liberal democracy. Equally important, the very fact that opportunity was *not* guaranteed (even for white citizens) served to obscure the power and pervasiveness of white democracy. Indeed, examples of white failure, poverty, and underperformance could be interpreted as proof of the system's fairness, reinforcing the conviction that one's achievements were personal rather than simultaneously racial and historical. In an experience that felt less like privilege and more like fairness, spaces of whiteness and racial domination (neighborhoods, schools, workplaces, territories) were experienced by white citizens as sites of freedom and opportunity where (white) mobility was encouraged, (white) equality was possible, and the rule of law and the values of constitutional liberalism prevailed. In this way, for many white Americans, the American Dream denotes a racialized sensorium whose possibilities feel genuine. Schools, neighborhoods, and community institutions were made white through racialized exclusions, violent practices of domination, and the denial of equality, opportunity, and protection under the law for nonwhite populations. Yet these racialized exclusions often went unacknowledged and unnamed.

At the same time, Herrenvolk democracy was about more than simply excluding nonwhite populations and hoarding resources. Herrenvolk democracy was, and is, also importantly about racial domination—about the violent freedom to both wield and exceed the law. The lynching, raping, defrauding, assaulting, and murdering of nonwhite populations were all practices that had the explicit and tacit consent of local, state, and federal governments throughout the Herrenvolk era. The tyrannical character of Herrenvolk democracy made it inevitable that white citizens would not simply desire unequal applications of the law, but they would also seek to *be* the law—to replace the rule of law with their own actions and judgements and to see racial domination as the practice of freedom. In sum, Herrenvolk democracy begets violence and teaches tyranny.

With passage of the Civil Rights Act of 1964 and the Voting Rights Act of 1965, Herrenvolk democracy was dealt an apparently lethal blow. Undercutting the legal bedrock of white supremacy, civil rights legislation marked the end of lawful racial discrimination and the sanctioned exercise of whiteness-as-standing. Because the law now prohibits racial discrimination, whites no longer have access to a state explicitly committed to ensuring their personal standing as white. Yet despite the official repeal of Herrenvolk democracy, Olson argues, whiteness continues to operate as "a form of social power," with many white citizens revealing "an interest in and an expectation of favored treatment in a polity whose fundamental principle is that all men are created equal." Today, white advantage is now reproduced "via norms" that operate as a system of "tacit and concealed racial privileges." Such norms are "reproduced less through overt forms of discrimination" and more through "everyday practices" that presume white advantage as the "natural outcome of market forces and individual choices" (Olson 2008, 709).

Today, for citizens still drawn to the politics of whiteness, the end of Herrenvolk democracy is experienced as a form of political loss and the diminishment of freedom. For nativist voters drawn to the politics of whiteness, access to whiteness as standing appears both tantalizingly conceivable yet legally (and often morally) disavowed. Experienced as an increasingly unattainable promise, citizens invested in the politics of whiteness exist in a state of enraged betrayal, attached to forms of whiteness they feel entitled to, yet find increasingly difficult to attain.

It is here—in this political context—where Latinx migrants emerge as a particularly potent target for nativist desire, rage, and fear. I argue that that migrants (with or without legal sanction) represent the rare population that offer nativists an administratively endorsed opportunity to access and revisit the power and pleasures of Herrenvolk democracy. As noncitizens, migrants are vulnerable to both state-sanctioned *and* extralegal practices of violence and terror. Witnessing and describing violent and authoritarian policies makes nativists feel stronger, freer, and more agentic, transforming acts of racialized violence into feats of heroism, democratic redemption, civic engagement, and virtuous sovereignty.[11] And just as with Herrenvolk logics of the past, such violence inevitably exceeds its boundaries, as nativists seek to both wield and exceed the law, denying rights and deploying violence against not only unauthorized migrants but legal immigrants and Latinx citizens as well.

In sum, my argument is *not* that racism reveals the hypocrisy of a nation that espouses the ideals of freedom, equality, and democracy. It is that American conceptions of equality, freedom, and democracy have historically been *constituted through* white supremacy. In other words, the *experience* of democracy, equality, and freedom cannot be detached from the political project of whiteness in the United States. My contention is that oppression and American democracy have been "mutually constitutive rather than antithetical" to one another (Olson 2004, xv). Appreciating how race has fundamentally shaped our conceptions of sovereignty, tyranny, and the rule of law, this essay echoes Lisa Lowe's call for a

"critical genealogy of liberalism" that explores how liberalism's abstract promises "were produced through placing particular subjects at a distance from the
'human'" (Lowe 2015, 167). While critics like Adam Serwer (2018) have rightly
argued that when it comes to the bond between Trump and his supporters, "the
cruelty is the point," my claim is that such cruelty is not only an experience of
collective pride and delight; it's also a particular type of civic experience. The
simultaneous experience of public happiness and racial tyranny is precisely what
freedom and equality feel like in the context of Herrenvolk democracy. In other
words, whiteness needs reconceptualization not only as discriminatory practice,
but as a *democratic* practice—a mass-based, participatory practice of exclusion
and performative membership with fellow (white) citizens. For those invested
in an ideology of whiteness, racial exclusion and domination *produces* a sense
of membership, creating a common-sense understanding of community, opportunity, futurity, and possibility.

Yet in seeking to deepen our understanding of the relationship between Mexicans, migration, and the politics of whiteness, my analysis also takes seriously
the complicated relationship that Latinxs and other racialized populations have
to the politics of immigration and the politics of whiteness. From the original
Naturalization Act of 1790, which limited naturalization to "free white persons,"
to the Chinese Exclusion Act of 1882 to Mexican Repatriation in the 1920 and
'30s, much of US immigration law is a history of racialized assaults on segments
of the US immigrant population. Such attacks on nonwhite immigrants are a
significant reason why the story of immigration has long been a story of various populations trying to either claim whiteness and/or assert themselves as
not-Black in order to claim rights and standing and avoid the state-sanctioned
violence and exclusions typically visited upon populations deemed nonwhite.
While Latinxs have been victims of white supremacy and white democracy,
some have also worked to claim whiteness, seeking the privileges and pleasures
of a polity that denies rights and dignity to those deemed nonwhite.[12]

Historically, Mexican Americans have been enmeshed in a complex racial
order based not only on Euro-American colonialism but also on a preexisting Spanish colonial order that led to complex racial dynamics in relation to
questions of Indigeneity and settlement. During Spanish colonial rule, some
Mexicans participated in the enslavement of Indians while others claimed alliances with tribal populations. After 1848, Mexican elites "accommodated, contested, and negotiated their position in the new American racial order" (Gómez
2018, 5). At times, this process involved claiming white status and distancing

themselves from alliances with tribal populations. As Gómez notes, in places like New Mexico, American colonizers were able to co-opt those Mexican Americans willing to trade in on their mestizo, part-European heritage in order to "divide Mexican Americans from their Pueblo neighbors" (119).

As Latinx studies scholars have long noted, such practices of colonial authority and co-optation highlight the historically ambiguous racial position of Mexicans, exemplifying the fact that Latinxs "have no simple positioning in the U.S. racial order" (Bebout 2016, 4; see also Gómez 2018; Hattam 2007; Mora 2014). Latinxs have been characterized at various times as white, nonwhite, Indigenous, Black, and not-Black. As HoSang and Lowndes argue, "While racial subordination is an enduring feature of U.S. political history, it continually changes in response to shifting social and political conditions, interests and structures. . . . Race performs dynamic and often contradictory work, continuing to produce hierarchy and exclusion while also articulating new forms of mobility and incorporation" (2019, 5–6). I argue that the internal diversity and racial indeterminacy of Latinxs actually makes certain forms of violence *more* feasible and defensible. In a political era where state-sanctioned racism is prohibited by law and de facto (if not de jure), racial equality prevails, the racial ambiguity of Latinx populations in relation to whiteness offers nativists the opportunity to deploy racist and dehumanizing representations of nonwhite "illegals" within a sanctioned legal discourse defined in terms of criminality, sovereignty, legality, and fairness. Opposition to immigration from Mexico and Latin America is the rare issue that combines the pleasures of violent white domination (Herrenvolk practices) alongside color-blind assertions of the rule of law.

For citizens who long to revive the politics of whiteness as standing, the practices of Immigration and Customs Enforcement (ICE) and the Customs and Border Protection (CBP) offer citizens the right to use the law to police populations, to impose tyranny while participating in forms of violence that feel like freedom—the freedom to economically exploit particular populations, the freedom to enforce the law, and the frontier freedom of engaging in practices of settler sovereignty characterized by forced removal and transfer. For those enamored of whiteness as standing, the power and value of ICE, CPB, and volunteer militias also lies in the *spectacles* of racialized violence and cruelty they offer their fellow nativists. Pictures of children in cages, families running from tear gas at the border, masses of incarcerated Latinx men in detention facilities, images of ICE agents arresting migrants, pictures of children crying— such visions of Herrenvolk violence offer nativists confirmation that those in charge are finally "doing something" about the scourge of illegal immigration. Beyond visual spectacles of cruelty, newspaper accounts of the filth and stench experienced by migrants in overcrowded holding pens, immigration raids, mass roundups, and quotes from their political opposition expressing horror at the current situation offer vicarious pleasures and satisfaction to nativists longing to see the United States defending its sovereignty and inflicting harm on a population viewed as invasive, dishonest, destructive, dangerous, and criminal.

Nativists also had access to the democratic and participatory experience of the Trump political rally. Trump's rallies offered nativists access to a collective space of community—one in which they could gather together in a public, share in the pleasure of Trump's violent anti-immigrant oratory, and give voice to their own visions of violence, whiteness, and pleasure by wearing T-shirts with violent, misogynistic, and/or racist phrases, chanting slogans and yelling into the crowd. Offering nativists a chance to revisit elements of the white mob that citizens had access to in the Herrenvolk era, rallygoers got to cheer and chant phrases like "build the wall," "lock her up," and "send them back," while boo- ing the media (Crowley 2019; Flynn 2019; Timmons 2019). Performing a kind of lynching in speech, the Trump rally—galvanized by the president's Twitter feed—offered nativists the chance to publicly indulge their desire for freedom from restraint.[13] Indeed, as historian Amy Wood argues, it is the act of "witness- ing" that underlies the particular form of spectatorship linked to the practice of lynching (2009, 4). As a deeply embodied and sensory-laden practice, to act as a witness is to "play a public role, one that bestows a particular kind of social authority on the individual, at the same time that it connects the individual to a larger community of fellow witnesses" (4). Similarly, like spectators at a lynching, Trump rallies brought attendees together through a shared act of wit- nessing. Experiencing the "push of the crowd" while being "physically near the scene of the action and among a crowd of like-minded people," spectators at a Trump rally were united through a shared sensorium and in the belief that they were witness to something "important or extraordinary" (31). In sum, through racialized rituals of participation and performance, MAGA rally attendees got to revisit elements of white democracy that citizens had access to in the Herrenvolk era (Sonmez and DeBonis 2019; Samuels 2019).

Together, rally attendees created a right-wing counterpublic—one that al- lowed them to experience a collective sense of white peoplehood. Witnessing each other cheering for a world of racialized violence and removal, rallygoers were encouraged to imagine a society where migrants were treated with impunity—rounded up, arrested, punished, and deported at will.

At the same time, we witnessed a growing rupture between white citizens who supported the enhanced visibility of this right-wing counterpublic and its investments in the politics of white democracy and those white citizens increasingly appalled by racist and xenophobic appeals to whiteness that stoked white resentment. This divide among white citizens represents an underappreciated aspect of political polarization today. This political tension reflects our uncertain future—a space of both democratic dangers as well as possibilities.

A Desire for Land but Not People: Herrenvolk Democracy and the Violent Legacies of the Mexican-American War

Theorizing white democracy through the field of Latinx studies requires turning to the history of western expansion and the racial politics of the frontier to grasp how the legacy of anti-Mexican violence shapes the rage-infused politics of American nativism today. Engaging the work of Arnoldo De León, Greg Grandin, David G. Gutiérrez, María Josefina Saldaña-Portillo, Jason de León, Kelly Lytle Hernandez, and Monica Muñoz Martinez, this essay turns to the politics of western expansion, especially the participatory politics of Indigenous dispossession and the war with Mexico, to explore the relationship between contemporary border politics, antimigrant sentiment and an American conception of frontier freedom founded on conquest and the right to movement and expansion. Exploring the conjoined histories of the frontier and the border allows us to see how American conceptions of freedom, sovereignty, democracy, citizenship, and the law have been shaped by this racialized legacy of legal and extrajudicial violence.[14]

Building on a rich body of Latinx scholarship, I argue the Herrenvolk politics of the frontier and the US-Mexico border represent particularly significant sites for considering how the conjoined legacies of war, slavery, conquest, settler-colonialism, and white supremacy continue to define, distort, and circumscribe American conceptions of law, freedom, sovereignty, movement, democracy, and citizenship. The frontier offered white citizens the freedom to claim territory, challenge borders, and engage in Herrenvolk practices of removal, settlement, and displacement—while also acquiring wealth and participating in acts of political creation through settling the West. Moving between frontier freedom and frontier justice, settlers struggled to establish and extend white democracy—a process that often involved violent assaults on Mexicans and Indians. By "demonstrating [their] mastery over the unmastered wild," settlers saw themselves as involved in a violent and epic struggle for the future, willing to risk their lives in order to bring justice and civilization to a dangerous and savage world (Livingston 2016, 81).

The Mexican-American war (1846–1848) offers an underexamined example of how the legacy of white democracy has come to shape contemporary border politics. Indeed, in 1836, when Texas won its independence from Mexico, Andrew Jackson stated that annexing the republic of Texas would expand America's "area of freedom" and extend its "circle of free institutions" (quoted in Grandin 2019, 84). However, the conception of freedom being articulated by the Anglo settlers of the Texas republic was deeply racialized—not only were most settlers from the Deep South, many were also "land speculators, slavers, militia leaders, and Indian killers" (Grandin 2019, 85). Such racialized politics had a profound impact on class conflict and class politics in the United States. For example, in 1848 (the same year that war with Mexico ended) workers in multiple countries across Europe revolted, built barricades, established labor parties and unions and called for the "social-democratization of European politics" (Grandin 2019, 95).

By contrast, while the United States also had hungry, exploited workers, "instead of waging class war upward—on aristocrats and owners," white workers "waged race war outward, on the frontier." "'Prentice' boys didn't head to the barricades to fight the gentry," writes Grandin, but rather, "joined with the gentry to go west and fight Indians and Mexicans" (2019, 95). Exploring the conjoined histories of the frontier and the border allows us to see how American conceptions of freedom, sovereignty, democracy, citizenship, and the law have been shaped by this racialized legacy of legal and extrajudicial violence. I see this history of anti-Mexican politics not only impacting other Latinx populations, but revealing how racialized violence continues to influence today's aggressive nativist politics.

The war concluded in 1848 with the signing of the Treaty of Guadalupe Hidalgo, which provided official recognition of the United States' previous annexation of Texas and ceded to the United States one-third of Mexico's territory, including all or part of California, Arizona, Nevada, Utah, Wyoming, Colorado, Kansas, Oklahoma, and New Mexico for a payment of $15 million.[15] The war transferred to the United States a total of about five hundred thousand square miles, resulting in a permanent southern border, "running about two thousand miles from Brownsville, Texas, to San Diego, California" (Grandin 2019, 92–93).

Home to over 115,000 Mexicans who eventually became US citizens (Gómez 2018, 1), the newly annexed land was made up of a diverse population that included "old-line Spanish families, who could trace their land claims back generations, centuries even; their mestizo and mulatto servants and ranch hands, along with other laborers; thousands of migrants in California, prospecting for gold; and scores of indigenous peoples, including Apache, Navajo, Pueblo, Ute, Yaqui, and Tohono O'odham" (Grandin 2019, 92, 94).

The war made the United States a continental power while also exacerbating tensions between free and slave states. In 1836, William H. Wharton, an American colonist, diplomat, statesman, and advocate for Texas's complete independence from Mexico, described the reasons why Americans should support the Texas revolution. He argued that a just and benevolent God would forbid that Texas "again become a howling wilderness, trod only by savages" and "permanently benighted by the ignorance and superstition, the anarchy and rapine of Mexican misrule" (quoted in De León 1983, 2–3). Describing the task of Texas settlement, Wharton characterizes it as a project that is as racial as it is republican:

> The Anglo-American races are destined to be forever the proprietors
> of this land of *promise* and *fulfillment*. *Their* laws will govern in, *their*
> learning will enlighten it, *their* enterprise will improve it. *Their* flocks
> will range its boundless pastures, for *them* its fertile lands will yield their
> luxuriant harvests; its beauteous rivers will waft the products of *their*
> industry and enterprise . . . in the possession of homes fortified by the
> genius of liberty, and sanctified by the spirit of a beneficent and tolerant
> religion . . . the wilderness of Texas has been redeemed by Anglo-American
> blood and enterprise. The colonists have carried with them the language,
> the habits, and the lofty love of liberty that has always characterized and
> distinguished their ancestors. (quoted in De León 1983, 2–3; emphasis in
> original)[16]

Wharton's words exemplify Olson's point that "racial subordination" both "constructs democratic ideals as well as violates them." In the case of Mexico, we can see how white supremacy limits the possibilities for full democracy while

making white democracy possible. For Wharton, the language of white supremacy is utterly enmeshed in the civic language of liberty, popular sovereignty, industry, and religious tolerance. Moreover, "if Mexicans are lazy, disloyal, savage,
and immoral, then whites 'as mirror opposites' are hardworking, loyal, civilized,
and moral beings—ideal citizen subjects" (Bebout 2016, 43).

In this depiction of Anglo-American "promise and fulfillment," we can see
what Lee Bebout has characterized as "whiteness on the border"—the "discursive and ideological constellation in which representations of Mexico, Mexicans, and Mexican Americans are deployed to construct . . . white identity
as American identity" (2016, 2). Whiteness on the border "suggests a linkage
between the U.S.-Mexico border region and imaginings of U.S. national racial
identity" (24). Moreover, as Bebout notes, this vivid imaginary of a "Mexican
Other" is a "long-enduring, prevalent, and dynamic component of the U.S.
racial project" (71).

Frontier freedom on the border was also a project invested in rescuing the
region from both Indians and Mexicans. Conquest served a double function,
rescuing the region from "Mexican misrule"—a failure of governance defined
in part by the Mexican inability to restrain the presence of Indigeneity, turning
the territory into a "howling wilderness, trod only by savages." As Laura Gómez
and María Josefina Saldaña-Portillo have noted, both Mexicans and Indigenous
communities contended with a double colonization imposed by Spain and the
United States. This combination of conquest alongside the imposition of US law
upon the preexisting Spanish and Mexican colonial racial order created complex
new racial dynamics for both populations. As Gómez has demonstrated, a central paradox of 1848 was "the *legal* construction of Mexicans as racially 'white'
alongside the *social* construction of Mexicans as non-white and as racially inferior" (2018, 5). Both the Spanish and American racial systems sought to enlist
Mexicans in the management of the territories, leading Mexicans to become
"agents in the reproduction of racial subordination" even as they were also victims of it (121). Moreover, as Saldaña-Portillo demonstrates, while seeking to
enlist Mexicans in territorial administration, the political and racial identities of
Mexicans also have their roots in racially produced geographies of colonial governance that were mediated by notions of Indigeneity and "Indianness" that developed under Spanish, Mexican, and US rule (2016, 8). The Mexican-American
war and its aftermath created an "infelicitous boundary between indigenous and
Mexican" racial identities (191). Even before the US war against Mexico, "it was
Mexicans' 'half-bred' status, their barbarous core, that required U.S. conquest

for the proper administration of the frontier." Anglo settlers saw the frontier as "horribly mismanaged" and in need of rescue in order to "release its democratic potential and develop its indigenous resources" (Saldaña-Portillo 2016, 225).

The power of these racialized images and assumptions had a significant impact on how the United States approached Mexican land annexation and political incorporation. As Reginald Horsman shows, the "bitter dispute concerning annexation of Mexican territory was primarily an argument not about territory but about Mexicans" (1986, 241). Charles Bent, the first civilian governor of the territory of New Mexico proclaimed that "the Mexican character is made up of stupidity, obstinacy, ignorance, duplicity, and vanity" while Edward Hannegan, an All Mexico Movement senator from Indiana, characterized Mexicans as "utterly unfit for the blessings and restraints of rational liberty, because they cannot comprehend the distinction between regulated freedom, and the unbridled licentiousness which consults only the evil passions of the human heart" (quoted in Grandin 2019, 92). In a similar vein, John C. Calhoun, Andrew Jackson's former vice president and an eventual senator from South Carolina, cautioned against the possible incorporation of a large number of Mexicans, arguing that "Mexicans represented a motley amalgamation of 'impure races, not [even] as good as the Cherokees or Choctaws.'" Calhoun asked: "Can we incorporate a people so dissimilar to us in every aspect—so little qualified for free and popular government—without certain destruction to our political institutions?" (Gutiérrez 1995, 16).

Such characterizations were already familiar to Americans through wartime accounts in newspapers, colonial historiographies, and political writings. In the period of 1821–1845, Mexican natives were regularly described as a form of "degraded humanity"—"uncivilized" and "beastly" (De León 1983, 5). Such portrayals of Mexican depravity and violence represent an assemblage of lasting stereotypes that continue to influence the contemporary politics of race and immigration in the United States. Today, the trope of the "violent, savage, Mexican" has yet to dissipate because "it serves so many functions," particularly in its ability to "justify and obscure white violence" (Bebout 2016, 42, 62).

Yet alongside depictions of Mexican savagery and unassimilable difference were also redemptive accounts of Anglos bringing enlightenment to a backward people in need of advancement. As Arnoldo De León notes, Anglo settlers saw themselves as "freedom loving" frontiersmen who entertained "a strong belief in themselves and the superiority of their way of life" (1983, 2). Supporters of the All Mexico Movement stated that Mexicans would "learn to love her

ravishers," while columnist and editor, John L. O'Sullivan argued that the influx
of white Americans into recently conquered territory would lead to both uplift
and absorption (Grandin 2019, 151). Sullivan described an "irresistible army of
Anglo-Saxon[s]" bringing with them "the plough and the rifle . . . schools and
colleges, courts and representative halls, mills and meeting houses" (quoted in
Gutiérrez 1995, 15). As Gutiérrez puts it, supporters believed this influx would
ultimately lead Mexicans to "simply melt into American society as they experienced the benefits of American civilization" (15).

Here again, we see how the language of conquest and annexation depicts
Mexicans as having something of value (land, gold, silver) but the presence of
Mexicans and/or Indigenous populations is described as an obstacle to be eliminated or overcome. Following the war, Mexicans were often imagined as "disappearing" — Mexicans were given the option to either self-deport and "recede"
into Mexico or lose their "Mexican character" by experiencing the "ennobling"
benefits of American civilization and citizenship. In other words, American
citizenship was portrayed in the Treaty of Guadalupe Hidalgo as a process of
"unbecoming Mexican" (Saldaña-Portillo, 2016, 195).[17] Grandin describes editor
of the *New York Herald* James Gordon Bennet's take on this assimilation: "just
as indigenous 'barbarism' had 'receded before the face of civilization,' the 'im-
becile' Mexicans were 'sure to melt way at the approach of Anglo-Saxon energy
and enterprise as snow before a southern sun" (2019, 91). In sum, despite their
differences, what Wharton's, Dana's, Bent's, Hannegan's, Calhoun's, O'Sullivan's,
Cass's, and Bennet's arguments all share is a belief that the nature and character
of the United States would not — and should not — be changed by the incorporation of Mexicans and Mexican territory.

Mexican racial indeterminacy had the paradoxical effect of making racialized
violence against Mexicans both *more* justifiable *and* more defensible. Because
Latinos have a historically ambiguous relationship to whiteness, attacking them
appears as a less overt racist act than an attack on a racial population widely
understood to be nonwhite. Herrenvolk attacks on Mexicans were legitimated
through depicting them as enemy soldiers, bandits, or revolutionaries. Today, it's
my contention that the category "illegal" does similar work. Long-standing racist
tropes characterizing Latinxs as violent, dirty, duplicitous, lazy, criminal, and
unfit for citizenship serve to legitimate violence against Mexicans. At the same
time, because Mexicans and other Latinx populations exist across a racial spectrum that includes being socially characterized as an inferior race while often

being legally classified as white, those attacking this population can claim their rhetoric and actions are about status (criminals, illegals, etc.) rather than race.

Ultimately, anti-Mexican violence reflects this long-standing desire for labor and land, but not people. White citizens had been reassured during the war that the nature and character of the United States would not change; instead, the dream of white settlers in the Southwest was a dream of absence or absorption. This desire for erasure was complicated by the fact that although incorporated through war and conquest, Mexicans *were* eligible for citizenship. Yet alongside their membership were enduring racial tropes of Mexicans as suspect subjects— potential threats to the cultural, economic, and civic character of the nation. White politicians, journalists, military leaders, ranchers, and business interests never articulated a vision of shared membership where Anglo and Mexican American citizens would collectively rule each other as equals. The promise of 1848 imagined Mexicans as either a perpetually disappearing presence or a population to be treated instrumentally. Of course, the problem for Anglos in the Southwest is that Mexicans did *not* disappear—not only did they continue to migrate, but they also continued to claim social, political, and cultural space, enduring as a visible presence in their communities and on land they had long inhabited.

Conclusion: Migrants' Futurity, Stunted Imaginaries, Divided Whiteness, and the Authoritarian Turn

Violence against migrants creates what I've characterized as a kind of Herrenvolk loophole for nativists—offering them the experience of imposing tyranny over a nonwhite population while ruling themselves democratically. Yet such pleasures ultimately fail to satisfy the desire for whiteness as standing. Today, whiteness no longer possesses the same economic and political guarantees it once did. Indeed, many white citizens (particularly conservatives) are melancholic over what they perceive as an increasingly dismal and limited future. For while white citizens used to personally enjoy standing over nonwhite populations (including the collective right to legally enforced segregated spaces and institutions) today, whiteness is now privileged more at an aggregate than an individual level (Olson 2004, 709). So, while nonwhites still experience racial profiling, police violence, redlining, educational inequalities, dramatically higher levels of incarceration, and other race-based disadvantages, there is no guarantee that any individual white citizen will personally benefit from the fact that whites as a group are statistically "much more likely to go to college, buy a house, and be gainfully employed" (Olson 2004, 709). Today, such possibilities are "probabilities, not guarantees" (Olson 2004, 76). Interestingly, as Olson observed, the troubling paradox inherent in the recent shift from white *standing* to white *normalization* is that it "perpetuates white advantage while also creating new forms of white insecurity and resentment because such benefits are less certain" (Olson 2004, 709).

Making the racial situation more fraught, this dynamic of white advantage alongside lost status is also occurring in the context of four decades of privatization, deregulation, and regressive tax policy (HoSang and Lowndes 2019, 11). As numerous scholars have detailed, the United States "is undergoing the most massive upward transfer of wealth it has experienced since the Gilded Age of the late nineteenth century" (HoSang and Lowndes 2019, 6; see also Brown 2017). Over the last forty years, the middle and working classes have been subject to static or declining wages. In an era of capitalism in stagnation characterized by low growth and increasing inequality, today more people "are working longer hours for less and less, and have seen state support in the form of social services evaporate" (HoSang and Lowndes 2019; see also McClanahan 2019). Moreover, the institutions that seek to guard against the upward redistribution of wealth — the labor unions, progressive income and wealth taxation policies, social welfare programs, consumer protections, and civil rights and anti-discrimination laws — have all faced sustained attacks that have left them dramatically weakened (HoSang and Lowndes 2019, 6). And finally, changes in immigration policy (such as the Immigration and Nationality Act of 1965) eliminated the use of national-origin quotas, moving US immigration policy away from its racialized and restrictionist focus on European immigration, changing the demographic profile of the United States (Gjelten 2015).

This combination — a legal transformation away from Herrenvolk democracy, a shift in the dynamics of US immigration policy, and a massive upward transfer of wealth away from middle- and working-class Americans — is occurring in the historical context of a nation whose civic identity has long been enmeshed in the politics of whiteness and white supremacy.

Given this confluence of historical and economic forces, it is no surprise that today, a people who defined freedom through a violent and racialized sense of movement and futurity would view migrants with an intense mix of envy, impotence, and rage. Because today, it's *migrants* who are on the move, struggling against the forces of limitation, crossing borders, and transforming their futures through movement. Resolute in their efforts to fight for new futures where they can prosper and thrive, today, it is migrants who are now widely recognized as engaged in an epic quest for freedom—a group understood to be risking their very lives in order to begin anew and claim opportunity for themselves and their families. For nativists, to see populations that are *supposed* to be both removable and disposable wield and exceed the law in order to achieve freedom and escape repression and subjugation, and to see their fellow US citizens viewing such movement with sympathy and/or admiration, is galling. Indeed, nativists see such actions as a brutal assault on their own futures. Citizens drawn to the politics of whiteness can only imagine cross-border movement as a practice of settler sovereignty—as a form of dispossession and violent domination. Limited by a scarcity logic in which migrant flourishing means citizen hardship, nativists in the thrall of whiteness presume that migrant movement will invert the practices of white democracy and settler citizenship, causing whites to "lose their country" as Latinx migrants inflict a vengeful politics of invasion, replacement, and racial conquest.

As scholars like Leo Chávez (2013) and Otto Santa Ana (2002) have shown, threat narratives of replacement, conquest, invasion, and infestation are not new. What *is* new is how this rhetoric is being promulgated by a particularly influential set of forces that has included a white nationalist president, a formidable conservative media ecosystem, and a growing number of anti-immigrant and alt-right organizations, often undergirded by a persistent gun culture (Benkler, Faris, and Roberts 2018; Exum 2018; Southern Poverty Law Center 2019). On June 19, 2018, the president tweeted: "Democrats are the problem. They don't care about crime and want illegal immigrants, no matter how bad they may be, to pour into and infest our Country, like MS-13. They can't win on their terrible policies, so they view them as potential voters!" (quoted in Simon 2018). A little over a year later, a twenty-one-year-old white Texan named Patrick Wood Crusius drove ten hours to El Paso, where he then entered a Walmart and carried out a mass shooting, killing twenty-two people and injuring twenty-four others. Telling the police that he was "targeting Mexicans," the El Paso shooter committed one of the deadliest hate crimes ever against Latinx people in the United States (Esquivel et al. 2019). In a 2,300-word manifesto posted to the web forum 8chan shortly before the attack, the shooter echoed the rhetoric of Trump and the hosts and contributors on Fox News, stating:

This attack is a response to the Hispanic invasion of Texas. They are the instigators, not me. I am simply defending my country from cultural and ethnic replacement brought on by an invasion. . . .

. . . Due to the death of the baby boomers . . . and the ever increasing Hispanic population, America will soon become a one party-state [*sic*]. The Democrat party will own America. . . . They intend to use open borders, free healthcare for illegals, citizenship and more to enact a political coup by importing and then legalizing millions of new voters. . . .

Statistically, millions of migrants have returned to their home countries to reunite with the family they lost contact with when they moved to America. . . . This is an encouraging sign that the Hispanic population is willing to return to their home countries if given the right incentive. An incentive that myself and many other patriotic Americans will provide. This will remove the threat of the Hispanic voting bloc. . . . This will also make the elites that run corporations realize that it's not in their interest to continue piss off Americans. . . .

My whole life I have been preparing for a future that currently doesn't exist. The job of my dreams will likely be automated. Hispanics will take control of the local and state government of my beloved Texas, changing policy to better suit their needs. They will turn Texas into an instrument of a political coup which will hasten the destruction of our country. . . .

America can only be destroyed from the inside-out. If our country falls, it will be the fault of traitors. This is why I see my actions as faultless. Because this isn't an act of imperialism but an act of preservation. (Crusius 2019)

Although the shooter's manifesto can rightly be characterized as a factually flawed and historically inaccurate racist screed, I quote it at length here to illustrate not only its Herrenvolk logics, but to highlight how the logic of white supremacy has stunted and deformed America's political imaginary. Echoing the history of the Texas Rangers, Border Patrol, and paramilitary militias, the shooter approaches the border as a site where one can go and act with impunity. Moreover, as a white American, the shooter understood himself as possessing not only a natural right to self-preservation but also a natural "right to violence" (Grandin 2019, 54; Rogin 1975, 42). And like earlier conceptions of the frontier, for the shooter, traveling to the border to engage in mass murder was an act of "frontier freedom"—a chance to engage in a civilizational struggle characterized by retribution, domination, and loss (Grandin 2019, 116).

As scholars of whiteness continually remind us, white citizenship has left a tragic and lasting mark on the American democratic imagination (Baldwin 1964; Morrison 1993; Olson 2004). Emphasizing standing and status rather than polit- ical participation and collective action, white citizenship continually constrains the meaning of both democracy and political freedom (Olson 2004, 129). Rather than envisioning a multiracial democracy where we engage in collective forms of self-rule characterized by freedom, justice, plenitude, meaningful work, soli- darity, justice, pleasure, and joy, Herrenvolk logics can only envision democratic citizenship, freedom, prosperity, and popular sovereignty through racialized narratives of deprivation, denigration, exclusion, suffering, and removal. Rather than envisioning a better and more beautiful world, white democracy's vision is defined by scarcity. In the logic of racial replacement, social goods can only be imagined within an economy of exclusion and democratic forms of denial. In the nativist imaginary, there is no expanding or inclusive visions of membership. If Latinxs are present and holding power, it marks the destruction of the nation, a "political coup."

Yet despite all the suffering and violence generated by the Herrenvolk imagi- nary, nativists cannot stop the reality that the United States future is multiracial. The United States has—and will continue to have—a rapidly growing Latinx population, both immigrant and native born. Despite Republican efforts to change the census or suppress the vote, the native-born Latinx population con- tinues to grow, migrants will continue to enter the United States, and their US- born children will continue to lay claim to America's future. Equally important, not all white citizens embrace an ideology of whiteness and white democracy. As philosopher Linda Martín Alcoff reminds us, today "whites themselves are increasingly politically polarized on a number of critical issues," from guns to healthcare to race (2005, 10).

We are seeing a growing rupture between white citizens who support the politics of whiteness and those white citizens who are increasingly alienated by racist and xenophobic appeals to white resentment. Indeed, the police murder of George Floyd, an African American man, in Minneapolis on May 25, 2020, and the massive protests that followed nationwide speak to the shifting and diverging politics of white identity (Remnick 2020; Stewart 2020). Across the country, the summer of 2020 saw a larger-than-usual presence of white people joining with communities of color to oppose racist policing and support the Black Lives Matter (BLM) movement.

It is my contention that this increasingly visible divide among whites remains an undertheorized element of the current debates regarding the illiberal and polarized state of American politics. Current studies by political scientists arguing that America's constitutional democracy is being endangered by an "authoritarian turn," "asymmetric polarization," and "hyperpartisanship" are correct—but their analysis will remain limited and inadequate unless they situate this antidemocratic behavior within a longer trajectory of white supremacy and Herrenvolk democracy. Theorizing whiteness and the politics of white standing is fundamental to understanding the GOP's unwillingness to defend the separation of powers, a free press, judicial independence, and constitutional protections. The Republican Party's current assaults on democracy through outrageous forms of gerrymandering, election tampering, and voter suppression—this is the legacy of white democracy. White supremacy *taught* white citizens to see themselves as both the defenders and beneficiaries of liberal democracy—claiming the rule of law while disregarding democratic norms in order to seize and retain power. Herrenvolk democracy's deep ideological and historical resources make citizens who remain invested in white democracy not only susceptible, but drawn to, a politics that promises them the freedom to deny rights not only to people of color, but also to the liberal whites who oppose white supremacy, characterizing them as members of antifa, an un-American left-wing mob bent on destroying America.

The Trump administration's assault on majority-white protesters in Portland, Oregon, by federal agents in July of 2020 is a vivid example of this dynamic. Dressed in camouflage and tactical gear and unleashing tear gas, the acting director of homeland security characterized the mostly white supporters of BLM as anticitizens, as "anarchists and criminals"—firing tear gas and pulling some of them into unmarked vans (Baker, Fuller, and Olmos 2020). Organized through the Department of Homeland Security, federal agents in Portland were part of "rapid deployment teams" that included two thousand officials from CBP and ICE (Olmos, Baker, and Kanno-Youngs 2020). That the same agents that violently apprehended and abused the rights of migrants would now be used to attack white and nonwhite protesters engaged in protest and civil disobedience should not be surprising. The ability to deny certain groups equality under the law while engaging in blatant acts of violence and deception—while still seeing themselves as law abiding and justified in their actions—this is the civic legacy of the Herrenvolk era. Today, we should not be shocked that the political party most invested in whiteness would also be the most willing to disregard democratic norms in order to seize and retain power. The authoritarianism we see today is not just Trump or some newfound willingness of Republicans to shatter norms. It is the tyranny that lies at the heart of white democracy.

Notes

1. When referring to nativism, I am drawing on political scientist Case Mudde's definition of nativism as "a xenophobic form of nationalism" that sees both non-native persons and their alleged ideas as a threat to the culture, security, and economic well-being of the nation-state. Yet nativism is not merely prejudice. As Mudde demonstrates, nativism reflects a set of beliefs regarding how the state should be structured, with nativists often seeking "a congruence of state and nation—the political and the cultural unit" (2017, 89). Today, nativism is a core feature of the radical right—with expressions of populism and authoritarianism tending to "pass through a nativist filter" (Friedman 2017).

2. See Varela 2020; Verza and Fox 2020; Rose 2020; Axelrod 2020; Rogers 2018.

3. While sometimes using the term "immigrant," this essay generally uses the term "migrant." The term "immigrant" generally refers to someone who has moved from one country to another with plans to relocate permanently. Technically, "immigrants" generally refers to legal permanent residents, those who hold visas, or have become US citizens. By contrast, "migrant" is a broader term that refers to anyone who is in the process of relocating to another country, as well someone who has already moved. The term is inclusive of refugee and asylum seekers as well as people who are still on the move or who have moved to a country but wish to eventually return to their home country. The term "migrant" also makes no reference to legal status. For more on the distinctions between the two terms, see Vore (2015). For more on the distinction between "migrant" and "immigrant" within the field of Latinx politics, see Gonzales (2016, 184).

4. Comparing the selection of "good immigrants" to dog breeding, King opined: "You want a good bird dog? . . . Pick the one that's the friskiest . . . not the one that's over there sleeping in the corner" (quoted in Thrush 2012).

5. As is widely known, the international movement of people has become a political flash point, both in the United States *and* throughout Europe. However, for the purposes of this chapter, my focus is on the United States and Latinx populations, particularly Mexicans and Mexican Americans.

6. The passage of the Immigration Reform and Control Act (IRCA) signed into law by Ronald Reagan in 1986 is often seen as pro-immigrant legislation,

providing amnesty for over a million undocumented immigrants and creating pathways to legalization that also allowed for family reunification (Chávez 2008, 7; Golash-Boza 2012, 37–38). As anthropologists Sarah Horton and Angela Stuesse (2016) describe, the law also sought to impose sanctions on employers, leading employers to devise "elaborate strategies to dodge federal oversight, consigning undocumented workers to a shadowy secondary labor market in which labor laws are routinely flouted." However, they argue, "criminalizing the employment of undocumented workers has done little to curb employers' appetite for such labors. Instead, employers have devised workarounds" that force undocumented workers underground and render them more vulnerable. Ten years later in 1996, Bill Clinton passed the Illegal Immigration Reform and Immigrant Responsibility Act, which made it more difficult for undocumented immigrants to adjust their status and become legal. Clinton also signed the Personal Responsibility and Work Opportunity Reconciliation Act, which sought to "end welfare as we know it." Part of this legislation also restricted *legal* immigrants' use of food stamps and Supplemental Security Income and barred *legal* immigrants from using Medicaid for five years after entry (Chávez 2008, 7). Clinton's policies also led to a significant increase in the number of people being detained and deported in the United States (Golash-Boza 2012; Goodman 2018).

7. For a more in-depth exploration of these questions, see Cristina Beltrán, *Cruelty as Citizenship: How Migrant Suffering Sustains White Democracy* (University of Minnesota Press, 2020).

8. Other scholars of whiteness and white supremacy I turn to include Du Bois ([1935] 1998), Wells-Barnett (2018), Baldwin ([1955] 2012), Roedigger (2007), van den Berge (1967), Mills (1999), Lipsitz (2006), Painter (2011) and Ignatiev (2008).

9. Of course, as numerous scholars have noted, it was initially Reconstruction that marked the first national effort to challenge Herrenvolk Democracy. Following the Civil War, the adoption of the Thirteenth, Fourteenth, and Fifteenth Amendments marked the effort to graft the principle of equality onto the Constitution, with the federal government (not the states) put in charge of enforcement. These three constitutional amendments abolished slavery, guaranteed due process and the equal protection of the law, and equipped Black men with the right to vote, respectively. Establishing the principle of birthright citizenship and guaranteeing the privileges and immunities of all citizens, the changes wrought by Reconstruction have been described as representing a "second founding of the United States" (Foner 2019). Unfortunately, Lincoln's successor, Andrew Johnson, along with many in the southern states, as well as the Supreme Court, all sought to actively undermine these newly established rights. A series of court decisions narrowed the rights guaranteed in the

amendments, states actively undermined them, and by 1877, Jim Crow laws establishing racial segregation were being established and Herrenvolk democracy had been revived (Du Bois [1935] 1998; Foner 2019).

10. Bound by contractual arrangements to serve a master as repayment for their ocean passage, indentured servants were generally Englishmen who served a master for a specified amount of time, usually four to seven years.

11. For a brilliant analysis of how American citizenship and conceptions of freedom, agency, and sovereignty have been shaped by narratives of victimization and vengeance, see Anker (2014). For more on how such affective investments shape Mexican and Latinx populations, see Bebout (2016), De León (1983), Gutiérrez (1995), Saldaña-Portillo (2016), Chávez (2013), Villanueva (2017), and Gómez (2018).

12. For more on the complex story regarding Latinxs and their relationship to whiteness, see Lukens (2012) and Haney López (2006). A growing number of Latinx studies scholars are exploring how Latinxs have sometimes claimed whiteness, negotiating not only the Black/white binary, but how they also inhabit categories like not-Black, off-white, etc. Of course, Latinxs may recognize themselves as white while also arguing for antiracist, pro-immigrant policies. But other white-identified Latinxs might display their own antimigrant narratives. Latinx police officers, ICE agents—all may (though not necessarily) have a close relationship to whiteness. Some may even fall prey to white supremacy (see Resto-Montero 2017 for more on this phenomenon). In sum, whiteness is a vexed category, even for the Latinxs who both claim and repudiate it.

13. Speaking at a rally in Florida in May 2019, Trump asked his Florida audience how to stop migrants from crossing into the United States. When a woman at the rally shouted "shoot them!" Trump only smiled, saying "only in the Panhandle can you get away with that statement." Three months later in El Paso, Texas, the United States experienced one of the deadliest hate crimes ever committed against Latinxs (Rupar 2019).

14. In claiming that a significant portion of conservatives exhibit intense affective reactions against Latinx citizens and noncitizens, I am not arguing that Latinxs are the *only* population facing visceral political, racial, and cultural hostility from the Right. Anti-Muslim hysteria is clearly producing particular forms of racialized hate speech and violent xenophobia, as seen in the persistent efforts of the Trump administration to ban individuals from a variety of countries in Africa and the Middle East. We've also seen an increase in anti-Semitic incidents, and anti-Asian sentiments are increasingly visible (ranging from long-standing anti-Asian hostility aimed at China and Japan to the racism against South Asians that often merges into Islamophobia). Transphobic and misogynist policies attacking the rights of women and sexual and gender

minorities have been frequent and ongoing. And of course, anti-Blackness and settler colonialism represent two of the most foundational and dominant racial logics circulating both historically and today. In placing Mexicans at the center of my analysis, I am not calling on political theorists to replace the Black-white binary with a new racial hierarchy that erases or sidelines the significance of other populations and histories. Instead, this essay is a call for developing deeper and more specific knowledge of the various populations that make up the American racial order. In this instance, rather than the all-too-common references to the racial subordination of "Blacks and Latinos," scholars should instead move beyond such cursory generalizations and provide deeper analyses of the *specific* historical and political dynamics occurring within various racialized populations (Smith 2016; Bebout 2016, 11).

15. If Texas is included, Mexico lost more than half its territory in the war (Gutiérrez 1995, 13).

16. For more detail, see William H. Wharton's full address, April 26, 1836, in Lamar (1921, 365).

17. As Saldaña-Portillo notes, article 9 of the Treaty of Guadalupe Hidalgo states the following:

> The Mexicans who, in the territories aforesaid, *shall not preserve the character of citizens of the Mexican Republic* . . . shall be incorporated into the Union of the United States and be admitted, at the proper time (to be judged of by the Congress of the United States) to the enjoyment of all the rights of the citizens of the United States according to the principles of the Constitution; and in the mean time shall be maintained and protected in the free enjoyment of their liberty and property, and secured in the free exercise of their religion without restriction. (quoted in 2016, 193; emphasis added)

Citing Early American scholar David Kazanjian, Saldaña-Portillo writes: "The fulfillment of the promise of article 9 formally required Mexicans to give up, to relinquish, the 'character' of Mexicanness in order to enjoy 'all the rights of the citizens of the United States' promised by the treaty.' As the first sentence of article 9 stipulates in the prohibition 'shall not preserve the character,' Kazanjian suggests, 'the first step on the road to becoming a U.S. citizen is a negation, a becoming un-preserved, disposed of, lost, wasted' (2003, 207). Becoming a U.S. citizen required the loss of a Mexican character that is at once national and racial, as the vernacular use of 'character' underscores." (194).

CHAPTER THREE

Deconstructing Trumpism

Lessons from the Recent Past
and for the Near Future

DAVÍD MONTEJANO

This chapter is written with the intention of explaining the phenomenon of Trumpism, which I see as a political movement based on Anglo-Saxon populism. Trumpism espouses a nativist worldview that calls for border walls, immigration restriction, and trade protectionism—an isolationist "America first" posture. These ideas and sentiments have deep intellectual roots that go beyond the tabloids, alt-right media, and the presidential tenure of Donald J. Trump. In identifying these ideas, I seek to describe how Trump invoked them to mobilize a movement that swept him to power. I also hope to identify points where intellectuals and activists concerned with the future of democracy might strategically intervene to stamp out or deflect such dangerous ideas.

The chapter has three parts. The first contextualizes our current historical moment. It provides a brief history of US policy and politics regarding Mexican immigration and explains the use of scapegoating as an effective political campaign strategy. The second part delves into the recurring themes in the nativist academic and mainstream literature regarding the Mexican presence in the country. I discuss how Trump's slogan and campaign to "Make America Great Again" reflected and amplified these themes. The final part examines the results of the 2018 midterm elections and addresses the possible futures we face.

Where Are We?

Imagine the following nightmarish scenario. A shoot-out between rival drug gangs in downtown Houston claims the lives of several bystanders, including a family with children. After weeks of tweeting about immigrant crime in the Southwest, the president of the United States seizes on this incident to declare an immigration emergency along the border. He sends thousands of troops to the Texas-Mexico border, and demands that Mexico immediately crack down on immigration and drug trafficking. The president of Mexico, portrayed previously in the American press as an anti-American leftist, declares that Mexico will no longer tolerate the threats of the past several years and recalls its ambassador. In the midst of mounting tensions, university students in Mexico City take over the American embassy. US intelligence in the meantime has intercepted communications between the Mexican president and known cartel leaders discussing de-escalation and social peace. Immediately upon receiving this intelligence, the US president calls a press conference to announce the discovery of "collusion" between the Mexican president and the drug cartels. Known for his dramatic and impulsive actions, the US president closes the border and threatens war unless the students end their occupation of the embassy, and the Mexican president resigns. The First and Second Marine Divisions mobilize for an imminent invasion.

This could serve as the "October surprise" that an unpopular president facing a reelection campaign might be springing. As surreal and shocking as the scenario may seem, elements of it did appear during Trump's years in the White House. Since the beginning of his first presidential campaign in 2016, Trump ranted about Mexican rapists and criminals. His rallies were punctuated with chants to "Build the Wall," his signature campaign promise. His travel stops regularly honored "angel moms," the mothers of those killed by immigrants. His right-wing advisors at Fox News constantly sensationalized immigrant crime and invited presidential retribution. Not surprisingly, in the days leading to the November 2018 elections, Trump tweeted an inflammatory ad about a twice-deported immigrant who killed two police officers, as well as footage of "angry, dangerous and violent hordes" crashing through borders (Bradner and Schouten 2018; Collinson 2018; Joseph 2018). A few months later, an impulsive Trump shut down the government over congressional refusal to fund his border wall. In February, he declared an immigration emergency and sent thousands of troops to the border. Then in June 2019, he threatened Mexico with prohibitive tariffs unless they halted immigration immediately. Mexico and an "uncontrolled border" had become ready scapegoats that Trump could use to rally base support and deflect attention from other problems. Trump used his "bully pulpit" and his executive powers as president to create the spectacle—in spite of ample contrary evidence—of a border under siege from criminal elements. He threatened a nationwide sweep of "millions" of immigrants. How far this mercurial commander in chief was willing to go could not be predicted. In dealing with Venezuela, Trump has hinted at a military invasion, noting that the Pentagon had a plan (Chait 2017; Douthat 2018a; Shear and Davis 2019). The Pentagon has long had a plan for Mexico as well.

The events leading to a breakdown of US-Mexican relations—the nightmarish scenario above—were described more than twenty years ago by Secretary of Defense Caspar Weinberger as a possible "next war" that the United States had to prepare for. Weinberger and his advisors had envisioned a possible future where Mexico would need to be "liberated" from its corrupt leadership and drug cartels. The contingency plan called for a propaganda campaign to justify the invasion of Mexico but most of the plan dealt with details of the military invasion itself. A map titled the *Operational Plan for the Liberation of Mexico* outlined the invasion routes. The "literary war game," Weinberger explained, was played by the Pentagon regularly in order to assess what weaponry would be needed to accomplish the mission. In the case of Mexico, Apache attack helicopters were at the top of the list (Weinberger and Schweizer 1996, 163–216).

Naturally, such dramatic scenarios about war with Mexico are unthinkable. However, when some elements of a fantasized war game become real or are plausible, it is a good time to take stock of how we got to this point. The actual state of US-Mexican relations may have evolved during Trump's tenure, but the point is that Mexico and Mexicans in the United States have long commanded wary attention from national security experts, academics, and politicians. Many of the ideas and policies promulgated by the Trump administration have been circulating in conservative circles for some time. Ivy League professors and national security advisors have long voiced alarms about the increasing Mexican presence in the country. In the 1980s and 1990s, the idea of a border wall with armed guards was discussed openly in mainstream journals and newspapers. Prominent politicians of the time proposed challenges to birthright citizenship (Langewiesche 1992, 68–69; Buchanan 2007). However bizarre and unnerving the Trump period has been, Trump has not been an aberration. His political rise was shocking, in good part because many pundits believed that the Obama presidency had ushered in a "post-racial" period when in fact it helped mobilize a nativist white backlash. In his own arrogant and vulgar style, Trump expressed what many national security experts and border politicians had long thought about the Mexican presence in the country: they do not belong in the United States.

Trump should thus be seen as the ugly, mature manifestation of deep-rooted anxieties, couched under the rubric of "national security" and patriotism, about the racial and cultural makeup of the country. The questions of citizenship and race lie at the heart of Trump's nativist worldview (Ganz 2018). Trump raised it doggedly when he questioned the birthplace of President Barack Obama. He raised it in his denunciation of immigrants from "shithole countries." And he raised it in his claims that he had the authority to deny citizenship to US-born children of undocumented parents. Still, even though Trump may be seen as nothing new, we need to know how we got to this point.

WE'VE BEEN HERE BEFORE

There have been periods when anti-immigrant, and specifically anti-Mexican, sentiment have reared their ugly heads. During the 1920s, in the wake of World War I, a nationwide populist movement to assert Anglo-Saxon identity swept the country. It was the time of the resurgence of the Ku Klux Klan and the creation of the Border Patrol, of general fear of southern and eastern European refugees and the disorder and cultural dilution they might introduce. There was a nostalgic longing to return to the "normalcy" of the past. So conscious was Congress of maintaining the Anglo-Saxon Protestant character of the country that the new immigration quotas reflected the ethnic composition of the nation thirty years prior, in 1890. Southern and eastern European immigration was thus severely restricted. Because of pressure from powerful western growers, Mexican immigration was not impacted; economic interests trumped racial-cultural concerns (Montejano 1987, 179–91; Ngai 2004).

Mexicans, however, did not escape the nativist hysteria of the period. A body of alarmist literature about the "Mexican problem" and its threat to rural America emerged. Doomsayers predicted the demise of the Nordic race; university professors lamented the transformation of prosperous rural towns by Mexican migrant workers and worried about a "second" racial menace. Prominent among the intellectual naysayers was Harvard-trained historian Lothrop Stoddard. Stoddard concerned himself with the "ebbing tide of white" against the "rising tide of color." The dikes of white civilization faced a "colored peril" with three facets: "the peril of arms, the peril of markets, and the peril of migration" (1920, 236). The Mexican represented the latter. Although cheap labor from eastern and southern Europe had been stopped, the Mexican "just slips quietly over" a thinly settled and lightly guarded border: "So the little brown peons keep swarming in and spread far beyond our southern border States—wherever, in fact, there is a call for 'cheap labor.' And everywhere the peon brings with him his ignorance, dirt, disease, and vice, which infect cities with slum plague-spots, depress wages, and lower the general tone of the community" (Stoddard 1927, 214–15). So rapid had this Mexican "peaceful penetration" been that Stoddard estimated their number to lie between one and two million. As he warned:

> Unless something is done, and that right soon, we shall have on our hands
> another race-problem of a very troublesome character. For the Mexican
> peon is about the most "alien," unassimilable creature that could be
> imagined. . . . Such a being, profoundly alien in blood, ideals, and outlook,
> can be only a destructive element in our national life. The Mexican must be
> kept out if grave dangers are to be averted. (216).

A few years after Stoddard's warning, with the onset of the Great Depression, between half a million to a million — estimates vary — Mexicans and their Mexican American children were repatriated to Mexico. Although welfare agency-sponsored "repatriation" trains catalyzed the deportation campaign, many of the repatriation caravans were sponsored by Catholic charities, local Mexican American communities, and the Mexican government. In other words, *self-deportation* took place (but see the introduction to this volume). Whether self-deported or government-deported, these were obvious and taken-for-granted statements that Mexicans were not seen as "American stock." That was the point of agricultural economist Paul Taylor, who studied the "Mexican problem" at the time, when he noted that Mexicans had very low rates of naturalization — among other reasons, they saw no benefit to it. Whatever American citizenship was being conferred to Mexicans, Taylor observed, was taking place through birth (Taylor 1930, 400; see also Montejano 1987, 188–91; Bernard 2018).

In the 1940s, the World War II emergency laid the foundation for the guest worker Bracero Program that endured through 1964. The need for labor again prevailed over cultural concerns about a Mexican presence. At the height of the program, approximately two hundred thousand braceros worked annually in the country, mainly in agriculture. But the demand for labor stimulated a parallel undocumented immigration of workers. In the early 1950s, in the midst of a recession and national economic anxieties, the Immigration and Naturalization Service (INS) launched a high-profile campaign to locate and deport "illegals." Called Operation Wetback, the sweep through the Mexican barrios of the Southwest claimed to have netted an estimated one million "deportable aliens" in 1954.

The operation was partly a public relations ploy meant to reassure an anxious American public, for many of those apprehended were simply enrolled in the Bracero Program. Nonetheless, Operation Wetback demonstrated the potential of military-style roundups in Mexican neighborhoods. It again highlighted the disposable status of Mexicans in the country (Hernández 2010).

The Bracero Program ended in 1964, never to be replaced. In an attempt to absorb the displaced labor, the United States and Mexico established border factories, or maquiladoras, through the Border Industrialization Program (BIP), the first of many initiatives that would continue to link the two economies. From the standpoint of the United States, the BIP was seen as a way of having access to Mexican labor without having a Mexican presence in the country. From the Mexican perspective, the BIP signified modernization and jobs. The result was a major internal migration within Mexico to the border cities. For example, while the country's population increased by 87 percent between 1950 and 1970, going from 24 million to 45 million, the population of Juárez grew from 122,566 to 424,135 during the same period, an increase of nearly 250 percent. The border cities of Matamoros, Reynosa, and Tijuana registered similar population increases. The success of the BIP, ironically, increased the labor force available along the border. The factory preference for young women workers further augmented the presence of surplus male labor. In other words, the end of the Bracero Program and the beginning of the BIP did not stem undocumented labor immigration. To the contrary, the Vietnam-related economic boom of the sixties attracted and required such labor. Starting with the BIP, the United States pursued a "contradictory" policy that sought to facilitate the flow of goods and capital from Mexico while blocking the movement of labor. The passage of the North American Free Trade Agreement (NAFTA) in 1994 enshrined this policy (Massey, Durand, and Malone 2002).

In the late sixties the Mexican presence in the country gained national attention with the Chicana and Chicano movement. Following on the heels of the Black civil rights movement, the US-born children of Mexican origin, now grown-up citizens, organized political challenges to the established Anglo power structure of the Southwest. The militancy of a previously "silent minority" startled politicians. These challenges alerted them and national security officials about the changing population makeup of the region. The "second racial problem" that Stoddard and others had warned about in the 1920s had finally erupted. In 1975, INS commissioner Leonard Chapman (1992), former commandant of the Marine Corps, warned of "a vast and silent invasion of illegal aliens" numbering some twelve million. Likewise, in 1978 former CIA director William Colby, predicting "an additional twenty million illegal aliens" in the country by 2000, asserted that Mexico was a far greater threat than the Soviet Union (Fagen 1979, 39; Langewiesche 1992, 68).

The threat was not that of tanks or missiles but of babies. The concerned governors of the southwestern states made this clear. In 1983, Bruce Babbit of Arizona commented that "in the War of 1848, we annexed the Southwest and now the Mexicans are taking it back" (quoted in Geyer 1983). According to Babbitt, the border had become more and more a juridical figment; it had dissolved in real terms. Babbitt was concerned about what this meant for cultural levels in education—and for the problem of birth control. Babbitt was worrying about dumb Brown babies. In his book *The Immigration Time Bomb*, Governor Richard Lamm of Colorado issued similar warnings in a more strident tone. Speaking of Blacks and Hispanics, Lamm said that "we are heading for an America in which we will have two angry, under-utilized and under-educated, frustrated, resentful, jealous, and volatile minority groups existing unassimilated and unintegrated without our borders" (1985). Lamm did not parse words. He urged that we regain control of our border and our inner cities. These warnings by government officials and politicians never made any distinctions between Mexican immigrants and American citizens of Mexican descent—both were Brown and Latinx and certainly not of commonly understood American stock (Lamm & Imhoff, 1985).

Finally, in 1986, in recognition of the broken immigration system, the US Congress passed the Immigration Reform and Control Act (IRCA), a compromise bill that granted legal status to millions of long-term undocumented immigrants while also enacting an employment verification program backed by financial penalties on employers. It was a bipartisan effort that Republican president Ronald Reagan championed and signed. It was the last time that Republicans and Democrats would agree on any significant immigration legislation. Since then, party politics have become increasingly polarized, making it unlikely that any significant reform will be forthcoming (Sierra 1999, 131–53).

HOW DID WE GET HERE AGAIN?

So, the anti-Mexican sentiment that Trump has aroused has a long legacy in American politics. And Trump as a political figure is not an anomaly or aberration. Southern political lore, in particular, hosts several celebrated populist demagogues. Governor Pappy Lee O' Daniel of Texas, a flour salesman who used his radio show and campaign rallies to great effect, could have been a precursor of Trump. Huey P. Long of Louisiana was known for his "fire and brimstone" oratory. Alabama governor George Wallace comes to mind. All were masters of the art of scapegoating during political campaigns. After identifying the threat posed by organized labor, communists, racketeers, or "negroes," they would present themselves as saviors or guardians of the common folk. This campaign style was effective in maintaining the hegemony of the segregationist Democratic Party in the South through the sixties (Key 1949).

A major change in partisan affiliation took place in the sixties when white southerners left the Democratic Party for the Republican Party. The 1964 campaign of Republican presidential candidate Governor Barry Goldwater of Arizona explicitly capitalized on the white backlash to the civil rights movement. Although Goldwater failed to gain any electoral votes outside the South, his campaign gave birth to a so-called Southern strategy. Nixon's modified use of Goldwater's Southern strategy worked successfully in 1968, and this provided the basis for Republican theorist Kevin Phillips's handbook on how to translate racial scapegoating into respectable "dog whistles." Phillips cynically argued that Black voting rights, so closely associated with Democratic Party policy, should be maintained in order to pressure white conservatives into switching to the Republican Party (Phillips 1969). The strategy proved successful in the victorious presidential campaigns of Reagan in 1980 and 1984, and the 1988 Bush campaign was infamous for its Willie Horton television ad, which played on the fear of African American criminality. The Republican Party assimilated the old Southern approach to politics and race (Davidson 1990).

The practice of scapegoating, of course, did not have to be limited to African Americans, especially if it promised electoral success. In fact, it is worth noting that Goldwater's Southern strategy was formulated in a southwestern context where Mexicans were the racial "other." In the 1980s, Latinos occupied an ambiguous place in Republican thinking. Economic conservatives among the party leadership "liked" Latinos. Reagan had praised immigrants for their work ethic, and the George Bush–Jim Baker wing of the GOP wished to recruit Hispanics, who were seen as receptive to a "family values" platform. The economic conservatives were also free traders and favored increased commercial ties with Mexico. On the other hand, cultural conservatives—the English-only, anti-affirmative action, fundamentalist wing of the party—readily identified Latinos as un-American. Many were the rank and file who had fled the increasingly multiracial and liberal Democratic Party in the sixties and seventies. They were also concerned about the loss of jobs to Mexico—that "giant sucking" sound that Ross Perot had voiced during his upstart presidential bid in 1992. From their nationalist standpoint, they were competing with cheap Mexican labor in Mexico as well as in their local communities (Brimelow 1992).

In 1992 and 1996 this division of opinion between economic and cultural conservatives over the question of immigration and free trade flared into the open at the Republican National Conventions. Presidential candidate Pat Buchanan explicitly opposed immigration that "diluted" America's European heritage and called for tightening the US-Mexico border (Buchanan 1991). Two of Buchanan's books, *The Death of the West: How Dying Populations and Immigrant Invasions Imperil Our Country and Civilization* (2002) and *State of Emergency: The Third World Invasion and Conquest of America* (2007), bluntly pressed the point. Describing Hispanics as a "strange anti-nation" within the United States, Buchanan blasted Republican courtship of Hispanics, noting that "Republican success with Hispanics, as with other minorities, is often at the expense of conservative principles" (2007, 44). Buchanan argued that Republicans would be better off in the long run if they wrote off the Hispanic vote and tried to restrict Hispanic immigration. The party leadership, firmly in control of the economic conservatives, attempted to contain its internal divisions. But serious cracks were beginning to appear.

CALIFORNIA, 1994: A SIGN

What happened in California with the campaign of the anti-immigrant Proposition 187 in 1994 is instructive. In California, the rise in anti-Mexican sentiment had been evident for some time. In San Diego County, the most spectacular example of Mexican bashing had been the Light Up the Border campaign, dating to November 1989, which attracted more than a thousand people who parked at sundown and trained their headlights on the border. As the California economy worsened in the early 1990s and unemployment reached near 10 percent, "citizen groups" began to spring up throughout the state to protest "street hiring" and to urge the Immigration and Naturalization Service (INS) to conduct raids. Proposition 187, a measure designed to deny public benefits (mainly medical and educational) to undocumented immigrants, had gained sufficient signatures to qualify as an item on the state ballot, and was generating momentum in early 1994. Incumbent governor Pete Wilson, up for reelection and with one the lowest popular ratings in memory, sensed a winning issue. As the former mayor of

San Diego, Wilson acted like a moderate Republican. But now he put himself at the head of the Proposition 187 campaign and cynically blamed immigrants for the state's budget difficulties and for problems with the schools, hospitals, and community services. Wilson's campaign featured dramatic film footage of immigrants rushing en masse past the San Isidro checkpoint; it was a startling suggestion of an uncontrolled border. Both Wilson and Proposition 187 coasted to easy victories (Montejano 1999, 245–46).

These dual victories set the template for future Republican campaigns in California: have the candidate champion ballot initiatives that appealed to the majority of white voters. In 1995–1996, driven by the need to galvanize support for a presidential bid, Governor Wilson led a successful campaign for Proposition 209, which banned affirmative action policies in the state. Proposition 209 passed, but Wilson's presidential campaign faltered. In 1998, Proposition 227—banning bilingual education in public schools—was the major plank of Republican gubernatorial candidate Ron Unz. Unz lost, but Proposition 227 passed (Chávez 1998).

In short, the passage of Proposition 187 of 1994 broadened the conservative assault on the civil rights gains of the sixties and seventies. Anti-immigrant sentiment had easily been redirected to other targets. The anti-immigration initiative, the opposition to affirmative action, the English-only movement— they all pointed to a "nativist" reflex in California that lacked only a legitimizing moment, that time when one of the major political parties or candidates made their cause a key element of a political campaign.

The passage of Proposition 187 set off a vigorous debate in the political science literature on whether the voting results reflected a response to a rapid demographic change—that is, an increase in the Latinx population. Much ink and many regression analyses were spent on discussing whether increased visibility and contact with Latinxs had resulted in "consensus" or "conflict." However, a cursory glance at the predominantly Anglo (non-Hispanic white) counties of rural northern California, where no significant increase in the Latinx population had occurred, would have suggested a more complex explanation. All voted overwhelmingly for Proposition 187, although there had been no demographic change of note. More to the point were the feelings of resentment in the region— about persistent high unemployment and neglect by Sacramento—that could be directed toward symbolic threats. The region, in fact, flirted with a separatist movement (Citrin and Highton 2002; Bowler, Nicholson, and Segura 2006).

In a region where discontent could be provoked by a variety of issues, an imagined Mexican threat was sufficient to stir anti-immigrant sentiment. In other words, the question about the impact of a Mexican presence, the question that consumed so much social science attention in assessing support for Proposition 187, was somewhat misplaced. The imagination stirred by political messaging was what mattered most.

More relevant was the framing of the Mexican presence as an economic burden and cultural threat by Governor Wilson's campaign. His victory further emboldened the cultural conservatives and highlighted the differences with the economic conservatives of the party. The contrast between California and Texas at this time is instructive. In 1990, the archconservative Federation for American Immigration Reform (FAIR), which had been lobbying Washington to restrict non-European immigration for a decade, ran commercials on six Houston radio stations linking immigration to such problems as homelessness, drug smuggling, and traffic congestion. The radio commercials, aired as a test for a national campaign, were withdrawn because of public protests. Texas governor George W. Bush told the State's Republican Party to not engage in anti-Mexican rhetoric. But in California, FAIR found an enthusiastic audience. Governor Pete Wilson was airing political ads featuring the storming of the San Isidro checkpoint by a mass of immigrants. While Wilson rode the coattails of Proposition 187 to reelection, Bush courted the Mexican American vote in halting Spanish. Bush was seen as a *simpático*, garnering as much as a third of the Latinx vote. Wilson and Bush offered different visions for the future of the Republican Party (Montejano 1999, 244–48).

Until Trump's surprising ascendancy in 2016, the Bush-Baker wing of the Republican Party was in control of party strategy. After the reelection of Barack Obama in 2012, an election that Mitt Romney lost even though he won 61 percent of the white vote, the party leadership had decided to embark on a campaign to recruit conservative Hispanics into the fold. Trump completely upended such thinking. In a field of Republican candidates seeking to appeal to a rising Hispanic electorate, Trump was alone in courting Republicans who "didn't want the party to remake itself, who wanted to be told that a wall could be built and things could go back to the way they were" (Klein 2018; see also Rapoport, Abramowitz, and Stone 2016). Trump's mix of economic populism and deliberate racial polarization was thought to be demographically doomed, but instead it won him precisely the midwestern white voters who had been overlooked in previous elections. His description of a country threatened by Mexican criminals and MS-13 gang members was ideal material for his demagoguery.

Trump's dramatic solution to the threat—initially seen as fantastical—was the idea of building a border wall along the US-Mexico border. According to Joshua Green, Trump's campaign advisors understood "the power of illegal immigration to manipulate popular sentiment," but they needed a "mnemonic device" to keep their boss on message. Thus, the idea of building a "big, beautiful wall" along the Mexican border emerged as a campaign promise. It appealed to Trump's ego—"I want it to be so beautiful because maybe someday they'll call it 'The Trump Wall.'" This pledge, repeated at every rally, became Trump's best-known policy proposal. Trump has acknowledged that when his rallies got "a little boring," he would just declare, "We will build the wall!" and the audience would go "nuts" (Green 2018a, 111; see also Borger 2019). Whether or not a physical border wall was practical or effective was immaterial. As a symbolic assertion of American identity, the idea of a wall was appealing to the Republican base.

Trump essentially did to the nation what Wilson did to California in the 1990s. He tapped into a fear or ignorance about Mexicans and the US-Mexico border and cast himself as a savior. Preparing the ground was the rise of the right-wing media, led by Fox News, that constantly raised alarms about securing the border. The attack of 9/11 and subsequent "war on terror" had also heightened a sense of national vulnerability to foreign threats. Building on this, Trump portrayed a country in economic decline because of unfair trade policies negotiated by previous weak administrations, a decline that only he, successful billionaire, could reverse. Most startlingly, his campaign ditched the Phillips handbook advice about respectability. The dog whistles were now bombastic chants of "Build the Wall" and howls about immigrant criminals.

Many commentators have been stunned at the remarkable transformation that Trumpism has brought about. The Republican Party has become the instrument of one man's will. Trump's popularity among Republicans stands (as of August 2018) at close to 90 percent. A similar percentage support his call to "build the wall" and for deporting all "illegals." In light of such base support, the Republican-led Senate tolerated Trump's abuse of his executive powers. There had been no opposition from Republican ranks to Trump's proposed wall. Trump embraced and empowered the cultural conservatives whose right-wing views and policies on immigration were presented as patriotic common sense. Many of these beliefs are rooted in crude, paranoid fantasies. Trump is said to have borrowed the theme of Mexican rapists from Ann Coulter's 2015 book *¡Adios, America! The Left's Plan to Turn Our Country into a Third World Hellhole.* Coulter's book, packed with material about Latin American rape culture, was published two weeks before Trump's campaign announcement. The views of Latinxs held by White House senior advisor (and speech writer) Stephen Miller, the architect of the Muslim ban, the family separation policy, and Trump's national emergency declaration, were formed at Santa Monica High School, where Miller first encountered Mexican American students. He remembers MEChA (Movimiento Estudiantil Chicano de Aztlán) as "a radical national Hispanic group that believes in . . . returning the southwestern United States to Mexico to create a 'bronze nation.'" Not surprisingly, Miller described former president George W. Bush's record on immigration as an "astonishing betrayal" (*Fox News Sunday*, February 18, 2019).

One of the unexpected ironies resulting from Trump's ceaseless campaigning and tweeting about Mexican immigrants was his according of *national* minority status to Mexican Americans. Mexican Americans are no longer a regional minority but a full-fledged American racial group that can rival African Americans as an existential threat. Much to the chagrin of many of us who have complained about the neglect of the southwestern borderlands, for the foreseeable future, the region will be receiving more attention than ever imagined. The chant to "build the wall" will be around long after Trump is gone. The chant, of course, portrays Mexican and Central American immigrants as undesirable, but it also suggests that Mexican-origin Americans are suspect citizens. If Mexican immigrants are rapists and criminals, can the descendants of previous generations be much different? It takes only a small rhetorical step to raise the specter of an unassimilated, uneducated, and crime-prone nonwhite minority.

How to Scapegoat Mexicans

In the previous section, I noted that Trumpism—whether seen as a broad political movement or as the cultish following of a populist demagogue—is not an aberration; it has a long pedigree in American politics. White-identified populism has long been a powerful undercurrent of American politics, and Trump is only its latest reincarnation. Mexico, Mexican immigrants, and Mexicans in the United States have been easy marks for those who wish to portray themselves as saviors. Joining the list of scapegoats have been the recent immigrants from the "Mexican countries"—as one Fox News newscast labeled them—of Guatemala, Honduras, and El Salvador (Neuburger 2019). Although it is tempting to dismiss Trumpism as racist or nativist, it is important to dissect the major elements of its worldview as President Trump expressed it.

Trump boasted that he did not like to read, but it is clear that his worldview was informed by current and former right-wing advisors Steve Bannon, Stephen Miller, and the Fox News anchors who are familiar with the nativist discourse in academic and "mainstream" literature. In my survey of this literature, three themes or tropes—the declining position of the United States in the global order, the "Latinization" of the country, and national security concerns about Mexico—surfaced prominently. Examining these will illustrate the intellectual arguments underlying Trump's ideas about Mexico and Mexicans. I discuss each in turn.

AMERICA IN DECLINE

Trump's stunning victory led to a vigorous argument about whether his success was due to his appeal to white tribalism and xenophobia or to his economic populist appeal aimed at working-class voters impacted by deindustrialization. In other words, is Trumpism primarily about race or economics? In a sense, there is no reason to disentangle these when Trump's campaign to "Make America Great Again" effectively merged the economic and cultural concerns of many. In the context of Trump's race-based, nationalist vision, the slogan has been a patriotic appeal for the "good old days" of prosperity and Anglo-Saxon cultural hegemony. The slogan, according to several commentators, tapped the resentment of many who felt left behind or burdened in some way (Bort 2018; Douthat 2018a). Since Trump supporters generally had little if any direct competition with Mexican labor, the connection had to be drawn explicitly. Trump made the connection in countless tweets and numerous rallies.

In the nativist literature, no diatribe against immigrants is complete without reference to their negative influence on US jobs and wages. Yet some caution must be drawn about who experiences "economic anxiety" and who expresses "racial resentment." One study found that Republicans making more than $100,000 per year were more dissatisfied than Democrats making less than $20,000 per year. Another found that Trump's Republican supporters had an average annual income of $70,000. In other words, there need be no direct personal experience with competition with Mexican labor in order to support building a border wall or rounding up "illegals." An abstract portrayal of such competition and the consequent displacement of American workers proved effective. In this regard, some conservative pundits cynically expressed concern about the "struggle for the bottom rung" between "blacks and browns" (Klein

2018; Miles 1992; Beinart 2016). These laments echoed the warnings of the 1920s about a second race problem.

The economic argument against immigrants also invariably points to the fiscal burden they impose on schools and hospitals. A prime example can be drawn from the early days of the anti-immigrant Proposition 187 initiative. Commentator Jack Miles (1992) asked the readers of the *Atlantic Monthly* to imagine the specter of a school-funding collapse in a severely depressed economy—specifically, that the Los Angeles Unified School District, faced with a $400 million cutback in state funding, could conceivably go into receivership. "In such an unthinkable crisis unthinkable remedies might suddenly be thought of," he wrote. In such a climate, Miles concluded, the imposition of a citizenship requirement for elementary and high school education might acquire the aura of civility. This, of course, would signify denying noncitizens any public services, and would be only a small step away from Governor Wilson's call to deny citizenship to their US-born children.

The economic trope in the nativist literature also deals with the notion of the relative decline of the United States in the world order. In fact, the "browning" of the country has come to signify decline. Yale historian Paul Kennedy, for example, argued that the military cost of maintaining a Pax Americana has allowed for the emergence of new economic centers that can challenge American economic standing. The consequent loss of well-paying manufacturing jobs, coupled with the high birth rates of American minorities, made it "unwise to assume that the prevailing norms of the American political economy would be maintained if the nation entered a period of sustained economic difficulty" (Kennedy 1987). Kennedy was later more explicit about the matter. Describing the implications of the "browning" of America—the result of differential birth rates and immigration—he pointed out, in a characteristically grim assessment, that "the mass migration at the moment is only the tip of an iceberg. We have to educate ourselves and our children to understand why there is going to be trouble" (Kennedy 1992, 20). The demographic combination of "browning" with some "graying" would pose a "troublesome mismatch" for states like California, where most children would soon be Latinx and most elderly Anglo. Any fiscal crisis, brought about by the exhaustion of Social Security and health care funds, would assume an ethnic-racial character. In short, predicted Kennedy, the forthcoming decline portended serious difficulties—difficulties of a racial nature—in preserving the US political consensus (Kennedy 1993; Hayes-Bautista, et al. 1988).

Anglo-Saxon nativism, in other words, has an economic trigger. In the Southwest, the alarmist discussion of uncontrolled borders and uncontrolled streets surfaces every time the United States enters a period of economic difficulty.

THE "BROWNING" OF AMERICA

That "cultural conservatives" see Latinxs as a racial threat becomes quite evident when addressing the question of American culture. The dominant theme in nativist literature of the past thirty years has emphasized the unassimilable and alien character of Latinx immigrants. The discussion has mimicked that of the 1920s, when Americans also felt anxious about their identity. In the 1990s, the fin de siècle assessments of the country manifested much concern and even fear about this growing Latinx presence. An April 1990 issue of *Time* put the matter bluntly: "What will the U.S. be like when whites are no longer the majority?" The question betrayed an anxiety over whose history, values, language, and identity would count in the future. The "crowded lifeboat" became the metaphor of choice for anti-immigrant pundits. The *National Review* and other archconservative journals argued that the "melting" dynamics of the past no longer applied: "Many passengers might have climbed aboard the lifeboat safely; one more may still capsize it." It was time, in the opinion of the *National Review*, to announce that the United States was no longer an immigrant country. The "American ethnic mix" had been upset because "in 1960, the U.S. population was 88.6 percent white; in 1990, it was only 75.6 percent white—a drop of 13 percentage points in thirty years" (Brimelow 1992). This alarmist analysis, rendered in 1992, echoed the apocalyptic calculations of the 1920s about the disappearing white race. The lifeboat metaphor remains a favorite anti-immigrant argument, as illustrated recently when Trump publicly told asylum seekers from Central America "to go away. We're full. There is no room for you" (Trump 2019b).

An apocalyptic tone clearly characterizes the work of Harvard professor Samuel Huntington. Huntington was well known for his warnings that the country faced an external Muslim threat and an internal Latinx threat. He framed these threats as a "clash of civilizations," a phrase that Trump occasionally uses at his rallies (Huntington 1996). For Huntington, Mexicans basically represented an unassimilable ethnic element that would bifurcate the country with two languages and cultures. Thus, continued Mexican immigration represented an existential threat to the country. Salvation lay, according to Huntington, in a patriotic recommitment to "Anglo Protestantism," the cultural core of the country

(Huntington 2004b). Huntington would have embraced Trump's association of a return to American greatness with the building of a border wall (Montejano 2004).

Although Huntington lamented the failure of assimilation, he was actually more concerned that Latinxs would in fact assimilate and become active citizens. In that eventuality, Huntington—like Kennedy, Buchanan, Coulter and others— raised the possibility of an "exclusivist" scenario, where a political movement of "native white Americans" revives an America that excludes and suppresses those who are not white or European. As evidence, he noted the California referenda of the 1990s against undocumented immigrants, affirmative action, and bilingual education, and the movement of whites out of the state. Then he added ominously, "As the racial balance continues to shift and more Hispanics become citizens and politically active, white groups may look for *other means* of protecting their interests" (Huntington 2004, 40; emphasis added).

Trumpism may have in fact been be the nativist movement envisioned by Huntington. Basically, through his vulgar, angry denunciations of immigrants, Trump as president gave license to his supporters to verbalize their racist thoughts and threats in the name of "Americanism." The Nazi rally at Charlottesville, the attack on the Pittsburg synagogue, and the shooting at El Paso's Walmart may be the "other means" adopted by the most extreme elements of Trumpism. Trump himself expressed a cavalier attitude about violence and pain. He joked publicly about shooting immigrants and opined that soldiers could shoot them if they threw rocks. According to presidential staffers, Trump often talked privately about fortifying a border wall with a water-filled trench, stocked with snakes or alligators, prompting aides to seek out cost estimates. He also wanted the wall electrified, with spikes on top that could pierce human flesh (Shear and Davis 2019; Russell 2019). It seems clear that if the national political consensus broke down, as Kennedy and Huntington warned, the threat would likely come from a nativist right-wing movement restoring America to "greatness."

The immigration restrictionists have naturally understood that extreme measures might be necessary to preserve the "American ethnic mix." A May 1992 *Atlantic Monthly* assessment of large-scale Mexican immigration, after concluding that "these newcomers may indeed be the ones we cannot accommodate," noted that the border could be sealed "with a large-scale deployment of the U.S. armed forces and the creation of free-fire zones. It would not require much killing: the Soviets sealed their borders for decades without an excessive expenditure of ammunition. The simple fact that there existed a systematic policy of shooting illegal immigrants would deter most Mexicans" (Langewiesche 1992, 68–69). Long before Donald Trump mused about an electrified border wall and armed guards, Russian-inspired ideas about border control were floating around in mainstream discourse (see Gonzales, this volume).

Since cultural conservatives view Mexicans in the United States as unassimilable and culturally alien, the question of demography looms large. Their worries, verging on hysteria, are that sometime in 2042 or 2044 white Americans will lose their majority status. In 2030, immigration will overtake new births as the dominant driver of population growth. Demographic change has been framed in a zero-sum calculus with attendant negative consequences. The only group projected to shrink, according to the Census Bureau, is the non-Hispanic white population (Miller 2018; Saenz 2018; Poston 2019; Herman 2019).

Some demographers have questioned the assumptions the Census Bureau is making about race, especially at a time when the categories themselves seem to be shifting. People of mixed race or ethnicity have been counted as minorities, which has had the effect of understating the size of the white-identified population. Sociologist Richard Alba has likened this to the one-drop rule. Alba and others have noted that the meaning of "whiteness" has changed over time. Immigrants from eastern and southern Europe in the early twentieth century were not initially seen as white or were seen as "lesser whites" but eventually gained entry into whiteness. Are not Asians and Hispanics following the same path toward eventual assimilation? More than a quarter of Asians and Hispanics marry outside their race (Alba 1990). Until Trump came along, Latinx scholars were wondering whether Latinxs would accept the "racial bribe" of whiteness (Guinier and Torres 2003; see also Haney López 2004).

Yet perception of race is what matters. The spatial-visibility experiments of political scientist Ryan Enos at both the micro level (train platforms) and macro level (county) suggest that the Latinx presence can illicit negative responses. Enos argues that the biggest gains Trump made over Mitt Romney's performance were in places where the Latinx population had grown most quickly. He cites the example of Luzerne County in Pennsylvania, which saw a 600 percent growth in the Latinx population between 2000 and 2014, and which gave Trump 12 percentage points more than given Romney in 2012 (cited in Tavernise 2018). Again, the problem with this line of reasoning is that Trump undoubtedly outperformed Romney in similar fashion in counties that saw no significant increase in the Latinx population. This is not to say that the thrust of Enos's argument is incorrect; it is to say that it is limited. A populist movement driven by constant campaign rhetoric about Mexican rapists and MS-13 gangs and rallies highlighted by chants to "build the wall" does not need Mexicans to be present. Real and *imagined* Mexican threats to an American way of life are sufficient to mobilize the politics of resentment.

Ezra Klein notes that a majority of Americans—though not of Republicans—believe the browning of American to be a good thing. States like California and Texas have become majority-minority states without falling apart. The problem, as Klein (2018) put it, is that the conversation about a browning America will not be driven by demographers but by "ambitious politicians looking for an edge, by political pundits looking for ratings, by outrageous stories going viral on social media."

DEMASIADO CERCA A LOS ESTADOS UNIDOS

A third recurrent theme in the nativist literature had to do with US-Mexican relations. Since World War II, Mexican emigration, the maquiladora industry, automobile supply chains, and agricultural exports and imports—to mention only a few economic links—have inextricably bound the two countries. Such market flows of labor and commodities have been largely mediated through treaties and based on stable, friendly relations between the two. Under Trump, the economic arrangements that were once seen as beneficial to both have become pressure points that he can threaten to squeeze. From Trump's nativist viewpoint, Mexicans did not have to be present in the country to be a threat. Trump promised anxious workers in the Midwest that he would prevent plant relocations to Mexico, and blasted the NAFTA agreement with Mexico and Canada as a "terrible deal" for American workers. Trump has used the threat of tariffs to force Mexico to adjust its border policies. He may intervene in other policy areas as well (Alexandrov 2019; Blitzer 2019).

The old saying "poor Mexico, so distant from God and so close to the United States" was never more relevant than under Trump. His nativist rants about Mexican immigrants and his views about trade treaties have jeopardized long-standing economic and political relations. His outrageous proposal to build a two-thousand-mile-long, thirty-foot-high wall along the US-Mexico border expressed the nativist desire to secure the country as an Anglo-Saxon nation. Trump and his media allies at Fox News regularly portrayed the border as a divide between order and criminality, with Immigration and Customs Enforcement (ICE) as the "thin green line" protecting the country from chaos. Ann

Coulter whipped up her anti-immigrant base when she cited drug-related violence in Mexico and concluded that Mexicans "specialize in corpse desecration,
burning people alive, rolling human heads onto packed nightclub dance floors,
dissolving bodies in acid, and hanging mutilated bodies from bridges" (quoted
in Beinart 2016). Like fears about an "American decline" and a "browning America," the negative images of Mexico and Central America function as ready-
made tropes for exclusionary foreign and domestic policies (Beinart 2016).

Such negative images of Mexico and Central America were tapped to support
immigration restriction and all sorts of border barriers. News about disappearances of women in Juárez, murders of journalists throughout the country, gun
battles in Mexican border towns, and the massacre of immigrants and targeted
families—obviously something has been terribly amiss in Mexico. The question
of whether Mexico should be considered "a failed state" has been raised. The
fragility of the Mexican state has been evident for some time. Among the symp-
toms and causes have been ingrained government corruption, immiseration and
repression, and emigration. A representative assessment from the late 1980s was
that of concerned historian Kennedy, who described Mexico as "on the verge of
economic bankruptcy and default. Its internal economic crisis forces hundreds
of thousands to drift illegally to the north each year. Its most profitable trade with
the United States is becoming a brutally managed flow of hard drugs, and the
border for all this sort of traffic is still extraordinarily permeable" (1987, 517). Unfortunately, the violence within Mexico, most of it drug related, provided Trump
the basis for his caricature of Mexican immigrants as criminal. Coming from
"shithole" countries, they were not "meritorious" (quoted in Shear and Davis 2019).

National security advisors have long cited Mexican drug traffic as a major
concern. According to the National Drug Intelligence Center, Colombian and
Mexican drug trafficking organizations have operations in at least 1,286 US cities. The smuggling generates between $18 billion and $39 billion in wholesale
drug proceeds. Almost all of it comes from marijuana sales. The American pro-
hibitionist campaign to stamp out the drug trade has resulted in significant
collateral damage in Mexico. When the Mexican presidential administration of
Felipe Calderón initiated a campaign against drug trafficking at the beginning
of his term (December 2006), one of the consequences was a rise in the level
of violence as drug cartels were forced to compete, as a congressional report
put it, "for control over territory, markets, and smuggling routes." By the end of
Calderón's term six years later (December 2012), between forty-five thousand
and fifty-five thousand drug-related deaths had been recorded (Lake et al. 2010).

The violence has escalated since then. The year 2019, with seventeen thousand killings counted between January and June, was one of Mexico's most violent years. It exceeded the civilian death toll in Iraq at the height of the war in 2006(Lake et al. 2010). US and world attention was drawn to this crisis of violence in November 2019, with the massacre of nine members of the LeBarón family, dual US-Mexican citizens, in Sonora. The killings have renewed talk about a Mexican "failed state" (Stephens 2019).

The Mexican crisis generated concern among US policy makers about the possibility of "spillover violence" along the Southwest border. Given the attention paid to Mexican immigration and the Mexican border, it should not be surprising that they have considered options for dealing with "spillover violence" (Weinberger and Schweizer 1996). The Pentagon, as noted earlier, has drawn up contingency plans for an invasion of Mexico, if necessary to bring about peace and order. If a crisis ever erupted along the US-Mexico border, the US president does have the authority to declare "an immigration emergency." In that case, Homeland Security would carry out plans to seal off the border and control "alien terrorists and undesirables." These plans were designed by a multiagency government group back in the 1990s, long before 9/11 and the ascendancy of Trump (Dunn 1996).

Although the situation along the border falls short of the Pentagon's literary war game, Trump has already invoked an "emergency" in order to circumvent congressional approval for his wall. As Trump tweeted (January 13, 2019), the border is "going to be militarized and defended or the United States, as we know it, is going to cease to exist." In response to the massacre of the LeBarón family, President Trump tweeted (January 14, 2019) that he would designate Mexican cartels as "terrorist organizations," thus opening up the possibility of targeted military intervention (Shear and Davis 2019; Vazquez 2019; Semple and Jakes 2019).

If Trump had thought that such intervention represented a winning presidential strategy, he might have considered it in 2019 and 2020. Trump would not have shied away from transforming elements of Pentagon fiction into reality. Instead, confident of a victory over "sleepy Joe," Trump embarked on a reelection campaign of mega-rallies that stayed away from any serious border bashing and focused on his charisma and the need to keep America great. Trump repeatedly claimed that only a fraudulent election could cost him the presidency. After Trump lost the election, his determination to remain in power was reflected in the shocking assault on Congress at the US Capitol by pro-Trump mobs on January 6, 2021. The assault included several white supremacist groups and exposed a "blind spot" in the national security thinking about threats to American democracy. These were the extralegal "other means" that Huntington and Kennedy had hinted at in their laments about a declining and "browning" America.

What Now?

All three themes—a declining United States, the Latinization of the country, a fragile Mexican state—have an element of reality. The United States is no longer an uncontested world power: New Brunswick, New Jersey, is now more than 50 percent Mexican, and Mexican society continues to be plagued with drug-related violence. The key lies in the framing of that element of reality. Should the United States be the sole police agent of the world? How has the Mexican presence impacted New Jersey? Is the new president of Mexico making progress in dealing with corruption? The negative and questionable assumptions behind these questions have to be unmasked, interrogated, and contested. The fictions of Trumpism have to be confronted.

The 2018 midterm elections offered hope about a course correction in the near future. In the days before the midterms, Trump sent army troops to the border to repel a Central American caravan and tweeted a political video accusing Democrats of helping Central American invaders overrun the nation with cop killers. CNN called the video ad "the most extreme step yet in the most inflammatory closing argument of any campaign in recent memory." The fear mongering did not work. Trump voters did in fact stand by Trump in the midterms; there were just not enough of them. Republicans gained about 46 percent of the vote, more or less the same percentage that Trump pulled in the presidential election. Trump's identity politics helped him consolidate his base, but it also cost him a fair number of voters. Despite an electoral map that favored Republicans, and despite a vibrant economy at full employment, Republicans lost forty congressional seats and control of the House, the greatest shift in party affiliation since 1974 (or Watergate). Democratic pollster Stanley Greenberg described the results of the 2018 midterm elections as "transformative." According to a post-election survey, Trump succeeded in making immigration and the border wall a top voting issue for the Republican base, but it backfired among other voters. "Mr. Trump declared war on immigrants—and on multicultural America—and lost" (Greenberg 2018; see also Douthat, 2018b).

The Latinx reaction to Trump's demagoguery about Mexican immigrants and the border was also made clear. Of the forty seats that flipped from Republican to Democrat, twenty were in districts where Latinx turnout was critical to the outcome. The UCLA Latino Policy & Politics Initiative analyzed official election results of more than twenty thousand precincts across eight states—California, New Jersey, New York, Texas, Florida, Arizona, New Mexico, and Nevada—and compared 2014 to 2018. Overall, the study concluded that the Latinx vote increased by 96 percent, or doubled, in that period, compared to a 37 percent increase in the non-Latinx vote. The investment of the Democratic Congressional Campaign Committee in voter turnout among the Latinx communities paid off, as turnout matched levels normally seen in presidential elections. In California, Latino voters comprised 21 percent of the voters and were critical in flipping seven districts and shattering the Republican hold in Orange County. In terms of turnout, about 60 percent of registered Latinxs voted, compared to about 30 percent in the previous midterms. In Texas, Latinxs cast 19.1 percent of all votes and more than doubled their turnout compared to 2014. Latinx turnout increased 128 percent but, because of gerrymandering, only flipped two seats (Irby 2019; UCLA 2019).

The recent history of California and Texas suggests two possible contrasting futures for Latinxs. Even though Latinxs in California and Texas have basically the same share of statewide voters, the differences in political representation could not be sharper. Democrats control all the statewide offices in California while Republicans do so in Texas. Such influence has obvious political and policy consequences. One telling example: California is a sanctuary state while Texas *requires* law enforcement to ascertain the citizenship status of all motorists who may be pulled over.

In California, the Republican Party's championing of the anti-immigrant Proposition 187 and the other exclusionary initiatives of the 1990s moved Latinxs to political activism within the Democratic Party. Up until that point, Latinxs voted for Republican candidates in substantial numbers. During the Reagan and George H. W. Bush years, Latinxs had been drifting toward the Republican Party. Governor Wilson himself won 47 percent of the Latinx vote in 1990. But that changed after the GOP began targeting Latinx immigrants. In 1994, the Republican gubernatorial candidate received 27 percent of the Latinx vote, and in 1998 20 percent. Latinxs now constitute almost 40 percent of the state population and more than 25 percent of eligible voters. Democrats control every statewide elected office and make up close to two-thirds of the state senate and assembly, along with almost three-quarters of the congressional delegation. Latinxs are represented at all levels of government. Several have been assembly leaders and lieutenant governors. The Republican Party in the state has basically atrophied (Beinart 2016; Gamboa 2019).

In Texas, the cultural conservative wing of the Republican Party was held in check while George W. Bush was governor and later president. Bush's "compassionate conservatism" regularly won him 40 percent of the Latinx vote. Succeeding Governor Rick Perry initially continued Bush's moderate policies—early on he signed college tuition legislation friendly to DACA (Deferred Action for Childhood Arrivals). However, once Bush left the presidency, Perry succumbed to the Tea Party–inspired Republican surge in Texas. The Democratic decline in the state was also linked to the blatant gerrymandering engineered by former congressman Tom DeLay. Gerrymandering and skewed maps of one design or another have continued to be mainstays of Republican strategy. The various gerrymandering schemes have been challenged in court several times (by the Mexican American Legal Defense and Educational Fund and others). Currently, for example, the Austin metroplex, perhaps the "bluest" spot in the state, remains divided among six congressional districts.

The saga continues. The Republican legislature passed strict ID voter registration laws that disproportionately impact Mexican Americans and African Americans. Since 2011, nine federal court rulings have arrived at that conclusion. Texas state attorney general Ken Paxton actively combed voter registration rolls for fraud. In January 2019, Paxton tweeted, to much fanfare, a "VOTER FRAUD ALERT" that approximately 95,000 noncitizens were on voter registration rolls and that 58,000 of them had voted in the midterms. County registrars were urged to begin purging these 95,000 people, demanding proof of citizenship within thirty days or canceling their registrations. Trump joined the action, tweeting on January 27 that voter fraud was rampant and that the numbers were just the tip of the iceberg (Stern 2019).

Paxton was taking a page from Republican playbook of shock and awe: declare a wildly inflated claim of noncitizen voting, then use the ensuing panic to justify mass disfranchisement. The purge list was created using a profoundly flawed method. Based on Department of Public Safety records dating back to 1996, the secretary of state had identified noncitizens who had obtained or renewed driver's licenses, and then cross-referenced them with voter rolls to come up with the figures of 95,000 registrants and 58,000 active voters. A major problem: 50,000 Texas residents are naturalized each year, and when they become citizens, they are not required to inform the Department of Public Safety.

Paxton's dramatic action was meant to intimidate Latinx voters, who comprise over half of all naturalized citizens in the state. In a parallel move, Homeland Security announced that it was investigating the citizenship status of Texas border residents who had been delivered by midwives (Contreras 2019; *Houston Chronicle* Editorial Board 2019).

Essentially, voter intimidation and repression in Texas has been the Republican response to what happened in California. The recent senate contest in Texas offered an optimistic note: reactionary Ted Cruz survived an impressive challenge from young, charismatic Beto O'Rouke, winning 50.9 percent to 48.3 percent, or around 220,000 votes out of 8.33 million cast. It was the best showing for a Democrat in decades (Tomasky 2018). Demography also favors increased Latinx influence, but again demography is not destiny. A repressive political order, based on making Texas great again, is a possibility. Much will depend on what happens to Trump and Trumpism.

Donald Trump has made the Republican Party his own. An energized ideological minority now controls the party apparatus. Trump embraced and empowered the "cultural conservatives" whose right-wing views and policies are now presented as patriotic common sense. If Trump had been reelected, the policies of Anglo nativism would have been advanced. A two-thousand-mile-long border wall would have been built and the border area further militarized, there would have been a movement toward repealing birthright citizenship and severely restricting the naturalization process, and more obstacles to voter registration and participation—perhaps English literacy tests—would have been imposed. The country would have gone the Texas route.

Even though Trump was not reelected in 2020, nativist ideas exist in the American imaginary, ready to be invoked by any ambitious politician willing to stoke the racial fires. Trump's anti-immigrant mantras have raised the question of the place of Latinxs in the country. The proximity of Spanish-speaking Latin America renders the situation of Latinxs in the United States unlike that of any other immigrant or minority group. Negative images of Mexicans and Central Americans do not stop at the border, and are transferred easily to Latinxs because of appearance and ethnicity. Throughout the country, Latinxs are suspect citizens, subject to police interrogation, voter-identity laws, the constant need to demonstrate loyalty, and, along the southwestern border, interior checkpoints.

The 2020 presidential election has determined, for a time, that the country will follow an inclusive path that encourages active citizenship and welcomes immigrants rather than an exclusionary one that severely restricts immigrants and their citizen look-alikes. But this path was won narrowly, with a margin of only nine million votes. Trump received slightly more than seventy-two million votes, an indication that exclusionary nativism will remain a potent political force in American life.

CHAPTER FOUR

Reckoning with the Gaze

MICHELLE GARCÍA

"Who do you like more, the country or the Hispanics?" President Donald Trump asked supporter and National Hispanic Advisory Council member Steve Cortes during a rally in Rio Rancho, New Mexico, in 2019. With the audience staring in his direction, Cortes selected the option that conveyed loyalty to the nation and, in response, Trump shouted into the microphone: "He says the country. I don't know. I may have to go for the Hispanics, to be honest with you (ABC News 2019.)

It was a scene that simulated a Border Patrol checkpoint, with Trump functioning as the green-uniform-wearing agent guarding the borderline—the entrance to the nation—and empowered to impose a litmus test of patriotism. In the public performance, Cortes's social citizenship is scrutinized, with his ethnicity and nation presented as mutually exclusive options, and, like a checkpoint, his credentials questioned, verified, and then disputed. Unlike a physical Border Patrol checkpoint, the location of which is determined by its distance from an international boundary, the checkpoint of social citizenship is mobile, appearing anywhere, even at a president's rally.

The performance typified a presidency that has seized the border wall as its symbol and "build the wall" as a motto. It also represented a form of political surveillance toward Latinxs that the Trump presidency has exploited. Latinxs that agree and promote his border security measures and cruelty toward asylum seekers and migrants are honored and praised, while dissenters are deemed foreign, not American.

During the 2020 State of the Union Address, Trump momentarily paused his vilification of asylum seekers and other migrants to recognize one Latinx: Raúl Ortiz, the newly appointed deputy chief of Border Patrol, a servant of the surveillance. However, in 2018 Trump, in an effort to discredit the civil fraud lawsuit against Trump University, said that US District Court Judge Gonzalo Curiel— a US-born citizen of Mexican descent— was incapable of fairly adjudicating the case because, "he's a Mexican." Trump argued, in an interview with the *Wall Street Journal* that Curiel's ethnicity posed an "absolute conflict" (Sullivan 2016). The comments were denounced across the political spectrum as racist because Curiel's ethnicity was the basis for Trump's argument that the federal judge was unqualified. Unacknowledged and scrutinized, however, was racist tactic itself: invalidating Curiel's citizenship by subjecting his ethnicity and identity to Trump's judgmental gaze.

In his assault on Latinxs, Trump seized on an unexamined feature of American cultural and political life, what I, following others, call the "gaze." With this entitled, scrutinizing gaze, a deeply entrenched surveillance has emerged—a social panopticon (Foucalt 1983) similar to the network of binoculars, cameras, and drones stationed across the US-Mexico border. The Trump era has promoted a nation of unofficially deputized Border Patrol agents operating checkpoints across the country. Through a culture of surveillance, a willing public performs a version of national identity that empowers them to sit in judgment of Latinxs. Nearly 38 percent of Latinxs reported to Pew Research Center in 2018 that they had been told to "go back," chastised for speaking Spanish, or been on the receiving end of offensive names in the previous year. Since Trump assumed the presidency, Latinxs have increasingly reported feeling worried "about their place in American society," from 41 percent to 49 percent between 2017 and 2018, among both foreign- and US-born Latinxs (López, González-Barrera, and Krogstad 2018).

Through political, cultural and legal surveillance, a violent gaze, Trump has leveraged politicians, past and present, to exact obedience and submission from Latinxs, and particularly Mexican Americans living in Texas. Rather than a political aberration, the Trump era represents a violent culmination and naked expression of a gaze that took shape with the founding of the nation. With its roots in colonialism, Native American genocide, and American slavery, the gaze has been a reliable weapon to define, subjugate, and dehumanize, an expression of white supremacy. In the nation's violent push westward, the gaze, which reduced people to property and deemed Native Americans savages, became an essential feature of western expansion, and the justification for the campaign of imperialism behind the Mexican-American War, which characterized Mexicans and later Mexican Americans as a vicious enemy and the outsider (see Montejano and Beltrán, this volume).

The gaze of the eighteenth and nineteenth centuries never disappeared, I contend. It burrowed deep, finding new ways of expression through culture and politics. Its violent expression toward Black Americans is largely recognizable and the focus of study and reflection is an essential element of American life. In his seminal work, *The Soul of Black Folk*, W. E. Burghardt Du Bois describes a "double-consciousness" created in the Black psyche in response to the white lens of racism. "One feels his two-ness,—an American, a Negro; two souls, two thoughts, two unreconciled strivings; two warring ideals in one dark body, whose dogged strength alone keeps it from being torn asunder. It is a peculiar sensation, this double-consciousness, this sense of always looking at one's self through the eyes of others, of measuring one's soul by the tape of a world that looks on in amused contempt and pity" ([1903] 1995, 45).

Time did little to erode the imposing, entitled gaze. "The white gaze, the only valid one, is already dissecting me. I am fixed," Frantz Fanon writes in *Black Skin, White Masks*. "I am overdetermined from the outside" (2008, 95). The gaze is not unique to the United States. Fanon was not writing about the United States specifically, and indeed wrote of the internationalism of the white gaze. Decades after the US civil rights movement, the unstated and influential power of the gaze can be heard in public outcry for racial justice catalyzed through the repeated calls of "Black Lives Matter." Unstated but understood is the object of the statement: matters to whom, and whose gaze must change?

Since its inception, the gaze conferred power, positioning whites within a now-familiar role of sitting in judgment over Black and later Brown people, and nowhere is the empowered gaze more obvious than the sight of crowds chanting, "Build the Wall." With the border as a reliable site from which judgment is legally meted out, the violent gaze is masked by the legitimacy of immigration law. Acting as the arbiter of reality, the gaze succeeds at repackaging violence against Latinxs, citizens, and noncitizens, as political and policy debates of "immigration" and "border security."

In response, critics have predictably attacked the border wall and the chant as expressions of xenophobia and nativism, as described by politicians and the press. Left unquestioned is the source of the vitriol; left unscrutinized and therefore legitimized is the hate itself. Until now.

Analyzing the gaze of the Trump era requires an examination of its earliest expressions, where the border, which functions as a geographic symbol of the gaze, first took shape, and where Mexicans and Mexican Americans long have been its object: Texas. For Mexican Americans in Texas, the gaze can be traced to the nineteenth century, to the era that saw insurgents remade as heroes at the Alamo and the tiny presidio granted outsize influence as a symbol of lost causes, "true grit," and Texas itself. Upon first contact between whites and Mexicans, the hateful, violent attitude behind the gaze was recorded in everything from official documents to popular literature. The new frontier of Texas was described by William H. Emory (1857) in a United States and Mexican boundary survey, as a "vast country uninhabited by civilized races, and infested by nomadic tribes of savages." As Arnoldo de León writes, "The English conceived of them as degenerate creatures. English writers put together a portrait that turned the people of Mexico into a degraded humanity" (1983, 5).

The portrait permeated the national consciousness, mixing with the smoldering rage from the Mexican-American War, in which "most hawks and doves agreed that Mexicans were racial degenerates" (Johnson 2005, 10). The scalding contact between Mexican Americans and whites resulted in two narratives seemingly parallel to each other, with histories that seemed completely divorced from each other. When confronted with the gaze, some Tejanos seemed bewildered by the references to them as lesser people, a "mongrel race," or foreigners. The Tejano statesman José Antonio Navarro wrote in the 1850s, two decades after the Alamo, "Why do we appear like foreigners in the very land of our birth?" (quoted in Ramos 2019). What Navarro and countless others were unable to reconcile was their self-image and the gaze imposed upon them.

Established Mexican Americans confronted a gaze that solidified with vicious warfare and violence in the form of land grabbing and lynching that were pervasive only one century ago. Theirs was a pastoral culture that came under siege by outsiders. Such a perspective was evidenced in *El Mesquite* by Elena Zamora O'Shea, which chronicles the arrival of Spanish colonists into present-day South Texas and the seemingly bucolic subjugation of Indigenous people, a way of life abruptly upended by incoming whites. Told through the perspective of an old mesquite tree, the loss of belonging and citizenship is memorialized by the tree asking, "If they were Spaniards when governed by Spain and Mexicans when governed by Mexico, why can they not be Americans now that they are under the American government?" (1935, xxiii).

Contained within these episodes and fueling the gaze is an American rage and hate, the echoes of which are heard in the Trump era. In the past and present, they have been reliable weapons of surveillance to quell dissent and prevent rebellion against systemic racism and racist violence. During the nineteenth and early twentieth centuries, the gaze enabled lynching, land grabbing, and extrajudicial killings of Mexican Americans to be legitimized and celebrated by whites. "Texas archives contain photographs of the forgotten dead, hogtied and dragged behind horses," writes Villanueva). "In the tradition of lynching, the perpetrators collected souvenirs as trophies" (2017, 135)

Within this climate, English- and Spanish-language newspapers across the states published a message on June 19, 1916, from Texas governor James Ferguson in the form of a Loyalty Proclamation:

> To Texas Mexicans: At this time, I want to say a word to citizens of Mexican parentage residing permanently or temporarily in Texas. The state of Texas demands of all persons while in her borders absolute obedience and respect to her laws and constituted authorities. If Texas Mexicans will aid by words and deeds the various peace officers in Texas to carry out this demand they need have no fear of bodily harm and they will receive protection of our laws. If they do not in some manner show their loyalty to this state and nation, they will bring trouble upon themselves and many crimes will be committed which cannot be prevented. (quoted in Villanueva 2017, 149–60)

Villanueva focuses, rightfully so, on the demand for loyalty and unquestioned obedience at a time of intense repression. More insidiously, the proclamation made clear to ethnic Mexicans that they were the subject of the gaze; their actions were closely monitored, and even their intimate sentiments were subject to scrutiny.

At the time of Ferguson's proclamation, the Texas Rangers maintained a "blacklist" of ethnic Mexicans—that is, Texans of Mexican descent. Even the mere suggestion that an ethnic Mexican had landed on the list was enough to cause him or her to gather their family and flee. They had been labeled, named, and made the target of monitoring and the hostile gaze. "The proclamation was significant at the time in that Latinos and Anglos understood the government had the power to do and say [anything] about assimilation and showing your allegiance to the United States," Villanueva told me. "It demanded that you assumed to be a threat" (personal communication, 2018).

Decades later, and before Trump occupied office, the confrontation of the gaze and its violent intent had formed a recognizable and formative moment in the lives of Mexican Americans. For Richard Flores (2002), that moment came during a childhood trip to the Alamo, the Spanish-built presidio and legendary battle site of the 1835 uprising by mostly white immigrants from the United States (known as Texians) against Mexico, which governed the lands. But on the tour

Flores's friend turned to him and accused him and other "'meskins" of killing the Texian heroes in battle. John Morán González confronted the gaze on family drives, at the US Border Patrol checkpoint, eighty miles north of his childhood home in Texas's Rio Grande Valley, when each member of the family had to answer the question, "Are you a US citizen?" (2009, ix–x).

For both men, encounters with the gaze engraved deep and powerful memories, which were made apparent decades later when they referenced those incidents as the premises of their scholarly work. "It is not that I didn't know I was Mexican, I couldn't escape it," writes Flores (2002). "I just hadn't realized the liability it was in the eyes of my best friend." In Flores, echoes of nineteenth-century Du Bois can be heard: "Then it dawned upon me with a certain suddenness that I was different from the others; or like, mayhap, in heart and life and longing, but shut out from their world by a vast veil" (Du Bois 1897). He muses on the confrontation with the gaze and the almost-indescribable loss he experienced that day: "Innocence? Certitude? Identity?" (2002, xiii).

Just as Flores described feeling the brunt of the gaze at the Alamo as a child, its violent intent was experienced from the friend who cast it upon him. "When violence leaves its ineffaceable mark," writes Guidotti-Hernández, "everyone involved, spectators, enactors of violence and the recipients of violence, is differentiated through her or his role in these processes" (2011, 9). On that day, Flores's "friend" asserted his right to a gaze that has functioned as whip and censor to define, confine, and marginalize Americans of Mexican descent.

To craft a response to the Trump era requires a reckoning with the varied responses by Mexican Americans to the gaze, some of which validated and perpetuated the gaze. Historically, when confronted with violence and exclusion, some of the most powerful and influential Mexican Americans, meaning also the wealthiest, responded with a concerted campaign of resistance. Molina writes that Mexican Americans fought exclusion by "joining labor unions, choosing not to naturalize, and hoping that their children would not assimilate American ways, which they perceived as too permissive" (2014, 23).

In Laredo, Texas, for example, Jovita Idár and her family denounced the oppression in their newspapers and formed solidarity with Mexican activists and thinkers in Nuevo Laredo, Mexico (Martínez et al. 2017). Mexicans and Mexican Americans in South Texas fomented revolution inspired by the ideology of the anarchist Flores Magón brothers in Mexico. The Magonistas in Texas rightly identified the root of oppression as race and white supremacy. They located their struggle within the common experience of Native Americans and African

Americans (Johnson 2005). Indeed, some Mexican Americans understood what Molina states directly: "*Racialized groups are linked across time and space*" (2014, 6–7; see also 22, 88; italics in original). Such groups are not connected by a shared culture or identity but by the gaze and its resulting oppression and violence.

Our history contains examples of such resistance by redirecting the gaze back at the unnamed observer who wields the power. In 1954, the case of Hernandez v. Texas reached the US Supreme Court. This cased argued that Latinxs, who were legally designated as "white," were treated socially and politically as a class apart, and as such, juries should reflect their ethnic identity. During oral arguments, the justices attempted to identify the class status of ethnic Mexicans in Texas. "They call them greasers down there, don't they," asked one. "Are they citizens?" Lead attorney for the plaintiff, Gus García, responded by taking direct aim at the gaze itself: "If there is any assimilating to be done, it seems to me the other people have to do it," said Garcia. "After all, General Sam Houston was nothing but a wetback from Tennessee."[1]

Legendary journalist Rubén Salazar (1970) began in a column for the *Los Angeles Times* begins his dissection of the term and identity of "Chicano" by addressing the gaze itself: "A Chicano is a Mexican-American with a non-Anglo image of himself." But this worldview coexisted with Mexican Americans responding to marginalization, oppression, and brutality in twentieth-century Texas by pleading for recognition of citizenship and accommodation of the gaze. In response to Governor Ferguson's Loyalty Proclamation in the early twentieth century, ethnic Mexicans sent letters to the governor expressing unbridled loyalty to Texas. With those letters and the proclamation, Tejanos were made aware that they existed within the confined space of a critical gaze.

The racist violence against Texas Mexicans was a determining factor in the creation of the League of United Latin American Citizens (LULAC), which held the first meeting of its Ladies LULAC council in my hometown of Alice, Texas, in 1933. LULAC formed a platform that was decidedly uncritical of the forces of oppression. Instead, writes Benjamin Márquez, "LULAC's politics was that of assimilation and accommodation, with the major goal to reform American society and fit in with the white majority" (2014, 1). LULAC's position was undoubtedly influenced by anti-Mexican violence that wracked the region in the preceding decades. They were concerned with the basic survival of Mexican Americans, who in previous decades had been the victims of thousands of lynchings and extrajudicial killings. Their approach was to become the most strident of patriots. "Its members cherished the ideals upon which the United States was founded;

their writings and public statements were filled with praise for U.S. political institutions as well as the American system of free enterprise," writes Márquez (2014, 1). The result was a platform that promoted aggressive assimilation, while seeking to preserve their Mexican heritage.

The position of accommodation extended far beyond LULAC's South Texas as the organization gained a national reach. It undoubtedly influenced and undermined Latinx culture, identity, and citizenship by contributing to the festering violent gaze that has flourished in our current moment. It ceded power to the gaze without question. Much scholarship has centered on the elitist, classist sensibility of LULAC's founding members—aspirational businessmen more interested in advancement than transformative change. Citizenship was an essential currency and it came at the cost of buying into a white vision of a racial hierarchy. But, as another historian has found, "Mexicans also fought to be recognized as white because whiteness afforded them certain rights. They were not challenging the terms of the debate but rather saying that they were on the right side of the color line" (Molina 2014, 40).

To be sure, Mexican immigration in the early twentieth century and the creation of the border helped to define Mexican Americans as perennial immigrants (see Jiménez, this volume). Generations of Mexican Americans undertook the bureaucratic process of obtaining citizenship and, concurrently, set out on the futile and circular errand of pleading for recognition of full citizenship—socially, politically, and culturally.

In his seminal work, *With His Pistol in His Hand*, Américo Paredes deconstructs the image of the Texas Mexican that emerged from the white gaze. "In the conflict along the Rio Grande, the English-speaking Texan (whom we shall call the Anglo-Texan for short) disappoints us in a folkloristic sense. He produces no border balladry. His contribution to the literature of border conflict is a set of attitudes and beliefs about the Mexican that form a legend of their own" (1970, 15). Some of the so-called "truths" cited by Paredes about the Texas Mexican from that gaze are echoed in the Trump-era discourse about Latinxs, and Mexicans specifically as "bad hombres" and rapists and criminals:

1. The Mexican is cruel by nature. The Texan must in self-defense treat the Mexican cruelly, since that is the only treatment the Mexican understands.

2. The Mexican is cowardly and treacherous, and no match for the Texan. He can get the better of the Texan only by stabbing him in the back or by ganging up on him with a crowd of accomplices.

3. Thievery is second nature in the Mexican, especially horse and cattle rustling, and on the whole he is about as degenerate a specimen of humanity as may be found anywhere. (16)

Paredes, writes Morán González (2009) powerfully constructed a response to the gaze of white supremacy and the attempt to construct a colonial vision of the Texas Mexican. However, in a critical assessment of Paredes's early-Texas narrative, José E. Limón (1994) argues that Paredes overlooked the impact that regional and geographic difference made on Mexican Americans' perception of their new position as the object of the white gaze. The result, according to Morán González's reading of Limón, was for Mexican Americans to "assign blame for the modern fracturing of the Texas Mexican culture to working-class *fuereños* (Mexican immigrants from outside the immediate border region) whose susceptibility to mass culture (in contradiction to folk) culture enabled the ultimate triumph of Anglo-Texan culture" (130).

Among the responses to the hateful gaze was accommodation and an adoption of its agenda for political advantage. An example is the report titled *What Price Wetback?* (American GI Forum of Texas and the Texas State Federation of Labor, 1953) based on a survey of unauthorized Mexican migrant workers. The middle-class Mexican American authors noted that the survey and report were drafted in response to a "wetback invasion." "The wetbacks" they wrote, "are a problem and a threat to our security and standard of living" (1.) The report, replete with photos of Mexicans working in the fields, living in abysmal conditions, and in line to be processed by Border Patrol, was published jointly by the Texas Federation of Labor and the American GI Forum, an organization representing Latinx war veterans.

The American GI Forum, which deployed the investigators to conduct the survey included in the report, made clear their reasoning for contributing to the anti-Mexican sentiment. The migrant workers were blamed for depressing wages in the crop-picking jobs. Over 80 percent of migrant farm laborers were American citizens of Mexican descent. Some 100,000 Mexican Americans worked as farmworkers within Texas. In 1951, an additional 65,666 traveled out of state on the farmworker trail toward fields in the north. Most of the Mexican American farmer workers, according to the survey, owned their homes or a small acreage, as well as their own vehicle. They were described as "solvent citizens, devout, interested in community projects—first class citizens in every respect" (56), except for possessing the citizenship that entitled them to upward mobility.

Missing from the report was any reason to explain the large number of Mexican Americans—third- or fourth-generation Americans—who toiled in one of the most exploitative industries. No mention was made of the abhorrent lack of educational opportunities and the rampant discrimination faced by Mexican Americans that kept them in the fields, generation after generation. Unnoted but glaringly apparent were the workings of the American gaze or racism.

The investigators and their cohort were soon disabused of any notion that citizenship, on paper, shielded them from the violent and brutal gaze. In the report, the authors noted that before its publication, Attorney General Herbert Brownell Jr., supported by President Dwight D. Eisenhower, "would spotlight the wetback problem as a national issue" (1). Eisenhower is remembered for executing Operation Wetback, which the government claimed resulted in the deportation of more than 1 million Mexicans, including 300,000 US citizens, according to historian Kelly Lytle Hernandez (2017).

Decades later Trump cited Operation Wetback as a successful and model approach to immigration and border security. Likewise, in Texas some Latinxs adopt the same assimilationist and white-dominant attitudes toward immigration, albeit with a more humane edge. Latinxs support tighter border security and demand that immigrants speak English, despite the fact that English adoption is well documented. What we see are Latinxs embracing, or at least adhering to, a paradigm of Americanness, of citizenship, one that is powerfully imbued with racist undertones and not centered on their own experience.

To this day, Mexican Americans react to criticism, racism, and challenges to their citizenship by making the case for their acceptance rather than taking on the roots and nature of the gaze inflicted upon them. Case in point, in January 2019, Tom Brokaw, the veteran NBC journalist, said on *Meet the Press*: "I also happen to believe that the Hispanics should work hard at assimilation. . . . You know, that they ought not be just codified in their communities but make sure that all their kids are learning to speak English" (quoted in García 2019). Predictably, many Latinxs responded by making the case that they had, in fact, assimilated. Tellingly, Latinx journalists responded by tweeting statistics about the prevalence of English use among Latinx families and their own families' "assimilation stories." Others denounced the statement by saying that speaking Spanish was part of a modern global culture. Rep. Joaquín Castro (D-TX) (2019) slammed the comment as an expression of "xenophobia" and referenced the widespread practice of teachers physically punishing children for speaking Spanish in school.

Such responses, however, did not examine or analyze the violent and, in this case, hardly subtle intent contained within the message. Brokaw said whites had expressed to him an anxiety, perhaps even fear, over whether they "want brown grandbabies" (quoted in García 2019). "Want" in this context is misleading. "Tolerate" is the underlying message.

In contrast, Yamiche Alcindor, a Black journalist and the White House correspondent for *PBS News Hour*, told Brokaw during the discussion, "And the idea that we think Americans can only speak English, as if Spanish, and other languages, wasn't always part of America, is, in some ways, troubling" (quoted in García 2019). Her comment struck at the gaze and its legacy of violence as expressed in Brokaw's statement. Even more, Alcindor asserted, it shifted the focus from citizenship—about which Latinx pleaded that they had "done their part, as Brokaw asserted"—to the perception, assumptions, and ideology contained in his statement.

The same response is found, for example, in the work of James Baldwin, who locked on to the gaze toward Blacks and exposed it as a corruption of the viewer, not the viewed. "What white people have to do," Baldwin said once, "is try to find out in their hearts why it was necessary for them to have a nigger in the first place. Because I am not a nigger. I'm a man. If I'm not the nigger here, and if you invented him, you the white people invented him, then you have to find out why. And the future of the country depends on that. Whether or not it is able to ask that question" (quoted in Peck 2016).

In the novel *Black No More* George Schuyler (2011) argues that Blackness must exist for whiteness to exist. Latinxs know this to be true. A whiteness predicated on the Latinx other has resulted in a library of works and political statements. The matter of Latinx citizenship and the legitimacy of Latinxs' standing is simply the end result of the needs of the gaze. Like a child who becomes aware of its own existence by observing the reactions of others to their actions, so does whiteness fortify itself by the presence of Latinxs. Even more, whiteness is then reinforced when Latinxs perform the "American act" to gain acceptance while doing nothing to acknowledge, much less challenge, the American rage behind the gaze.

The challenge for Latinxs is not simply to trade a citizenship argument for a race argument. What is needed is an American narrative centered on the experiences of Mexican Americans that contains an overt challenge to the gaze cast upon Latinxs (see Valenzuela, this volume). Simply narrating the Latinx experience without reckoning with the gaze reinforces the notion of the "other," occupying a parallel experience, the alternative person, the object performing for the gaze.

More than fifty years after attorney Gus García responded to the justices of the high court in Hernandez v. Texas, Justice Sonia Sotomayor, in an opinion regarding the Trump administration's attempt to end Deferred Action for Childhood Arrivals (DACA), reminded Latinxs, of all backgrounds, of indifference to the hostile gaze, even by the "liberal" justices. In her separate opinion, Justice Sotomayor (2020) enumerated Trump's public statements, contained in the lawsuit, that compared undocumented immigrants to "animals" and labeled Mexican immigrants as "criminals, drug dealers [and] rapists" and she chastised her colleagues, writing, "the plurality brushes these aside as 'unilluminating,' 'remote in time,' and 'having been made in unrelated contexts'" (2, 5). By dismissing the relevance of Trump's statement, the justices ignored the discriminatory intent of the policy; just as important, by ignoring the characterization of Mexicans through a well-worn image, the justices, in their opinion, foreclosed the possibility of challenging DACA based on the constitution's equal protection clause. Although the lawsuit centered on immigration policy, Sotomayor wrote, "I would not so readily dismiss the allegation that an executive decision disproportionately harms the same racial group that the President branded as less desirable mere months earlier" (3). In the opinion, Sotomayor applied a racial lens, one rooted in history and time, by exposing the workings of a gaze that has been imposed on Latinxs, both foreign and US born.

Demographic changes may force a long-needed reckoning. The millennial generation has eclipsed baby boomers in numbers. In Texas, more than half of youth have at least one parent who is an immigrant, according to an analysis for the Texas-based Jolt Initiative (Arce, Ramírez, and Pulido 2018). For this generation, said Manuel Pastor, a sociologist at the University of Southern California, the massacres and lynching that gave rise to LULAC are not their historical touchstones; instead, they reference the border wall and the "show me your papers laws" (personal communication, 2019), public policies that overtly reveal the hand of white supremacy.

For this generation, the nexus of race, the gaze, and citizenship is unavoidable. Nearly two hundred years after the Treaty of Guadalupe Hidalgo, which marked the official end of the Mexican-American War, conferred citizenship status to Tejanos, it may be that Latinxs gain full social citizenship through the efforts of those who intimately live the anti-immigrant demonization.

Leading up to the 2020 election, grassroots groups, without stating so explicitly, targeted the gaze as an obstacle to organizing and mobilizing Latinx voters. The Trump era promoted a vision of the nation that Latinxs know all too well, Antonio Arellano, acting executive director of Jolt, told me. "You need to prove you are worthy of this country, you have to prove that you are worthy of the American Dream," said Arellano. "That's not the American Dream; it is come as you are." Arellano says that harnessing the power of Latinx voting requires working with Latinxs to "paint themselves in the country to see themselves in the quilt of this nation" (personal communication, July 26, 2020). Crystal Zermeno, director of electoral strategy for the Texas Organizing Project, echoed that sentiment, saying that the imposing gaze that has taught Latinxs to see themselves as the "other" has dampened turnout. In focus group studies, they found that Latinxs "feel like voting is the other, it's not where they belong," Zeremeno told me. "Latinos think that voting is, 'whatever, that's for other people'" (personal communication, n.d.).

No one strategy can challenge the gaze. Its form and expression vary, its presence undefined by specific situations. To be sure, the gaze manifested as extremism is easily identifiable and just as easily dismissed as the work of outright racists, as the exception rather than the norm. Equally dangerous and insidious, however, are the workings of the gaze contained in softness, cloaked in the veneer of tolerance, a term that bestows the right of one to render judgment on another.

Not long ago, during the editing process for an article about the border, the editor for a well-known liberal publication attempted to cast the border region as inherently progressive because it is racially vibrant. Communities where Latinxs reside are often described in seemingly positive terms as "vibrant" or "diverse" enclaves. In the case of my article, such descriptions actually served to shift the attention from the expressions of white supremacy, which was my point, to the description of the border towns. A familiar foreboding came over me, one that I had been unable to articulate for much of my career. The problem itself seemed indescribable. What I came to realize was that I was peering straight into the gaze. Friendly and "politically progressive" to be sure, but a gaze that asserted its position to judge and define.

To make my point, I argued, essentially that if we say the border is significant because it is a diverse community, it implicitly centers and privileges whiteness. It says that what is significant is that these people exist at all, and it reinforces the presumption of the border and the United States as white.

The point was well received and the necessary adjustments were made. More significantly, by exposing and naming the gaze, I had gained something that had long seemed elusive and scarcely definable: I had claimed the ground beneath me. I had asserted the right to narrate—to occupy the center—and disarm the gaze.

Note

1.   John J. Herrera, letter to the editor, *Houston Post*, Feb. 22, 1972, 27, setting out details of the case (box 2, folder 24,Houston Metropolitan Research Center). See also Haney López and Olivas (2008) for additional context.

CHAPTER FIVE

Artist versus Ideologue

Two American Dystopias

RENATO ROSALDO

On June 16, 2015, as he was riding down an escalator, Donald Trump announced that he was running for president. He then falsely said of immigrants to the United States from Mexico, "They're bringing drugs. They're bringing crime. They're rapists. And some, I assume, are good people" (2015a). This alarming message was not surprising. After all, Trump's bigotry was as much his brand as was his lying. Trump later made it clear that he was as prejudiced against US citizens of Mexican descent as he was biased against Mexican nationals who were not US citizens, when he declared that the Mexican heritage of Indiana-born (US citizen) judge Gonzalo Curiel made him unfit to adjudicate about Trump University. American citizens of Mexican ancestry were, in his view, second-class citizens of the United States.

Trump's escalator remarks made visible his adherence to a social order that a number of scholars, notably including Cristina Beltrán in this volume, have called a Herrenvolk democracy, which is a racial hierarchy where the dominant white group rules over a subordinate nonwhite group (in this case, Mexican Americans). In elucidating the dynamics of this racial hierarchy, consider the notion of *whiteness*, as explored by Beltrán. Though it also applies to the United States, the notion of *whiteness* was developed in South Africa under apartheid as a race-based ideology in which the dominant white group took pleasure in inflicting acts of cruelty and terror on dark-skinned subordinate groups. Beltrán says, "Scholars have sometimes referred to [this] form of white democracy as Herrenvolk democracy, 'a regime that is democratic for the master race, but tyrannical for subordinate groups.'" She adds that Mexican "migrants (with or without legal sanction) represent the rare population that offer nativists an administratively endorsed opportunity to access and revisit the power and pleasures of Herrenvolk democracy."

In invoking the concept of Herrenvolk democracy, as Beltrán does, it is cru-
cial that social analysis consider two groups, the prey and the predator—the
dominant white group and the subordinate nonwhite group. I have chosen to
focus here, for a portrayal of the subordinate group, on the Mexican American
people as depicted in artist Helena María Viramontes's novel *Their Dogs Came
with Them* (2007). How do the Mexican-Americans live their subordination?
What is their subordination in existential terms? To what extent and in what
ways are they being subjected to systemic cruelty and terror as predicted by
the Herrenvolk concept? In the second part of this chapter, I will review the
manifesto of the conservative ideologue Samuel Huntington, which portrays the
dominant Anglo-Saxon group. Pairing Viramontes and Huntington is telling in
the current moment of Trumpism.

Viramontes's novel is usually read as pure realism, as a historical novel that
uses gritty prose to depict life, as it was actually lived, during the 1960s in East
Los Angeles, a predominantly Mexican American area of the city. The front
material announces a complex chronology for the novel. It devotes a page to the
declaration, set in bold, that the novel takes place in the decade of 1960–1970.
The novel depicts a decade of Mexican American life in East Angeles under a
Herrenvolk democracy that includes state-sanctioned cruelty and terror. On the
opposite page is the novel's epigraph, taken from Aztec accounts of the Spanish
conquest of Mexico in 1519. It says that the Spaniards "terrified everyone who
saw them. Their dogs came with them, running ahead of the column. They
raised their muzzles high; they lifted their muzzles to the wind" (vii). Thus, the
novel thematizes, without chronicling it year by year, the domination, both colonial and imperial, that the Mexican American population of East Los Angeles
endured for five hundred years.

This dystopian novel is organized thematically more than chronologically. It's
not plot driven. Instead, it is organized around the lives of four young female
protagonists, who endure gendered cruelty, and it traces their partially overlapping personal networks. The four protagonists are Ermila, who has lived with
her grandparents ever since her parents abandoned her; Turtle, born a girl and
refashioned as a boy to join a street gang, the McBride Boys; Ana, who cares for
her mentally challenged brother; and Tranquilina, the daughter of missionaries
who minister to the urban poor in East Los Angeles. The novel is laced with a
sense of profound loss. It tells of subjugation and coping. It speaks more from
the point of view of the prey than of the predator.

The initial period of the novel, set in the early 1960s, tells of the construction of the freeways through East Los Angeles, which results in the displacement, disappearance, and removal of Mexican Americans from their homes. Viramontes vividly terms this process as having "amputated the streets" (33), precisely a form of state-sanctioned cruelty characteristic of Herrenvolk democracy. The novel metaphorically suggests that the bulldozers used in freeway construction resembled the Spanish attack dogs of 1519, but now, rather than accompanying soldiers, they were leading columns of automobiles-to-come, in the brutal conquest and colonization of an urban East Los Angeles. The bulldozers of the early 1960s echoed the dogs of 1519 ("their muzzles high . . . their muzzles to the wind"), in the following manner: "The bulldozers had started from very far away and slowly arrived on First Street, their muzzles like sharpened metal teeth making way for the freeway" (6). Chavela, a neighbor, remarks that "displacement will always come down to two things, earthquakes or earthmovers" (8). Bulldozer-led displacement, in other words, is like a force of nature, like an earthquake, devastating for those who undergo its effects. Contrary to fact, the cruelty inflicted by freeway construction appears to have no human author. No person or group was held accountable for the devastation it caused, yet there were decision makers who saw the Mexican American people of East Los Angeles as expendable in the face of "progress" and what Jean Franco (2013) has called "cruel modernity." After Chavela herself disappeared, her "blue house looked as empty as a toothless mouth" (8.).

The astute observer of and commentator on this displacement is Ermila, at the time a six-year-old child. In a home nearby, Turtle looks out from the porch "to see the blue house like all the other houses disappearing inch by inch just like Chavela and the other neighbors. In its place, the four-freeway interchange would be constructed in order to reroute 547,300 cars a day through the Eastside and would become the busiest in the city" (169). What the reader has until this moment learned piecemeal is a sanitized version of the process of freeway construction and the amputation of the Mexican American community in East Los Angeles. It is now spelled out here by the narrator in its brutal quantitative magnitude.

The final period of the novel is set in the late, rather than the early, 1960s. This period is dominated by a fictional entity, the Quarantine Authority, that subjects the Mexican American people of East Los Angeles to a number of state-sanctioned forms of cruelty, including roadblocks, meticulous checkpoints, sharpshooters, and shots fired from armed helicopters. At that time "roadblocks enforced a quarantine to contain a potential outbreak of rabies" (54).

This dubious outbreak of rabies never occurs in the novel. Quarantine Authority troopers laboriously check the identity cards that Mexican Americans are required to present after curfew in order to get around their own neighborhoods. These cards resemble the pass cards required for Black people to travel in South Africa under apartheid. Quarantine Authority troopers are visible, hence known as the authors of their actions. Some, like Ulysses Rodríguez, are dark-skinned Mexican Americans (289), yet they inflict cruelty on their equally dark-skinned neighbors. In Viramontes's depiction, these officers are magnified in ways that make them resemble generic storm troopers, whether German or from Star Wars: "They bulked, all of them, not from the muscle of workouts or academy-regulated exercise, but from the loads of cartridges and pistols they carried in their waistbands, plump with the weight of batons and flashlights, choke chains, handcuffs, and Mace spray" (288). They are the enforcers in a Trumpist Herrenvolk democracy that inflicts cruelty on the subordinate Mexican American population. As it depicts this period, the novel becomes science fiction about a dystopian future set in the past: "Ermila watched the Quarantine Authority helicopters burst out of the midnight sky to shoot dogs not chained up by curfew. Qué locura, she thought, the world is going crazy" (77).

By this point in time, the late 1960s, roadblocks and armed helicopters evoke the horrors of the Vietnam War. Thus, the Quarantine Authority embodies the repressive arm of the state apparatus. It inflicts state-sanctioned cruelty and thereby transforms Mexican Americans into aliens as they walk their own neighborhoods, in a future that, like much science fiction, is a heightened depiction of their present-day condition in the United States. This is a dystopian vision of a dispossessed community.

At Garfield High School in East Los Angeles, Ermila and her girlfriends plan to participate in the blowouts, the famous militant student walkouts of the Chicana and Chicano movement, and ditch school, "everyone else thinking they held up banners or raised fists to demand a better education, declare Chicano Power" (50). As Ermila lies restless, in bed but not yet asleep due to the distant sound of bullets, the flashes of floodlights cut through the blinds. Ermila approaches a dog her grandmother acquired as protection and "asked herself: Why even bother? Why bother to lift her head from the pillow, sit on the bed to stare at the dog scratching ticks . . . ?" (175). By that time in Viramontes's narrative, dogs have grown abundant and degraded. A pack of wild dogs, what the narrator calls "asphalt jungle dogs," hurtles into the thick of freeway traffic. "All of the dogs howled and growled in devoted vengeance in response to the hooting and catcalls from the drivers who found themselves in their own gregarious herd of cars" (277). The packs of dogs resemble, in the reader's imagination, youth gangs, not unlike the McBride Boys. The people in East Los Angeles follow the path of the dogs, becoming increasingly degraded in response to predation from the Quarantine Authority.

Cruelty inflicted from an external source produces cruelty within the Mexican American community. It is as if a man has been yelled at by his boss and, in a displaced act of frustration and retaliation, kicks the dog as he enters his home. In the meantime, Ermila runs to warn her cousin that he is in mortal danger from the McBride Boys, but she does not reach him before the novel ends.

At that time, one of the McBride Boys offers Turtle a lift in his Pontiac Bonneville, but she feels in danger. She knows the rule: gang members who go AWOL (she went missing while wandering homeless) get beaten as the price of readmission to the gang. As a Quarantine Authority helicopter sets off in hot pursuit of its prey, Turtle feels she has no choice but to leap into the car. As the story develops, "The copter circled in on the Bonneville in a military maneuver, blinding Turtle with the fluorescent explosion of iris-burning light" (271). The car unexpectedly escapes the helicopter and in celebration of their escape the driver gives Turtle a joint laced with angel dust (PCP). Nearby, Ermila "turned to see if she recognized the car chased by the beams of the helicopter and wondered about Big Al. He was never the pursuer, but always the one being pursued" (294).

In the meantime, Ana enlists Tranquilina to help search for her brother. They run into Ermila's cousin, Nacho, at the bus depot and speak briefly with him, asking if he's seen Ana's brother. The novel's ending then becomes a convergence of three of the four protagonists, who meet face-to-face. Until then they live in parallel social networks that do not met. The final chapter of the novel resembles the ending of a Shakespearean tragedy, with bodies strewn on the stage. A storm of biblical proportions erupts during the apocalyptic conclusion, as torrential rains include a blazing bolt of lightning that strikes Ermila's cousin: "Nacho never knew what hit him" (320). Still in the Bonneville, Turtle is utterly dissociated from having inhaled the PCP-laced marijuana and sees herself, as if from the outside, vomiting, being pushed out of the car, being thrown away, and abandoned by the McBride Boys. In protest against the animalization of the Mexican Americans of East Los Angeles, Tranquilina roars to the Quarantine Authority sharpshooters, "Stop shooting, we're not dogs!" (334). But they keep shooting. With Ermila's cousin Nacho, Turtle, and Tranquilina strewn on the ground, the narrator comments on the emotional impact of the final scene by saying it consisted of "sorrow so wide, it was blinding" (325). A Herrenvolk democracy, as Beltrán argues, is tyrannical and, I would add, tragic, for the subordinate group. A repercussion of the state-sponsored cruelty toward the subordinate group (for example, Tranquilina's being shot) is that it also produces cruelty within the subordinate group (the deaths of Nacho and Turtle as they were being pursued by the McBride Boys).

The consideration of Herrenvolk democracy in the United States requires an analysis, not only of the subordinate Mexican American group, but also of the dominant white group. A major antecedent for white nationalism and for Trumpism is Samuel Huntington's manifesto, *Who Are We?* (2004). The central assertion of Huntington's book is that the United States is on the verge of splitting into two hostile camps: white Anglo-Saxon Protestants versus Mexican Americans. This claim, which I find hallucinatory, is designed to bring fear to the hearts of the dominant white population.

Huntington was one among a number of authors who have claimed that Mexican Americans are a threat to the dominant white population. In so doing, he revitalizes a long-standing characterization of the presence of Mexican Americans as somehow capable of eroding the virtues of the Protestant ethic. This anti-Mexican portrayal dates at least from before the Mexican-American War of 1846–1848, as a result of which the United States seized Mexican territory that now comprises the states of Texas, California, New Mexico, Arizona, Nevada, and Colorado.

Huntington (2004a) published an essay called "The Hispanic Challenge," in which he summarized *Who Are We?* Critics pointed out a plethora of evidence indicating that, in fact, the transition to English was widespread and accelerating (Portes and Rumbaut 2001, 2014). Huntington's scholarship, in short, is shoddy.

In "The Hispanic Challenge," Huntington endorses the view of what he could have called Herrenvolk democracy, but what he in fact calls the new white nationalism, which asserts "that the shifting U.S. demographics foretell the replacement of white culture by black or brown cultures that are intellectually and morally inferior" (41). This statement is astonishingly offensive and an incitement to cruelty on the part of white people in ways that, reading Huntington through the lens of Trumpism and Herrenvolk democracy, arguably informed the chants at the infamous torchlight marches in Charlottesville, Virginia, on August 11–12, 2017 ("You/Jews will not replace us"). Lest one think my reading of Huntington is forced, it may help to underscore a passage in his larger book, in which he speaks of the need for dominant white national identity groups to define themselves in opposition to a despised "other." To support this argument he cites Joseph Goebbels, the Nazi minister of propaganda (1933–1945) as follows: "Do they also need an enemy? Some people clearly do. Oh, how wonderful it is to hate," (2004b, 25). When I first saw Goebbels cited as a credible source, I was horrified that anybody would be guided by these words and that Huntington could expect his readers to be convinced by them. It appears that Huntington is giving white nationalists their genealogy.

In reading Huntington, it is important to consider how he characterizes his project. Otherwise, the reader may be puzzled that he is not weighing evidence and coming to a judgement about accuracy or truthfulness. He is not writing a work of scholarship as an academic scholar might be expected to do. His book is instead an exhortation directed at white citizens, instructing them about the acts of cruelty that will give them pleasure in a Herrenvolk democracy, instructing them on how to behave like members of the so-called master race.

At the beginning of his book *The Clash of Civilizations and the Remaking of World Order* Huntington clarifies matters when he says, "This book is not intended to be a work of social science. . . . It aspires to present a framework, a paradigm, for viewing global politics that will be meaningful to scholars and useful to policymakers" (1996, 13). Early in *Who Are We?* Huntington speaks about his shift in identity, from scholar to ideologue: "If I think of myself as a scholar, I will try to act like a scholar. But individuals also can change their identities. If I begin to act differently—as a polemicist, for instance—I will suffer 'cognitive dissonance' and am likely to relieve the resulting anguish by stopping that behavior or by redefining myself from a scholar to a political advocate" (2004b, 22). Put otherwise, Huntington is an ideologue who masquerades as a scholar. In so disguising himself, it no doubt helps that he is a Harvard professor. His project is to produce ideology and act as a warrior engaged in ideological battles.

But Huntington is part of a larger enterprise, not a solitary warrior. The editor of *Harper's Magazine*, Lewis Lapham (2004), described the larger enterprise that Huntington draws on in an essay called "Tentacles of Rage: The Republican Propaganda Mill, a Brief History." The essay builds on the analysis of Rob Stein, a former advisor to the chairman of the Democratic National Committee, which shows the systematic character of the right-wing propaganda mill, built on foundations, think tanks, and mass media distributions that have funded students and scholars. Lapham lists Huntington's book, *The Clash of Civilizations*, along with seven other books as examples of this ideological production, including works by such authors as Milton Friedman, Charles Murray, and Dinesh

D'Souza, who have been funded by such foundations as the Olin Foundation, the Lilly Foundation, and (Huntington's funders) the Bradley Foundation and the Smith Richardson Foundation. Huntington was part of a larger and systematic right-wing enterprise promoting ultraconservative economic views, racist understandings of intelligence testing, and attacks on multiculturalism.

Huntington shaped the ideas of an influential group of anti-immigrant scholar-activists whose members studied under his direction at Harvard. One of his early students was Cuban-born George Borjas, described in the *Miami Herald* as an "avowed conservative" (Dorschner 2017), which was not surprising for a Cuban American of the era. Borjas encouraged state and local governments to enact anti-Mexican measures when he became a professor of economic and social policy at Harvard's Kennedy School. He also was the primary advisor for Jason Richwine's (2009) PhD dissertation in public policy, entitled "IQ and Immigration Policy." Richwine held a post at the Heritage Foundation, which he was later forced to resign because of the controversy around a major assertion of his thesis: that Latinx immigrants are, and will remain, less intelligent than comparable US-born whites.

From 1984 to 1988, Huntington served as adviser to Kris Kobach, then a Harvard undergraduate, who later described himself as a nationalist. Kobach worked hard to convince state and local governments to enact hardline anti-immigrant policies to control Mexican immigration. He then became the secretary of state of Kansas from 2010 to 2018. The links from Huntington to Kobach to Trump became apparent in late March 2019, when Kobach was considered by Trump as a candidate to be his immigration czar. His views proved so extreme that he was deemed unlikely to receive congressional approval for this position. Huntington, as a "white" nationalist, and Borjas, as a "Latino" white nationalist, both had ties to John Tanton, the white nationalist founder of the Federation for American Immigration Reform (FAIR), which was eventually designated as a "hate group" by the Southern Poverty Law Center. Borjas contributed to and participated in events sponsored by Tanton's Center for Immigration Studies (Shorman 2017).

On August 8, 1997, Tanton wrote a letter to Huntington (now archived in the Bentley Historical Library at the University of Michigan in Ann Arbor), in which he clearly expected agreement to the following: "The situation then is that the people who have been the carriers of Western Civilization are well on the way toward resigning their commission to carry the culture into the future" (quoted in Beirch 2008). Tanton would have found Trump's 2020 rally speeches reassuring.

In June 2005, *Miami Herald* columnist Andres Oppenheimer placed Huntington alongside right-wing commentators Lou Dobbs of CNN and Bill O'Reilly of Fox News, as perpetrators of the false view that Hispanics were "taking over" the nation. Carlos Lozada (2017), a Pulitzer Prize–winning book critic for the *Washington Post*, connects Huntington to Trump and white nativism in the following manner: "Huntington both chronicles and anticipates America's fights over its founding premises, fights that Trump's ascent has aggravated. Huntington foresees—and, frankly, stokes—the rise of white nativism in response to Hispanic immigration." Lozada calls Huntington, "a prophet for the Trump era"

Huntington spoke of culture and civilization as if they could be reduced to national character. A cardboard notion of assimilation, for example, is at the heart of *Who Are We?* To counter this notion, I draw on a fine essay by Asian American studies scholar David Palumbo-Liu, "Multiculturalism Now: Civilization, National Identity, and Difference Before and After September 11." The essay linked Huntington's views to earlier studies of national character conducted in support of the national mobilization during World War II:

> Dealing with the enemy, as well as discovering the constancy of American identity, required particular attention to the notion of "culture." "Culture" would serve to explain and define what was then called "national character"...
>
> ... After the war, there was a persistence of such interests in defining the American character as that thing which was "exceptionally" American. It was to be something essential and enduring, despite having to respond to external factors such as immigration and social and political change. (2002, 111–12)

Huntington argued that civilizations were cultural entities, but he in fact reduced them to the level of nation states.

Huntington further argued for the primacy of national identity and the need for coherence and purity at that level. A corollary of this argument was that contestation within nations was divisive, but wars between nations were not. Palumbo-Liu comments as follows:

> *The Clash of Civilizations* subordinates economic concerns to a purely cultural thesis that argues that multiculturalism is the bane of America's existence. Indeed, his long book spends three hundred pages organizing

the world according to civilizations [Sinic, Japanese, Hindu, Islamic, Western, Latin American, and possibly African] in order to launch an attack on
domestic cultural politics. The basic thesis of the book is that in the post–
Cold War world, the great conflicts will not occur between nations nor
through ideological conflict (capitalism vs. socialism) but through "civilizational" conflict. . . . Civilization or religion, it all comes down to a belief in
the absolutism of national culture and identity. (118–19)

In *Who Are We?* Huntington extended his argument concerning the primacy
and purity of national identity as opposed to the subnational: "National identity
became preeminent compared to other identities after the Civil War, and American nationalism flourished during the following century. In the 1960s, however,
subnational, dual-national, and transnational identities began to rival and erode
the preeminence of national identity" (2004b, xv). It was but a short step from
the fear of subnational identities to targeting Latinxs as the dangerous, unassimilable ingredient in our national stew. Huntington itemized the following factors:
the shared border, the scale of migration, illegality, regional concentration, the
persistence of migration, and the historical claim to US territory that, until the
Mexican-American War of 1846–1848, was about half of the republic of Mexico.
These factors, he claimed, make Mexicans unwilling to assimilate for reasons
that he never makes clear.

Huntington heaped more factors on his pile. He measured assimilation, for
example, in terms of such factors as the persistence of Spanish, the lag in educational attainment, the persistence of poverty, and conversion to Evangelical
Protestantism. In his words, "Unquestionably, a most significant manifestation
of assimilation for Hispanic immigrants is conversion to Evangelical Protestantism" (2004b, 241). Evidently, he had never been to a Latinx Evangelical service,
nor heard of syncretism. He also spoke of relatively low levels of educational attainment and high rates of poverty in ways that are bizarre as measures of assimilation. He said, "The education of Mexican-origin people differs significantly
from the American norm. . . . What is clear is that the educational achievements
of subsequent generations of Mexican-Americans continue to lag" (232–33). He
also contested, "Compared with the American norm, Mexican-Americans are
poor and are likely to remain so for some while" (255). This use of the phrase
"the American norm" is simply laughable.

These claims are familiar to scholars of Latinx studies, but they usually appear
in the context of arguments about an underclass, subordination, discrimination,

or residential segregation. It is outlandish to call completing high school, or better yet, college, and enjoying a middle-class income the American norm. Failure to become middle class in the United States, according to Huntington, is a failure to assimilate to the national norm and become American rather than (as most researchers would have it) a failure to prosper, perhaps in the face of racial discrimination or some other variable. It would seem to follow that, for Huntington, white Anglo-Saxon Protestants among the rural poor in the United States have failed to assimilate and, culturally speaking, are not American.

In *The Clash of Civilizations* Huntington expanded his argument about internal divisions within the national in the following manner:

> Western culture is challenged by groups within Western societies. One such challenge comes from immigrants from other civilizations who reject assimilation and continue to adhere to and to propagate the values, customs, and cultures of their home societies. This phenomenon is most notable among Muslims in Europe, who are, however, a small minority. It is also manifest, in lesser degree, among Hispanics in the United States, who are a large minority. If assimilation fails in this case, the United States will become a cleft country, with all the potentials for internal strife and disunion that entails. (1996, 304–30)

In *Who Are We?* Huntington is more explicit about the enemy within. As he wrote, "For several decades interest groups and nonelected government elites have promoted racial preferences, affirmative action, and minority language and cultural maintenance programs which violate the American Creed and serve the interests of blacks and nonwhite immigrant groups" (2004b, 312–13).

Huntington sometimes described himself as a white nationalist and, more often, as a white nativist. He knew that nativism had a nefarious genealogy—most prominently, the Ku Klux Klan and neo-Nazis. In order to sanitize this genealogy, Huntington claimed that there was a new genteel white nativism afoot, one espoused by respectable, middle-class people, even educated men like himself. As he said, "The term 'nativism' has acquired pejorative connotations among denationalized elites on the assumption that it is wrong to vigorously defend one's 'native' culture and identity and to maintain their 'purity' against foreign influences" (2004b, 310).

In "The Hispanic Challenge" Huntington further defined his notion of white nativism. The following prophetic passage shows the slippery slope in Huntington's work, from description to prescription, as well as his shift in identity from social scientist to militant ideologue: "A plausible reaction to the demographic changes underway in the United States could be the rise of an anti-Hispanic, anti-black, and anti-immigrant movement composed largely of white, working- and middle-class males, protesting their job losses to immigrants and foreign countries, the perversion of their culture, and the displacement of their language. Such a movement can be labeled 'white nativism'" (2004a, 40). Lest there be any confusion about where Huntington stands, his white nativism is far from genteel. He, as I said above, dehumanizes so-called Black or Brown cultures in "The Hispanic Challenge" when he says that the people he then described as the new white nationalists "contend that the shifting U.S. demographics foretell the replacement of white culture by black or brown cultures that are intellectually and morally inferior" (41). These fighting words foretold and helped build the gratuitous cruelty that has flourished under Trumpism and its accompanying Herrenvolk democracy.

Huntington goes on to cite Carol Swain's 2002 book, *The New White Nationalists in America*, which asserts the following about this new group: "Cultured, intelligent, and often possessing impressive degrees from some of America's premier colleges and universities, this new breed of white racial advocate is a far cry from the populist politicians and hooded clansmen of the Old South" (2002, 15). Huntington conveniently erases noncitizens in order to preserve a pure white version of eighteenth-century American settler colonial communities: "The American people who achieved independence in the late eighteenth century were few and homogeneous: overwhelmingly white (thanks to the exclusion of blacks and Indians from citizenship), British and Protestant" (2004b, 11). It appears that Huntington is trapped in his own colonized imagination, a fantasy of the origins of his own national identity that does not consider the nineteenth-century building of the nation.

Huntington then brings his point home with what I'd like to call syntactic violence that builds on ignorance of Native American social formations. His words foretell and prepare the ground for the cruelty to come under Trumpism in the following manner: "The seventeenth- and eighteenth-century settlers came to America because it was a *tabula rasa*. Apart from Indian tribes, which could be killed off or pushed westward, no society was there, and they came in order to create societies that embodied and would reinforce the culture and values they brought with them from their origin country" (2004b, 40). What, in this context, is his vision of the ideal citizen in our democratic society?

In falsely condemning Mexican Americans for excessive retention of the

Spanish language, and what he deems as the refusal to learn English, Huntington overlooks the fact that Latinxs wish to learn English as well as to retain Spanish. He also overlooks the history of French and German in the United States and the fact that the United States has always been a multilingual nation. Because people retain Spanish, it does not follow that they are not learning English. This is a case of both/and, not a hydraulic model where, as one goes up the other goes down, the more English you speak, the less Spanish, or vice versa. If we are to think well about Mexican Americans in the United States, we must conceive of the bilingual citizen rather than of one person with one (and only one) culture and one (and only one) language (see Lozano 2018).

If one reads *Who Are We?* as a plan for action, the central theses are as follows: Mexican Americans should abandon Spanish and speak English only, becoming monolingual rather than bilingual; they should become Protestant; and, they should assimilate to the American way of life. Huntington targets Mexican Americans because their presence and sheer numbers threaten Anglo-American dominance in the United States. By reverting to an ideology of national identity that is more English imperial than American democratic, he has cleared the table for the Trump regime and its unapologetic bigotry.

Reading Huntington through the lens of Trumpism clarifies what's at stake when he insults, denigrates, or dehumanizes subordinated racialized groups. Huntington's words that seemed abstract at the time of his manifesto's publication now imply concrete acts of cruelty — emblematically, such acts as the separation of young children from their parents, the confinement of those children in cages, the tweet storms of gratuitous insults. When *Who Are We?* was first published, I was filled with foreboding, not because Huntington grasped our national situation so well, but rather because he was an insider among right-wing extremists and probably knew of plans on the drawing boards for policies of cruelty toward US Latinxs. At the time, I imagined mass deportations that were coming, because they had occurred during the 1930s and the Obama administration was setting further precedents for deportation. I did not then imagine Trumpism, but it has given new and fuller meaning to Huntington's words.

What remains puzzling is why Huntington was accorded such respect. Why weren't we tipped off by the violence of his language, or by his proudly saying he was a white nativist, or by his citation of Goebbels — the Nazi minister of propaganda — as a credible source? Trump certainly has learned from Huntington, and we too must take these lessons to heart.

Viramontes saw into her future, our present, and was able to imagine and depict in circumstantial detail how Mexican Americans were to experience the infliction of state-sponsored cruelty. Her characters experienced such cruelty in the early 1960s with the displacements and disappearances caused by the building of the East Los Angeles freeway interchange and in the late 1960s with the roadblocks and checkpoints administered and enforced by a fictional entity, the Quarantine Authority, with its storm troopers (in certain respects comparable to Immigration and Customs Enforcement under Trumpism). It is urgent to see the US version of Herrenvolk democracy from the viewpoints of both dominant and subordinate racialized groups, those who inflict cruelty on their racial subordinates and those who endure state-sanctioned cruelty and in turn inflict cruelty among themselves, which has induced "sorrow so wide, it was blinding."

CHAPTER SIX

I Won't Tell My Story

Narrative Capital and Refusal among Undocumented Activists in the Trump Era

ALYSHIA GÁLVEZ

Introduction

Around the time Donald J. Trump was elected president, a lot of the undocumented activists and artists I know fell silent.[1] While they remained engaged, and often commented vociferously, bitingly, and hilariously on national politics, debates, and discourses, they ceased to transmit their own stories to a broader audience. More and more often, they expressed a refusal to speak and instead stated a choice to stay silent. It was the end of an era.

In this chapter, I examine the refusal of undocumented activists to tell their stories. I argue it is a deeply political act, as well as a "theory of the political" (Simpson 2014, 21), that refuses the logic and reasoning of a state and a polity that would deny their humanity. Refusal, Audra Simpson argues, is premised on the "deep impossibility of representation and consent within governance systems that are predicated upon dispossession and disavowal of the political histories that govern the populations now found within state regimes" (2007, 18). While Hartman asserts "a right to obscurity" (1997, 36) and Glissant a "right to opacity for everyone" (1997, 194), hooks articulates a "space of refusal" as a productive margin, a space of openness that allows one to "say no to the coloniser, say no to the downpressor" (1989, 21). Moten helps us understand refusal as not simply a form of nonparticipation but as a politics, in the sense that politics at root is a negotiation about resources in the world: "This is a political imperative that infuses the unfinished project of emancipation as well as any number of other transitions or crossings in progress." He notes it is particularly important for the "the fugitive, the immigrant and the new (and newly constrained) citizen" who needs "to hold something in reserve, to keep a secret" (2009, 105).

Simpson calls for "ethnography that can both *refuse* and also take up *refusal* in generative ways" (2007, 78). McGranahan calls for anthropologists to "recognize and theorize refusal as an element of social and political relations" (2006, 320). Inspired by these frames, this essay seeks to both explore refusal and take up refusal in generative ways.

To make sense of refusal, I focus on citizenship, empathy, and change to understand stories as a kind of narrative capital, and to make sense of the refusal by many activists to participate in the moral economy in which narrative capital circulates. Theories of citizenship are useful for thinking about who has the right to speak—in Arendt's formulation "the right to have rights" (1973, 296)—but also the continual expectation of silence and docility by marginalized groups who, insofar as they are allowed to speak at all, are expected to speak in specific ways: in supplication, gratitude, or as an expression of pain. An exploration of empathy helps us understand and theorize narrative capital: to ask what is gained from first-person narratives, why they are valuable, for what, and to whom, and the bases of common understanding and empathy on which they rest. Finally, the narrative capital of stories depends on an expectation of change—that the telling of the story obligates the listener to act in the world as a result. I argue that in an age of "fake news" and Twitter bots and trolls, with four years of Trump as president, none of the agreements inherent in these conceptualizations of citizenship, empathy, and change is guaranteed or reliable. By refusing to tell their stories, undocumented activists are not simply protecting themselves. While some frame refusal as a kind of self-care, a refusal to do unpaid emotional labor, I assert that the implications are even more broadly and starkly political than that and constitute a critique of the white supremacist, settler colonialist foundations of the United States, placing those who refuse in a tradition well established by Black and Native Americans. As Tuck and Yang articulate,

> Settler colonial knowledge is premised on frontiers; conquest, then, is an exercise of the felt entitlement to transgress these limits. Refusal, and stances of refusal in research, are attempts to place limits on conquest and the colonization of knowledge by marking what is off limits, what is not up for grabs or discussion, what is sacred, and what can't be known. (2014, 225)

León is more graphic than Tuck and Yang, framing inquiry and a quest for knowledge as a kind of rape, describing artist Xandra Ibarra's art of refusal and opacity as "a defiant withholding, a refusal to offer access to the interiority that a penetrative gaze might crave" (2017, 370). León seizes on Glissant's critique of dominant "epistemologies of elucidation" and calls for collective refusals to be knowable, a right to opacity *for* everyone, an aesthetic and ethico-political response to the demands for transparency (378). Settler colonialism's obsession with borders and its current hypermilitarized, nativist, and neoliberal iteration in the Trump era are premised on weaponized positivism in which all is knowable and yet, nothing is to be believed, making research, journalism, and even the "backgrounding" politicians' aides do when writing legislation or speeches a kind of domination. Refusal to tell stories is a means of asserting rights that pushes back on the hubris of knowledge and knowability. Refusal to be knowable, *opacity*, is a strategy for resistance. By refusing to use their stories or cash in on narrative capital, undocumented activists open space for an articulation of rights that is less personalistic, less empathetic, and therefore, more categorical and, arguably, more radical.

Background

It was the first week of fall semester in 2010. In an honors seminar on immigrant Health and migration at Lehman College of the City University of New York, a young woman named Melissa raised her hand to make a comment about one of the readings, prefacing her intervention with the statement, "as an undocumented person . . . " Having taught for several years at that point, I had never had a student speak openly in class about their immigration status, much less the first week of the semester. That student and several of her classmates, all first-year students who were barely eighteen years old, were already working that semester to found the Lehman College DREAM Team, the first organization at CUNY and in New York City created by and for undocumented students to share their stories, find support, and advocate for their rights. That spring, undocumented youth activists in Chicago had coined the phrase "undocumented, unafraid, and unapologetic," and soon, around the country, undocumented youth were also "coming out of the shadows," holding events in which they would tell their stories publicly and speak into a microphone, in their campus quad or on the steps of city hall, often while wearing caps and gowns to signify their academic aspirations and achievements (Zimmerman 2012; Pallares 2014). Melissa and the other students who founded the Lehman DREAM Team were affiliated with the New York State Youth Leadership Council (NYSYLC), "the first undocumented youth led organization in New York [whose] goal is to give undocumented youth the tools and space to organize and create change in our communities" (NYSYLC, n.d.).

In narrating their stories of arrival, upbringing, and achievement in the United States, these activists were calling for the DREAM Act, which had, since 2000, been proposed every year before Congress and had yet to pass. Many of them were in the Senate Chamber in 2010 when, having passed in the House of Representatives, the DREAM Act moved to the Senate. Proponents failed to defeat the filibuster to bring it to a vote, and the bill was defeated. It was activism by youth that had kept the DREAM Act alive for a decade, and they did not stop when it was defeated (see Zimmerman, this volume, 2012, 2018).

When undocumented youth "came out of the shadows," in 2010, they were responding to efforts to silence them. While larger discourses of anti-immigrant sentiment, on the rise in the current era since Pete Wilson's Proposition 187 (see Montejano, this volume), held undocumented immigrants ineligible to participate in national civil discourse as interlopers (or another more pejorative "I" word), in the immigration rights movement of the early twenty-first century, undocumented youth were silenced even by allies. During that time, many major immigrant rights organizations pressured immigrant youth to remain quiet or to deliver prepared scripts (personal communications with activists, 2010–2017 Fernandes 2017) as part of an effort to control the narrative around immigration reform nationally. Immigration reform advocates told youth they should obey their recommendations and demand comprehensive immigration reform, partly under the logic that the "Dreamers" were so appealing, so unimpeachable as proto-Americans, that the victory of the DREAM act could easily happen and thus deflate momentum for a broader reform. When youth countered that "comprehensive immigration reform" meant a combination of legalization and enhanced border enforcement that would ensnare their family members in enforcement, they were chided that they were too young and innocent to know how politics works. Well-funded and large-scale advocacy organizations, sometimes deridingly referred to by the youth as the "nonprofit industrial complex," presented themselves as spokespeople for the movement, and encouraged those who were undocumented to stay "safe" by not speaking publicly (Domínguez Zamorano et al. 2010; see also Roy 2014).

But the organizations founded by undocumented youth, especially the more radical ones (and there were splits in this era between more conciliatory and more radical organizations), said they were always already at risk for deportation. They refused to allow others to speak for them, demanding to be the ones to tell their stories and making a calculus that they would be safer out of the shadows than in them. When they began to achieve some key victories — stopping imminent deportations, getting people out of detention, and fostering solidarity with the cause — this calculus was viewed by some as a correct one, even though it was still seen as terribly risky by many "allies." Thus, when in the wake of the defeat of the DREAM Act, and the stalling of immigration reform proposals, President Obama seemed to waffle on whether he could or should use executive authority to provide temporary relief to those who would have benefited from the DREAM Act, these same activist youth occupied his campaign offices with hunger strikes and sit-ins. In June 2012, Obama signed an executive order authorizing Deferred Action for Childhood Arrivals (DACA), protecting from deportation undocumented youth who met certain criteria. Undocumented activists claimed victory for nudging Obama to action and reminded those who had told them not to do it — not to make Obama uncomfortable, not to call him "Deporter in Chief" or shame him during his reelection campaign — that they would remember their efforts to silence them.

Undocumented youth centered their own stories and voices; they refused to be spoken for, shushed, or coached into beseeching an unwilling state to recognize them (see Zimmerman 2012, 2018; Pallares 2014; Bishop 2018). While their movement may have started with their wearing caps and gowns, the more radical activists soon rejected the term "Dreamer," the caps and gowns, and even the premise of the DREAM Act. They asserted that the centering of their academic achievements, mastery of English, and characterization as "more American than many citizens" did violence to their parents as well as their friends and siblings who did not finish school or were entangled in the criminal justice system. Some critiqued the Dreamer archetype as reinforcing neoliberal notions of the self-sufficient, upwardly mobile subject (Pallares 2014; Fernandes 2017). The DREAM Act, in theory, and DACA, in reality, did lead to non-Dreamers being criminalized and further marginalized, categorized as not "redeemable," becoming even more abject post-DACA than they were before. The "DACA-mented," rather than take the crumbs they were handed, called them crumbs, and then many stopped playing along.

DeGenova calls this phase of the movement "incorrigible," a proactive and strategic stance, but also a product of the inherently abject status of the migrant. For his theory of the abject, DeGenova (drawing on Kristeva) states that "the distinctly disruptive force of the abject involves that which 'disturbs identity, system, order. What does not respect borders, positions, rules. The in-between,

the ambiguous, the composite'" (2015, 104). If this seems to echo Gloria Anzaldúa's (1999) framing of the in-between space of the border as both wound
and productive in-between space, a *nepantla* perspective, it is not an accident.
Many of the most engaged activists in the undocumented youth movement
crossed the US-Mexico border on foot or in their parents' arms, and Anzaldúa
is an important part of their scholarly and activist formation. They frame the
border both as the arbitrary and illegitimate division that divides and harms — as
Anzaldúa does, along with Dunbar-Ortiz (2018) and others — but also as a productive space for challenging their status in ways not constrained by or confined
to conventional or historical definitions of citizenship. They articulate bases
of rights that are based on complex lived experiences, as shaped by belonging
as by exclusion. Denied access to their country of origin, relatives who stayed
behind, language and reassurances of continuity, they simultaneously embrace
and celebrate their hybrid identities, multilingual communication skills, and
multiple spatial and cultural frames of reference, while they also grieve the de-
territorialization, estrangement, and displacement that produced them.

In the years since, years in which Trump launched his campaign on a statement of hate and bias against Mexican immigrants and began a presidency
based on the same hate, the undocumented youth activists who fought for the
DREAM Act achieved state-level DREAM Acts in Illinois and California (and
only recently New York), and turned their sights on reframing the immigrant
rights movement as a whole. Many shifted to a focus on halting deportation and
detention through campaigns like Not One More, and broad-ranging solidarity
work that links mass incarceration to immigration enforcement. But the failure
to achieve their larger goals, in spite of how compellingly and honestly they
shared their stories, took a toll.

They observed how DACA was rescinded in the first year of the Trump administration amid a rapid proliferation of extreme xenophobia, characterized
by the implementation of policies previously viewed as unspeakably extreme
(building of a border wall, travel bans, family separation, detention of children,
curtailing of the right to request asylum, summary deportations, etc.).[2] During
the COVID-19 pandemic and in an election year, anti-immigrant policies became even more pronounced in year three of the Trump administration. As
Rubio and Alvarez forcefully argue, "To ask for citizenship or to so much as
desire it enters certain people into a Faustian bargain with the state. Here, to
seek inclusion or recognition from the state is to accept the terms and legitimacy
of one's own dispossession" (2019). Rather than double down on the model

immigrant myth, the notion that "immigrants get the job done," that immigrants deserve rights because of their contributions in the form of labor, and more, undocumented activists say, "Immigrants deserve rights."[3] Full stop. This is the notion that immigrants do not deserve rights because they contribute, or because they have family values, or because they've been here a long time, or because they are assimilated or assimilable, or because they share "American values." They deserve rights. *Punto.* This is a politics of refusal that opens space for other kinds of imagined frames for rights and belonging.

In the next sections, I will explore the three sets of ideas that underlie the notion of narrative capital and provide it its currency, and the ways that these ideas have crumbled, leading to refusal and silence as a solution. First, citizenship is the concept that undergirds how states conceptualize belonging and exclusion, but in ways that are always already vernacular. Empathy is, in contemporary US and global politics, envisioned as a precursor to social change and legislative reform, and one of the major currencies in which social movements and nonprofit organizations deal. And finally, change: how to foment it, and what drives it, are questions that dog activists and their movements. Narrative capital circulates in all three of these arenas, playing a role that can sometimes reinforce the status quo, rather than threaten it.

Citizenship

Citizenship, in the formal sense, refers to standing within the law, a norm of belonging and exclusion. But it is also inherently social, a "relation among strangers who learn to feel it as a common identity based on shared historical, legal, or familial connections to a geopolitical space" (Berlant 2011, 37). Renato Rosaldo and those he has inspired have theorized cultural citizenship as a way to understand citizenship vernacularly, how it feels as well as what it means to belong (1994, 402; Gálvez 2013; see also Rosaldo, this volume). While the original formulation of the idea was primarily focused on Latinx communities that have formal inclusion in the body politic, but nevertheless are made to feel that they don't belong, that they are "second-class citizens," it is equally relevant to thinking about people who might feel like they belong but lack juridical standing for such claims, like many undocumented immigrants. Cultural citizenship offers a way to think about and through the exclusions inherent in citizenship, the kinds of "second"- and "third"-class citizenship Rosaldo and the Latino Cultural Citizenship Group alerted us to (Rosaldo 1994; Flores and Benmayor 1997), and the "histories of subordinated groups that might not be covered by official legal or political narratives" (Berlant 2011, 38).

As a kind of "politicized intimacy," citizenship requires that people "must recognize certain stories, events, experiences, practices, and ways of life as related to the core of who they are, their public status, and their resemblance to other people . . . We can say that citizenship's legal architecture manifests itself and is continually reshaped in the space of transactions between intimates and strangers" (Berlant 2011, 37). Similarly, Niezen (2010) has theorized the expectation of "strategic representations" of suffering to distant audiences in his work on global human rights. The affective aspect of citizenship makes it messy because it belies any fiction that it is a transparent system of extending or withholding rights based on objectively available categories. Martín Alcoff (2005), Anderson (2016), and Dunbar-Ortiz (2014) are a few of the many authors that historically document the centrality of exclusion driven by white supremacism historically—rather than an exception, it is a rule that can be continuously traced in every reduction or ostensible expansion of rights in the United States. Conceptually framed limits to belonging are carved out—in historically specific ways—throughout the history of the republic, even while the larger narrative purports to assert the rule of, by, and for "the people." These persistent exceptions in the granting of rights by the state to members of different historically disenfranchised and marginalized groups alert us to the use of stories for achieving unfreedom, not only, or even mainly for, freedom. This leads us to ask, can citizenship be imagined without stories? And is it enriched or impoverished by its dependence on them?

Latinx populations in the United States have historically been treated as "other" and their centrality to the history of the country marginalized. Treated too often as always an emergent political force, a sleeping giant, they are framed as forever becoming, never arrived (Beltrán 2010). Nativist discourses gloss differences between populations, implying Latinx people are immigrants and immigrants are undocumented, and therefore draw into question citizenship rights of all (a theme throughout this volume). Difference is too often hailed by white nationalists as a rationale for denial of rights, with Latinx people framed by nativists as unassimilable, with divided loyalties, not loyal to the nation's creed (see Huntington 2004).

Stories have also been deployed as a way to reassert the humanity and assimilability of Latinx people (Brooks 2006; Dávila 2008). The emergence of the last major wave of nationwide activism for comprehensive immigration reform in 2005 and 2006 gave fuel to these assertions of the patriotism, work ethic, values, and assimilability of immigrants, who as a whole are comprised in their majority of Mexican-origin people. Many undocumented youth who later became activists witnessed immigrant mobilization at young ages. Some of them embraced the notion that narrative capital was important to the acquisition of support for citizenship rights. When they took the radical turn I describe in this chapter, they would come to the conclusion that no amount of narrative capital would be sufficient to overcome the notion that they—as immigrants, or Latinx people, or people of Mexican origin—could never fully "belong." So, belonging became less important to their framing of rights and their strategies for change.

Empathy

The efficacy of telling stories rests on assumptions that one will be believed, that one will be heard, and that hearing obligates the listener. Stories have been an increasingly powerful role in social movements and politics (Fernandes 2017; Polletta 2009; Bishop 2018). But today, this bargain is broken. Berlant argues that aversion is the counterpart of compassion:

> I have been struck by an undertone accompanying the performance
> of compassion: that scenes of vulnerability produce a desire to withhold
> compassionate attachment, to be irritated by the scene of suffering in some
> way. Repeatedly, we witness someone's desire to not connect, sympathize,
> or recognize an obligation to the sufferer; to refuse engagement with
> the scene or to minimize its effects; to misread it conveniently; to snuff
> or drown it out with pedantically shaped phrases or carefully designed
> apartheids; not to rescue or help; to go on blithely without conscience;
> to feel bad for the sufferers, but only so that they will go away quickly.
> (2011, 10)

In an era of fake news and internet trolls, personal narratives can be called lies, and rather than induce empathy, can produce aversion, debunking, and denigration. Narratives depend on a sequence of events: the story induces empathy, empathy leads to investment in amelioration of the suffering, and investment becomes a kind of solidarity and collaboration that can lead to larger gains for communities beyond the individual narrator. It is no longer safe to assume that hearing one's story will induce empathy. Empathy can no longer be assumed to lead to action, much less solidarity or gains for a larger collective. On the contrary, empathy for one notable narrator can deflate or distract from claims made by the collective. Indeed, what Childress (2009) calls "the empathy frame" can in fact serve to challenge and change attitudes about one person or a small subset of people, while leaving unaltered larger structures of white supremacism and inequality.

Telling stories is an act that fits into several overlapping traditions and techniques of affective social construction. In the Latin American context, first-person narratives, or *testimonios*, are a genre of narrative with a legacy related to radical social change and resistance. During the Central American civil wars, testimonios of survivors of massacres and human rights violations served to shed light on and also to focus international media and advocacy attention on the genocidal behaviors of the military regimes in El Salvador and Guatemala. Anthropologist Ricardo Falla refers to the role of receiving testimony as a quasi-sacred one: witnesses to testimony operate in a chain of annunciation of life (1994, 2). Falla turned his own ethnographic practice to the documentation and transmission of first-person narrative, recording first the testimonio of a refugee from the massacre at Ixcán, who crossed the border from Petén, Guatemala, into Mexico with blood stains still on his clothing. Testimonios delivered by refugees in churches and other spaces during the US-based sanctuary movement in the 1980s served to foster solidarity work and civil disobedience that helped protect migrants from deportation (Coutin 1993).

The central power of testimonio is its truth claim: that eyewitnesses can be trusted to tell their own truth. Polletta notes that the multivalent and complex nature of narrative is part of what makes it so compelling: "storytelling is appreciated, enjoyed and distrusted" (2009, xi). In the current post-truth, "fake news" era, it seems all claims are to be debunked, mocked, and derided. Telling stories is implicitly a trust exercise in which the story will be believed and the hearer of the story will be moved to act. Given the slippage between narrative and truth in the Trump era, risks inherent in telling one's story may no longer be outweighed by the potential benefits.

Yalda Uhls, a former movie producer and director of UCLA's Center for Scholars and Storytellers, wrote a blog post for CNN.com in which she unpacked the instantly viral image of a mother running from tear gas at the Tijuana–San Ysidro border on November 25, 2018. She noted, "Nonthreatening stories can contain messages which are smuggled in through a compelling narrative that appeals to emotion. And emotion combined with accurate information can be a powerful motivator to change social norms" (2018). In the photograph, a mother wears a T-shirt with images from the animated Disney movie *Frozen* and is trying desperately to pull along her twin daughters, toddlers who are wearing diapers and losing their sandals as they run. Uhls notes that "stories work on a cellular level." The image of a mother struggling to find safety and freedom for her daughters referenced the message of the movie that was featured on her shirt, about sisters seeking freedom from oppression. Uhls later reflected that her blog post, which she thought would be a compelling and humanizing reflection on a harrowing and gut-wrenching image of the current US policy toward immigrants and asylum seekers, had actually received many hate-filled comments from people mocking the mother and her twin daughters and wishing them ill (personal communication, March 17, 2021). CNN shut down and then hid the comments, but it is clear that the story of migrants seeking asylum at the border and the suffering they and their children experience, culminating with the spraying of tear gas, was not enough to elicit empathy from Trump supporters who seem to feed on the president's anti-immigrant ideology.

Change

If stories do not compel change, then why tell them? In refusing to tell their stories to a larger audience, undocumented activists are renouncing the traffic in narrative capital. As Luis Saavedra explained to me,

> In refusing to tell stories, undocumented folks/youth, I think, are forcing Americans to acknowledge oppressive policies, structures and institutions that they are part of (and have benefitted from) but only "saw" or "heard" through undocumented narratives. In essence, by refusing to tell their stories, undocumented folks are producing a deafening silence of oppression that allies and Americans are left to contend with—an uncomfortable silence/truth. How do you appeal to someone who has never lived or experienced oppression in some form? Well, you make it visible and not just "tell them" about it. (Personal communication, January 27, 2019)

Too long uncompensated, misappropriated, and misunderstood, their stories will not be put out there anymore by them. This is radical because it compels theories of change and of citizenship without empathy. If empathy is an unreliable and potholed path to lasting social change and social justice, what are we left with? Empathy, a sacrosanct concept in the liberal imagination, is premised on the notion that compassion can be evoked, that it is not exclusive to primal affiliations of family and clan, but rather can be transferred to others outside of one's own network of attachment. The liberal democratic project depends on this, the idea of the common good as the foundation for pursuing and sustaining equality, even at one's own expense. But we clearly are not in a moment for empathy. Over and over again, we see that those with privilege are willing to cede the commons if it means avoiding actually communing with others unlike themselves, whether white families in Prince Williams County, Virginia, who preferred to allow the public schools to shut down rather than desegregate in 1959, or portions of the Trump electorate that vote against their own economic interests to sustain white supremacism in the twenty-first century (Anderson 2016).

Even though demand for and consumption of the stories of undocumented immigrants are still the fuel that powers the web of nonprofit organizations advocating nationally for immigration reform, their viability appears ever more diminished as the Trump era continues. We can see compelling stories of personal suffering constituting one of the primary genres of "immigration stories" reported by the media, and often counterposed to quantitative statistical portrayals of the issue. But stories, even when they are believed, may do more to sustain the status quo and uphold white supremacist ideology than liberate its purported beneficiaries. Linda Martín Alcoff notes that "racializing perceptual practices are used to produce a visual registry of any given social field. . . . This field is organized differently to distribute the likelihood of intersubjective trust, the extension of epistemic credence, and empathy" (2005, 196). Lehman College graduate Luis Saavedra told me, "Stories are not effective against structures and institutions that are morally broken (have always been really, just took Trump and his rhetoric to make it visible to 'allies' and everyday Americans)" (personal communication, January 27, 2019). In a public Facebook post, activist and Yosimar Reyes wrote, "Let it be known that it was CITIZENS that fucked up on the messaging of our stories. THEY created this good immigrant bad immigrant narrative" 2016).

Without the compelling first-person narratives of immigrants, "allies" are obliged to reckon with the intransigence and unyielding nature of the structures that constrain immigrant agency and access to rights. Premised as necessary to achieving the larger goal of immigration reform, "damage-centered researchers" as Tuck and Yang call them, or what we might call damage-centered "allies," "may operate, even benevolently, within a theory of change in which harm must be recorded or proven in order to convince an outside adjudicator that reparations are deserved" (2014, 227). They argue that "settler colonial ideology, constituted by its conscription of others, holds the wounded body as more engrossing than the body that is not wounded" (229). If compassion is a requisite for the building of affective ties with those structurally and socially viewed as "outside" of the nation-state, and other, then perhaps the kind of citizenship it produces is an impoverished one.

Change

In conclusion, undocumented activists have realized that empathy is a poor substitute for justice. In the same way they calculated in 2010–2011 that telling their stories was safer than staying in the shadows, many have now calculated that no amount of storytelling will make this country love them enough to give them (full) citizenship. This clear-eyed assessment leaves advocates and allies in a lurch: without stories how does one make a claim for the laws to be changed? How will lawmakers be "moved" to advocate for immigration reform and mass legalization if not through empathy? We do not currently have a good model for rights that are categorical when the promises of the Bill of Rights, the Emancipation Proclamation, the Fourteenth Amendment, the Voting Rights Act, and more have yet to be fully enjoyed by Black citizens. Focusing instead on "protection of the well-being of communities . . . nurturing, organizing, creating, etc." (Saavedra, personal communication, January 27, 2019), many former activists are turning inward to their communities, families, and selves. In conversation with each other, they are now talking about radical self-care and #undocujoy. In a tweet, Louie A. Ortiz-Fonseca wrote "leave it to the muthafuggahs to tell it and they will have you thinking this country provided daca out of the kindness of their hearts . . . this is why we got to keep telling our stories to ourselves" (Ortiz-Fonseca September 6, 2017). In so doing, just as they took the mic several years ago, many are now passing the mic to see what the response will be on the part of citizens and the state. By refusing to tell their stories, undocumented activists are saying this problem is ours—those who enjoy juridical citizenship—to fix. In the meantime, they'll keep their stories to themselves.

Notes

1. Most of the people whose activism, commentary, art, and teaching that have
    inspired this paper reject the term "Dreamer," which is still often used for those
    who would have been eligible for the benefits of the DREAM Act, had it passed.
    They opted as early as 2011 for the term *undocumented youth*. Today, many
    comment that they should no longer be called *youth* because, they are mostly
    in their mid- to late twenties, or older, and the term *youth* is infantilizing or
    maybe inaccurate. Many also reject the term *activist*. Finally, some are no longer
    undocumented. So, terminology is complicated. They often say *undocument-
    ed people* or *folks* in referring to themselves as members of a collective. Some
    argue for different terms like *illegalized* (Sati 2017), or *illegal* and *alien* (Rubio
    and Alvarez 2019). All of the people whose words, ideas, and stories I reference
    in this paper have played — and in some cases continue to play — public roles
    in various mobilizations for immigrant rights, and have been core organizers,
    educators, and artists in radical branches of the larger immigrant rights move-
    ment. All are Latinx, mostly born in Mexico. While they reject terminology that
    differentiates or cleaves them off from their families, there is a set of characteris-
    tics, organizations, and moments conjuncturally shared by this particular subset
    of the larger population.

    Moreover, I struggled with an ethically adequate research methodology for
    this paper. It seemed unethical to ask activists to talk to me about not talking.
    In undocumented activist spaces, too many academics and reporters come
    and go, demanding data, interviews, confessions, time, energy, and space,
    and then they (mis)represent, (mis)interpret, and impose their own analyses
    on the stories they are told, writing books and articles, obtaining academic
    positions and accolades for their work. What I write about in this essay comes
    from accumulated observations as a result of a decade of concerted effort to be
    a worthy accomplice (not an "ally") and friend to undocumented youth, as a
    professor, a faculty advisor to the Lehman DREAM Team, the founding director
    of the CUNY Mexican Studies Institute, and an informal advocate for undoc-
    umented students in higher education. Out of a strong conviction that it was
    not my place, as a white US citizen and cis-hetero professor, to tell their stories,
    I have not conducted research related to this arena of engagement and did not
    plan to. However, the recent wave of silence has made me wonder whether it
    is not also a burden to expect undocumented people to do all the talking, even
    when the talking that needs to be done is to change the systems that they did
    not create and are not upholding the way I am, by taking a paycheck from a
    university that still does not serve undocumented students well. So, the way I
    have tentatively resolved this for this essay is to discuss the refusal to talk based
    on information that is available publicly, and my own interpretation of countless
    personal interactions, tweets, and Facebook posts. I only directly quote or
    reproduce social media posts that were publicly available when I captured them

(and may still be) or personal communication with people who authorized me to share their words. My purpose is to illuminate the ways that current debates surrounding immigration issues have failed to notice the decision to remain silent among many stakeholders, and the need we (nonimmigrants) have to be more observant, better listeners, and more capable of reforming the policies our elected officials have constructed, in keeping with the priorities of the directly impacted, rather than dated talking points and priorities.

2.   A judge for the United States Court of Appeals for the Ninth Circuit halted the implementation of DACA's rescission in 2018, so while new applications and renewals continue to be processed, the program remains in limbo.

3.   According to Lin-Manuel Miranda, "immigrants get the job done" is the line in his blockbuster, award-winning musical, *Hamilton*, that gets the most cheers from audiences. This phrase, and the sentiment behind it, is a rallying cry for many in the mainstream immigrant rights movement. Dunbar-Ortiz is currently writing a critique of this slogan, which she initially presented at the New School in November 2018.

CHAPTER SEVEN

How Did We Get Here?

Central Americans and Immigration Policy
from Reagan to Trump

ARELY M. ZIMMERMAN

In 2018, when thousands of Honduran migrants joined a caravan intended to go to the United States to claim asylum, Trump capitalized on the opportunity to reframe the journey of migrants as an "invasion," resorting to racialized stereotypes of Central American criminality.[1] "At this very moment, large, well-organized caravans of migrants are marching towards our southern border," Trump averred. "Some people call it an invasion. It's like an invasion. They have violently overrun the Mexican border. . . . So this isn't an innocent group of people. It's a large number of people that are tough," the president continued. "We have no idea who they are. All we know is they're pretty tough people when they can blast through the Mexican military and Mexican police. . . . I don't want them in our country," Trump concluded (quoted in Lind 2019).

Trump's depiction of Central Americans had its roots in a longer history of racialized constructions of Latinx immigrants as threats to the United States. According to Leo Chávez (2008), the "Latino threat narrative" has been discursively constructed through the circulation of images, stereotypes, and hegemonic truths reproduced in our society through the crafting and recycling of myths created by media pundits, politicians, and individuals about Latin American migration. The Latino threat narrative is used to justify immigration enforcement and spectacles of real and symbolic violence against Brown bodies. While Chávez refers to Latin American migration more broadly, his analysis is mostly centered on Mexican migration, and more specifically, the US-Mexico border as a site of racialized violence and exclusion.

President Trump, however, often used the specter of Central Americans — and racialized images of the Central American gang, MS-13, more specifically — in his public tweets and statements to prop up his immigration and border enforcement policies that extend down to Mexico's southern border with Guatemala. As in the statement about the Honduran caravan, Trump referenced that these migrants were not Mexican, and that they, in fact, violently overran Mexico's military and police.

Trump's references to Central Americans in the context of racialized foreign threats requires an expansion of our analytical apparatus to include Central American migration and other sites of border violence beyond the US-Mexico border. By examining the Central American experience, I argue that American immigration policy represents a continuation of a racial project in which good and bad immigrants are necessarily distinguished in a politics of citizenship and deservingness that justifies inclusion of some, and the exclusion of many. Central Americans, specifically Guatemalan, Salvadoran, and Honduran migrants, are most often characterized as undeserving of citizenship and, therefore, have been excluded from immigration reform legislation since they began migrating in large numbers. Thus, while Trump's flagrantly racist dog whistling with Central Americans in mind is certainly a concern, it is rooted in a much longer history of Central American exclusion, tied to US geopolitical, neocolonial, and neoliberal economic interests in Central America.

In this chapter, I trace the racialized threat narratives that deemed Central Americans "bad" immigrants, from the Reagan administration to the current era. I show how the cumulative effects of four decades of exclusion have left Central Americans particularly vulnerable under Trump's draconian policies. In the final section, I argue that given Central Americans' history of exclusion, comprehensive immigration reform proposals that set some undocumented immigrants on a path toward citizenship, but designate unprecedented levels of investment in border and immigration enforcement, hardly suffice for achieving full membership for Central Americans currently living in the United States.

Latino Threat Narratives and Central Americans

Citizenship is not only a function of formal legal status, but also of the different forms of belonging and representation in an imagined community (Oboler 2006; Rocco 2014). As such, Leo Chávez's notion of a "Latino threat narrative" captures the insidious ways that media and public discourse racializes Latinos, and the effects these processes have on the quality of citizenship for people of Latino/a descent (Chávez 2013). Produced by media pundits and politicians, the Latino threat narrative includes the belief in Latinos' unwillingness to learn English, their pathologically high fertility rates, their lack of desire to integrate into the social and cultural life of the nation, and their secret desires to "reconquer" the Southwest (Chávez 2013, ix). Decades of public discourse in the United States have constructed and represented the US-Mexican border as a place of danger and threat to U.S. society and culture, using metaphors and images to invoke crisis, time bombs, invasion, reconquest, floods, war, and border breakdown. In examining the militias of American "citizens" that patrol the border, "the discourse of invasion, the loss of U.S. sovereignty, and the representation of Mexican immigrants as the 'enemy' has . . . helped to justify increased militarization of the border as a way of 'doing something' about these threats to the nation's security and the American way of life" (Chávez 2008, 13; Gonzales this volume).

While Chávez's (2013) focus is on Mexico and people of Mexican origin, the Latino threat narrative is often generalized to all Latin American immigrants and at times to all Latinxs in the United States. For instance, at the height of Central American migration in the 1980s, President Ronald Reagan often cited Central American migration as evidence that the United States had "lost control of our own borders, and no nation can do that and survive" (Chávez 2008, 13). Even though Chávez fails to make mention of Central Americans specifically, it is a fact that Reagan used the Latino threat narrative to justify his immigration enforcement policies to target Central Americans as part of his Cold War strategy (Kahn 1996). On April 27, 1983, during a televised speech to Congress to request $6 million for military aid, training, and other assistance to El Salvador's regime, Reagan insisted that Salvadoran revolutionaries were on a mission to "destabilize the entire region from the Panama Canal to Mexico and to . . . eventually move chaos and anarchy toward the American border" (Reagan 1983). He also memorably warned that "terrorists and subversives [are] just two days' driving time from [the border crossing at] Harlingen, Texas," making the Central American threat imminent and probable (quoted in Kamen 1990).

Reagan characterized the "threat" of Central Americans as cultural. He associated them with an incipient communist takeover. In its faulty logic, the Reagan administration persisted in pushing the notion that communism would be more appealing to Central American migrants because communists would "feed on the anger and frustration of recent Central and South American immigrants who will not realize their own version of the American dream" (Dunn 1996). The Reagan administration's support for the Salvadoran and Guatemalan governments strongly influenced the low rate of asylum for Central Americans (Gzesh 2006). From 1984 to 1990, the United States granted asylum to 25 percent of the 48,000 asylum applicants from Nicaragua, compared with only 2.6 percent of the 45,000 claims from Salvadorans and 1.8 percent of the 9,500 claims from Guatemalans (Davy 2006). Most observers attribute this discrepancy to the US policy of supporting anti-communist activity. In the late 1980s, Nicaraguans were migrating from a socialist regime, while the United States supported the Salvadoran government against a Marxist insurgency. As a consequence of a discriminatory policy, a majority of Central American immigrants became undocumented, blocked from paths to legalization. Instead, asylum seekers were detained in what was the largest systematic detention plan since the internment of Japanese Americans during WWII. Immigrant detention was used, like it is now, as a way for the US government to discourage and punish select migrants (Kahn 1996).

In the midst of the US government's pursuit of Central American migrants, a major immigration reform bill was passed in Congress. The Immigration Reform and Control Act, also known as IRCA, is commonly remembered as an "amnesty" measure, but was also a response to the increasing worry over Latin American and Asian immigration (Calavita 1989). As the first comprehensive reform of US immigration policy since the McCarran-Walter Act of 1952 (also known as the Immigration and Nationality Act), the law included employer sanctions, worker verification systems, increased border security, and family reunification restrictions (45). While the law enabled millions of undocumented immigrants to become legal residents, the cutoff date ensured that the majority of Central Americans would not qualify, as fewer than half of Salvadorans and Guatemalans arrived prior to January 1, 1982 (Menjívar 2006). A majority of Central Americans were effectively left out of a major pathway to citizenship. In 1990, after a vigorous refugee rights campaign, Salvadorans were granted TPS (temporary protected status), but Guatemalans were not.[2] Even as a reprieve of deportation, TPS does not provide Central Americans a pathway to legal permanent status, which left more than a quarter of a million people vulnerable to the immigration policies of the Trump administration as he ramped up efforts to terminate TPS for Hondurans, Salvadorans and Nicaraguans (Capellari 2019).

In the subsequent decade, the threat narrative reappeared with vigor as justification for draconian anti-immigrant legislation at the state and federal levels. The Illegal Immigration Reform and Immigrant Responsibility act of 1996 (IIRIRA) expanded the grounds for deportation considerably and facilitated the removal of hundreds of thousands of immigrants, some retroactively (Stumpf 2006). Central Americans were disproportionately affected by the retributive dimension of the law (Menjívar and Abrego 2012), and had to prove that their deportation would cause them and their families "extreme hardship" in order to avoid it.[3] Unsurprisingly, deportations of Central Americans rose dramatically after the law's passage.[4]

IIRIRA was a major setback for Salvadorans, Hondurans, and Guatemalans seeking to remain in the United States because, at the time of its passage, the governments in these countries were transitioning to democracy, thus making it hard for nationals to seek asylum (Torres 2004). As a corrective, Congress enacted reforms for specific groups of undocumented immigrants who were longtime residents of the United States under the Nicaragua and Cuban Adjustment and Relief Act (NACARA). Yet again, however, NACARA privileged Nicaraguans over Guatemalan and Salvadoran immigrants by allowing them (as well as Cubans) to more easily apply for legal residency, while Guatemalans and Salvadorans were subject to arbitrary cutoff dates and discretionary decisions of the attorney general (Coffino 2006).

At the same time as immigration laws and policies emphasized internal removal of immigrants, the United States began to aggressively pursue border militarization and the construction of a transnational security apparatus. For example, the Mérida Initiative created a militarized southern border between Mexico and Guatemala, leading to increased risks for Central American migrants (Behrens 2009). With US funding through this security cooperation program, Mexico was incentivized to prevent Central Americans from reaching the United States by escalating their policing of migrants (Seelke and Finklea 2017, i).

In sum, the 1980s and 1990s were decades in which purposive legal interventions rendered Central American migrants illegal, undocumented, or temporary.[5] Even with immigration reform programs like IRCA and NACARA, the legalization of select immigrants came at the cost of increased border enforcement, militarization, deportation, and even detention. As Nicholas De Genova (2004, 173) points out in regards to the history of Mexican migration, citizenship and illegality are inevitably linked through an active process of inclusion through illegalization. In examining the Central American case here, I show that this process is not only driven by legal interventions, but also by discursive practices that designate certain migrants as deserving and others as undeserving of citizenship. Central Americans, as objects of racialized criminalization, have been cast as the embodiment of the unworthy criminal alien alongside Mexicans (see Gonzales, this volume). These decades set a historical precedent for how President Obama and President Trump have responded to the renewed spike in the cycle of Central American migration.

Contemporary Central American Migration

The alarmist tone over undocumented immigration defies the fact that there has been an overall decline in the immigrant population since the global economic crisis of 2007, due largely to a decline in Mexican immigrants.[6] Since 2007, however, the number of immigrants in the United States from El Salvador, Guatemala, and Honduras has risen by 25 percent.[7] The surge is due to increasing levels of violence in their home countries, among other factors. One year into Obama's presidency, a coup d'état against Honduran president Manuel Zelaya ushered in a new era of militarization that left a trail of violence and repression in its wake (Portillo Villeda 2016). The violence in Honduras quickly escalated, prompting a surge of migration (Blanchard et al. 2011). The state-sanctioned violence, coupled with the everyday violence of neoliberal economies, impunity, gender-based oppression, and corruption, marked the Northern Triangle countries as the most dangerous in the world.[8]

Central American migration has thus continued to swell, as many migrants undertake the perilous journey across multiple borders. Unsurprisingly, the majority of apprehensions by Border Patrol at the US-Mexico Border in 2014 and then again in 2016 were of Central Americans, many of whom were children that were unaccompanied by an adult or guardian (Krogstad and González-Barrera 2014). In 2014, at the height of media attention, there were approximately forty-seven thousand unaccompanied children hoping to claim asylum and/or reunite with family members already living in the United States (Negroponte 2014). The UN high commissioner for refugees noted that an estimated 58 percent of unaccompanied minors "raise potential international protection" claims, which are viable under international law (Wolgin and Kelley 2014).

President Obama declared the surge in child migrants a humanitarian emergency, yet Central Americans continued to face high denial rates of their asylum claims under his watch (TRAC 2017). In a public letter, President Obama stated that his "administration would address this urgent humanitarian situation with an aggressive unified coordinated federal response on both sides of the border," which included "fulfilling our legal and moral obligation to make sure we appropriately care for unaccompanied children." In the same letter he also stated that the Department of Homeland Security would be "taking aggressive steps to secure resources to our Southwest border to deter both adults and children from this dangerous journey, increase capacity for enforcement and removal proceedings, and quickly return unlawful migrants to their home countries"

(2014). Obama appealed to humanitarian values, while criminalizing the choice of migrant parents to place their children in harm's way and using immigrant detention as a deterrent. The infrastructure for immigrant detention expanded and thirty-two thousand immigrants were detained, two-thirds of them comprised of Mexicans and Central Americans (Kerwin and Lin 2009, 11).[9] Ultimately, even though the humanitarian frame was deployed, the threat narrative prevailed in guiding Obama's policy.

Moreover, another central part of Obama's immigration policy was interior border policing and enforcement. It was widely reported in news outlets that Central Americans would be targeted, apprehended, and deported in the wake of the media attention on unaccompanied minors. Over the course of two years, raids swept up many Central American migrant workers in Texas, North Carolina, and South Dakota (Edwards 2016).[10] By making a spectacle out of these raids, the Obama administration could assure the general public that the president was tough on immigration, while publicly espousing humanitarian concerns for Central American children. As part of his multilayered immigration policy, Obama also granted deferred action for children and the parents of children who migrated to the United States as children. DACA provided immediate deportation relief for many undocumented young people who had been lobbying for immigration reform and an end to deportations for over a decade. Yet, while many Central American youth stand to benefit, they are underrepresented as DACA beneficiaries (López and Krogstad 2017). That, coupled with the looming termination of TPS, may leave hundreds of thousands of families vulnerable to deportation.[11] Surprisingly, Obama's response to the surge in Central American migration did not differ much from that of his predecessors. On the contrary, the immigration enforcement infrastructure, especially around immigrant detention and interior border policing, was exploited by the Trump administration to dismantle the US asylum system altogether, and to shut out Central Americans from pathways to legal migration.

Central Americans in Trump's America

From the beginning of his campaign for the 2016 presidential election, Donald Trump made anti-Latinx racism central to his campaign, deploying the Latino threat narrative through public statements and campaign speeches. Once elected, he focused his attention on Central Americans as the most urgent threat to national security. On Twitter, his preferred social media platform, he regularly touted Mexico's efforts in apprehending Central American migrants and espoused Mexico as an ally in his war against them. Invoking MS-13, a gang that was formed in the 1980s in Los Angeles by Central American youth, Trump dog whistled to racist supporters. In February 2018, for example, he wrote that MS-13 gang members "are being removed by our Great ICE and Border Patrol Agents by the thousands, but these killers come back in from El Salvador, and through Mexico, like water. El Salvador just takes our money, and Mexico must help MORE with this problem. We need the Wall" (Trump 2018). In reality, MS-13 makes up less than 1 percent of all criminally active gang members in the United States (Rogers 2014). Using the stereotype of the Salvadoran gang member, however, proved useful for Trump, despite the relatively small size of the gang. It served to draw a meaningful distinction between "good" and "bad" immigrants, with Central Americans falling squarely into the "bad" category. On April 23, 2017, in an interview with the Associated Press White House correspondent, Trump stated, "We are putting MS-13 in jail and getting them the hell out of our country. . . . We are not after the Dreamers, we are after the criminals. . . . We are cleaning out cities and towns of hardline criminals, some of the worst people on earth, people that rape and kill women" (Trump 2017b).

By drawing a direct contrast between MS-13 and Dreamers — portrayed as innocent, high-achieving, and patriotic immigrant youth — Trump legitimized his administration's anti-immigration policies. With statements like these, Trump wielded Central American migration as a political strategy by using racialized criminalization to entrench the notion that Central Americans are subhuman predators prone to unrecognizable forms of violence and crime that necessitate tougher immigration policies.

In March of 2019, ninety-three thousand people were apprehended at the border, the highest monthly total in more than a decade. Most were families and asylum seekers from Central America.[12] Trump's Latino threat narrative was used as justification for his escalation and expansion of the anti-immigrant infrastructure that was in place under Obama, taking it to a deadly degree. Consider his statement conflating illegality with criminality: "They come from Central America. They're tougher than any people you've ever met. They're killing and raping everybody out there. They're illegal. And they are finished" (quoted in Balsamo 2016). In late 2018, when domestic and international media spotlighted the caravan of migrants from Honduras, Trump repeatedly threatened refugees with military action while decrying a legal system that prevented him from getting "rough" with migrants (Ward 2019). By October 2019, President

Trump had ordered about five thousand active-duty military personnel to the border days before the midterm election (Cloud and O'Toole 2019). The militarization of the US-Mexico border was not new, but it became a site of escalating violence, as border patrol as well as Mexican security forces fired tear gas and clashed with asylum seekers, including children (Averbuch and Malkin 2018).

Trump's policies effectively ended asylum for Central Americans. In a move clearly aimed at them, the Trump administration announced an end to all asylum protections for migrants passing through another country—in this case, Mexico—on their way to the United States (Long 2019). This mostly affects Central Americans, as they do not typically migrate to the United States with a visa or via air travel, and, even though the majority of undocumented immigration is attributable to persons who overstay their visa, such policies target and punish those who cross the border without a proper entry process and inspection (Warren 2019). Again, Trump designated Guatemala, Honduras, and El Salvador to enter into "safe third country" agreements, forcing asylum seekers to claim asylum in those countries before trying to seek refuge in the United States. In cases where the asylum seeker is already on US soil, they were to be deported to one of the three countries—but not their country of origin (Ibe 2020). The agreements effectively block migrants from accessing the US asylum system, forcing them to seek protection in countries that struggle with high rates of violence and poverty, lack institutions and infrastructure to assist large numbers of refugees, and grapple with severe sociopolitical, economic, and environmental issues (Ibe 2020).

Trump's policies directly targeted Central Americans, with the explicit goal of deterring migration from the region. Under Trump, more than 5,000 children were separated from immigrant parents under the zero-tolerance policy, and 38,000 migrants were detained in private prison facilities. Even amid the spread of the coronavirus, that number did not significantly decline (it dropped to 24,713) and the Department of Homeland Security continued to operate flights with deportees to Central America (Kerwin 2020).

The cumulative effects of Central American migrant exclusion over the past four decades resulted in a markedly vulnerable population that has very little recourse as a result of Trump's policies. While there has been public opposition to the images of children in makeshift tents in ICE detention prisons, there is little understanding of the causes of Central American migration, and the ways that Central American migrants' illegality has been the result of several decades of intentional exclusion. Moreover, the threat narrative has become a "commonsense" racial script, giving Trump license to push through various immigration and asylum policies that effectively waged war against migrants, dismantling the US asylum system altogether and violating several international treaties and norms (Amnesty International 2018). The resulting deaths of migrants and children held in detention should not have surprised observers; rather, they should have been expected as the result of a set of policies that have sought to discipline and punish migrants, and that have precedent in American history (Acevedo 2019).[13]

Lessons from the Central American experience: The Future of Citizenship

The experience of Central American migrants in the United States is instructive when considering the future of Latinxs' citizenship. As Rosaldo (1997) attests in his seminal volume on the topic, Latinxs have long used protest and public politics to defend their cultural identities, demand rights, and be recognized as full members of the American polity. Even as newer immigrants, Central Americans have a rich history of grassroots organizing for refugee rights (Perla Jr and Coutin 2012). Through social movement activism and everyday forms of resistance, Central Americans have won some important policy concessions. However, as I have shown here, the majority of Central Americans were left out of immigration reform efforts, especially the most vulnerable migrants from Guatemala (Menjívar 2006). These historical antecedents taught Central Americans important lessons about citizenship and inclusion. They continue having to consider how to confront the challenges that Trump posed to immigrant rights and to democratic inclusion. As the 2020 presidential election loomed, Democrats touted immigration reform as an alternative to Trump's anti-immigrant rhetoric. Yet many of these proposals offered legalization in exchange for the expansion of immigration enforcement. Immigrant rights advocates anticipated reform coming at a steep price. In early 2019, for example, after facing backlash for the partial government shutdown, Trump offered his solution: temporary protections for roughly seven hundred thousand young undocumented immigrants in exchange for $5.7 billion in funding for a wall along the southern border (Karni and Stolberg 2019). While the Democratic leadership recoiled at Trump's offer, the various iterations of immigration reform proposed over the last several decades have been similar in their approach in emphasizing enforcement while offering narrow legalizations (Gonzales 2013).

The consensus on immigration enforcement is rooted in Latino threat narratives that both major parties have upheld. This threat narrative presumes that immigrants must be detained and deported for noncriminal offenses, subject to indefinite detention, and even separated from their children to "deter" more migration from the region, willfully ignoring the structural dimensions that pull immigrants to the United States. By producing notions of good and bad immigrants, the Latino threat narrative simultaneously affirms the myth of America as an immigrant-friendly country.

From the perspective of Central American migrants, however, citizenship has been far from the political rite of passage that marks immigrants' pathway to becoming American (Plascencia 2012). Rather, citizenship has been a site of political, social, and legal exclusion, wherein national sovereignty is used to justify the curtailment of migrants' rights. Citizenship is also the mode by which the state makes citizens through schemes of surveillance, discipline, control, and administration (Ong 1996). Used by the powerful to produce consent, and to "establish the criteria of belonging within a national population and territory," citizenship designates those that have the right to have rights and those who do not (738).

Given this reality, many Central American refugee rights groups do not center citizenship as an organizing principle. For example, in 1988, Los Angeles–based Central American Resource Center's campaign, No Human Being is Illegal, was part of a broader effort to first end deportations of Salvadoran refugees and secure a legal status in the United States, and then to expose and put a halt to US backing of military operations in El Salvador (Coutin 2003). Many decades later, the Human Rights Alliance for Child Refugees and Families used "Freedom NOT Reform" as their slogan, rejecting migrant detention and family separation as commonsense policy (Human Rights Alliance n.d.). Their activism is rooted in a history of Central American political engagement that has seen refugees claim transnational rights while rejecting forms of migrant illegality and criminalization. From their perspective, legalization is only one dimension of a broader immigrant rights movement that includes decriminalization, the abolition of incarceration and immigrant detention, and opposition to US intervention in Latin America. These groups, collectively, are enacting contentious citizenship as a mode of rights, claims *delinked* from the nation-state and rooted in transnational networks of solidarity against the state security apparatus. These groups' capacity to resist and transform the current configuration of rights and citizenship will ultimately determine the future of American democracy.

Notes

1. There are important sociodemographic and cultural differences among Central Americans, including diverse ethnic and linguistic groups (Hagan 1994; England 2009; Pebley, Rosero-Bixby, and Hurtado 1997). Notwithstanding these differences, Guatemalan, Honduran, and Salvadoran immigrants' experiences of immigration and their context of exit and reception in the United States have been very similar, and thus, for analytical purposes I will consider them a structural group, noting contrasts between them when appropriate.

2. The secretary of Homeland Security has the discretion to designate a country for TPS for periods of six to eighteen months and can extend these periods if the country continues to meet the conditions for designation. Congress has also provided TPS legislatively. A foreign national who is granted TPS receives a registration document and employment authorization for the duration of the TPS designation. Over the years, the George W. Bush and Obama administrations extended TPS for Central Americans from El Salvador, Honduras, and Nicaragua on the rationale that it was still unsafe for their nationals to return due to the disruption of living conditions from environmental disasters (see Wilson 2020).

3. IIRIRA increased the level of hardship that aliens must prove, from "extreme" to "exceptional and extremely unusual" (see Coffino 2006).

4. According to Menjívar and Abrego (2012), the year before IIRIRA passed there were 69,680 deportations; this figure has increased every year, reaching a record of 392,000 in 2010 and surpassing it in fiscal year 2011 with 396,906 deportations. Between 2000 and 2009, 149,833 Guatemalans, 159,265 Hondurans, and 105,397 Salvadorans were deported. And whereas in 1998 these three Central American groups accounted for approximately 9 percent of total deportations, they made up 17 percent in 2005 and 21 percent in 2008, remaining in the top four groups (with Mexico) of deportees. This was done through the creation of two mechanisms of IIRIRA that (a) made it possible to deport legal immigrants who have been convicted of a felony at any time in the United States, even when they have already completed their sentence, and (b) created the 287(g) program, which allows local police to enter into agreements with ICE to target and detain "criminal illegal aliens."

5. De Genova (2004) refers to this process as the "legal production of illegality," referring to the case of Mexican migration.

6. By 2017, the undocumented immigrant population had declined by 1.7 million, or 14 percent. There were 10.5 million unauthorized immigrants in the United States in 2017, accounting for 3.2 percent of the nation's population (see Budiman 2020).

7.   About 115,000 new immigrants arrived from Guatemala, El Salvador, and Honduras in 2014, double the 60,000 who entered the United States three years earlier. Meanwhile, the number of new arrivals from Mexico declined slightly, from 175,000 in 2011 to 165,000 in 2014 (Cohn, Passel, and González-Barrera 2017).

8.   At its peak, Honduras registered 74.6 homicides per 100,000 residents and El Salvador and Guatemala were not far behind (Cohn, Passel, and González-Barrera 2017).

9.   The Obama administration also oversaw the highest rate of deportations — close to 3 million during an eight-year term. (Chishti, Pierce, and Bolter 2017)

10. Many of those who were detained had lost their asylum cases because they were unable to find adequate legal counsel; others were given deportation orders in absentia or through "rocket dockets" that are meant to expedite trials but in reality deny due process (Edwards 2016).

11. TPS, or temporary status, has only been applied to nationals from El Salvador, Honduras, and Nicaragua. Guatemalans have never been designated as beneficiaries except when Attorney General Janet Reno announced that she would temporarily suspend the deportation of nationals from El Salvador, Guatemala, Honduras, and Nicaragua because of Hurricane Mitch (Wilson 2019). In spring 2018, the US government announced it would end TPS, placing 57,000 people at risk for deportation in addition to 200,000 Salvadorans. In 2019, a federal judge blocked Trump's plans to terminate TPS (Lind 2018). The case will possibly be heard by the Supreme Court in the next year, while the lives of Central Americans remain in legal limbo. If TPS is terminated, however, those Central Americans will be subject to deportation (Wilson 2019).

12. In March 2019, US immigration authorities apprehended nearly 93,000 migrants at the border, the highest monthly total in more than a decade. Most were families and asylum seekers from Central America.

13. It is notable that the majority of migrant children who have died in detention have been of Mayan descent. Guatemala has a population of 15 million people, 40 percent of them Indigenous, according to the most recent census. In the past year, 250,000 Guatemalan migrants have been apprehended at the US-Mexico border. At least half of them are Mayans, and many speak little or no Spanish. According to the Department of Justice, Mam was the ninth most common language used in immigration courts in 2019, more common than French. Three Guatemalan Mayan languages made the top twenty-five: Mam, K'iche,' and Q'anjob'al (see Nolan 2020).

CHAPTER EIGHT

This Too Shall Pass

Mexican-Immigrant Replenishment and Trumpism

TOMÁS R. JIMÉNEZ

For the better part of a century, the American immigration landscape was heavily defined by Mexican sojourners. Each decade from 1910 through the first decade of the twenty-first century, with the exception of the 1930s, saw growth of the Mexican-immigrant population. That growth was particularly large in the last three decades of the twentieth century, and included a substantial unauthorized population. Meanwhile, US-born people of Mexican descent—Mexican Americans—were integrating steadily, even if discrimination prevented the same degree of integration that European-origin groups experienced (Jiménez 2010b; Telles & Ortiz 2008).

Colonization, continuous immigration, and integration have created an internally diverse Mexican-origin population with respect to legal status, linguistic ability, geography, and socioeconomic status. Yet popular portrayals continue to present people of Mexican descent as a foreign group whose ranks are filled with unauthorized immigrants seeking to do harm to the United States and its citizens. Today's primary purveyor of that portrayal is President Donald Trump. Then candidate Trump kicked off his presidential run by lashing out at Mexican immigrants, whom he described as drug smugglers, rapists, and criminals. Throughout his campaign and since his election, Trump has smeared layers of paint on to a portrait he renders of an out-of-control southern border that needs sealing off, and an imperative to expunge unauthorized immigrants—"illegals"—from the country.

The irony is just how off kilter this portrayal is relative to the facts. The era of mass Mexican migration and settlement appears to have ended. Over the last decade, Mexican migration to the United States has been net negative. In spite of Trump peddling the idea of a southwestern border out of control, the border has never been more *in* control (González-Barrera and Krogstad 2018). My aim is to try to make sense of what it means to be Mexican American in the United States today, given the combination of dramatically reduced levels of immigration and the heightened politicization of Mexican immigration in an age of Trumpism.

In doing so, I revisit the thesis of my book *Replenished Ethnicity: Mexican Americans, Immigration and Identity* (Jiménez 2010b), in which I argue that continuous immigration—"immigrant replenishment"—was a defining feature of what it means to be Mexican American, even for individuals whose families have been in the United States for many generations. In weighing the effect of continuous Mexican immigration, the book considered what was at the time of the book's publication a counterfactual: What would it mean to be Mexican American if Mexican immigration were to stop?

That counterfactual, now a reality, is the backdrop to the age of Trumpism. What does it mean to "become" Mexican American in an age of Trumpism and diminished levels of Mexican immigration? Both Trump's presidency and the changing patterns of Mexican immigration are significant now, and will likely shape what it means to be Mexican American for decades to come.

Mexican American History, Demography, and Identity before Trumpism

Well before Donald Trump was elected or seriously embarked on a political career, I undertook a study to understand what it meant to be Mexican American at the beginning of the new millennium. My interest in this topic came from my reading of the immigration and assimilation literatures, which showed that the third- and fourth-generation descendants of European immigrants developed a symbolic sense of ethnic identity (Gans 1979). They claim an ethnic identity, but those claims are accompanied by materially inconsequential connections to their ethnic ancestry. Their claims may come with consumption of the cuisine or sporadic celebrations of a holiday related to their ethnic ancestry, but their ethnic origins did not otherwise significantly structure opportunities or the way they made sense of themselves in the world (Alba 1990; Waters 1990). That depiction of assimilation was written without much consideration of non-European immigrant groups that were entering the United States near the turn of the nineteenth century.

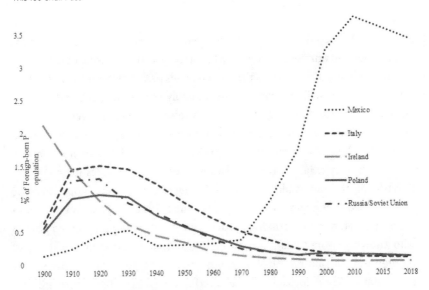

FIGURE 8.1. Foreign-born Mexican and select foreign-born European populations as a share total of US population, 1900–2018. *Sources: US Decennial Census and American Community Survey*

WAVES OF MEXICAN IMMIGRATION

Perhaps the most prominent of those non-European groups was Mexicans. Large portions of the contemporary Southwest once belonged to Mexico, and only became part of the United States at the conclusion of the Mexican–American war in 1848, when the two countries signed the Treaty of Guadalupe Hidalgo. In addition to the sale of land, an estimated seventy thousand Mexicans who resided in the territory became American citizens.[1] Mass Mexican immigration began in 1910, more than a half century after the signing of the treaty. As figure 8.1 shows, Mexicans begin entering the United States as immigrants in large numbers, during the Mexican Revolution, just as mass migration from Europe reached its peak.

Mexican immigration continued until the 1930s, when mass deportations sent some two hundred thousand Mexicans, and in some cases their US-born children, back to Mexico. The 1930s was the only decade in the twentieth century when there was a net decline in the number of Mexican immigrants in the United

States. Throughout the middle part of the twentieth century, when the United States and Mexico had a bilateral guest-worker program—the Bracero Program—Mexican immigrants continued to arrive, steadily growing the Mexican-immigrant population. In 1965, the United States passed sweeping immigration legislation that distributed visas more equitably across the globe and ended a virtual ban on Asian immigration. The law also put the first-ever cap on the number of visas for Latin American countries, including Mexico., narrowing the legal pathway for Mexican immigration, which by that time had a nearly fifty-year history (Massey, Durand, and Malone 2002). Clandestine migration thus became the only available option for many Mexicans if they hoped to come to the United States. Subsequent policies in the 1980s and 1990s sought to limit Mexican migration by fortifying border security, imposing fines on employers who knowingly hired unauthorized immigrants, and restricting the ability of immigrants, both authorized and unauthorized, to access certain forms of public assistance. These measures made entering the United States more difficult, dangerous, and expensive, as unauthorized migration increasingly required the assistance of a smuggler to traverse more dangerous terrain where detection by the Border Patrol was less likely (Minian 2018). When unauthorized immigrants reached the United States, they were reluctant to return, and instead settled north of the border. Their settlement created powerful anchors for subsequent Mexican migration (Massey, Durand, and Pren 2016).

In the meantime, the descendants of the earliest Mexican immigrants, who by the late nineteenth and early twentieth centuries were in the fourth and fifth generations since immigration, were exhibiting patterns of assimilation that, over time and across generations, resembled the assimilation of European groups, though not nearly to the same degree. On average, each generation received more education and more income, and was more likely to intermarry and live in neighborhoods less characterized by Mexicans; some were shedding claims to Mexican ancestry altogether (Alba, Jiménez, and Marrow 2014; Duncan and Trejo 2018; Jiménez 2010b; Smith 2003, 2006; Telles and Ortiz 2008).

More profound than differences in levels of assimilation between later-generation descendants of European and Mexican immigrants was that southern and eastern European immigration to the United States took place in a roughly four-decade period (between 1880 and 1920), while Mexican immigration proceeded virtually uninterrupted for a century. It was that demographic comparison, illustrated in figure 8.1, that led me to wonder whether the symbolic form of the ethnicity that emerged among later generation descendants of European

immigrants had anything to do with the end of immigration. The Mexican-
origin case was an opportunity to answer that question precisely because Mexican migration had been continuous. Of course, the Mexican-origin case differs
in many other respects. Perhaps the most important is that the original Mexican
Americans, those who were already in the contemporary US Southwest when
the Treaty of Guadalupe Hidalgo was signed, were incorporated through colonialism. And while they were considered legally white, which in theory conferred upon them the legal standing of a white person in a country where legal
whiteness was highly consequential, their de facto status was that of nonwhites,
and the terrors of racism have thus been visited upon them (Fox and Guglielmo
2012; Haney-López 2006; Montejano 1987).

IMMIGRANT REPLENISHMENT AND MEXICAN AMERICAN IDENTITY

In order to understand how Mexican-immigrant replenishment shaped what
it means to be Mexican American, I conducted ethnographic research, doing
interviews and observations with later-generation Mexican Americans (those
whose families arrived in the United States before 1940) in two historic and contemporary Mexican immigrant–receiving cities: Garden City, Kansas, and Santa
Maria, California. Garden City experienced an interrupted pattern of Mexican
immigration, with a large influx entering in the 1910s and 1920s to help build the
railroad, a long hiatus from the 1930s to 1980, and then a resurgence of Mexican
immigration in the 1980s and 1990s, when beef-packing plants entered the area.
Santa Maria, in contrast, experienced a continuous influx of Mexican immigration over that period. Mexican immigrants have always come to Santa Maria to
work in crop agriculture. The immigrant replenishment to both places washed
away differences I expected to find. Nonetheless, comparisons with what had
been written about the European case proved informative.

   Through the process of doing the interviews and conducting participant
observation, I learned that conventional aspects of assimilation—upward socioeconomic mobility, intermarriage, neighborhood integration—had occurred
among Mexican Americans, much as they had among European groups. While
these dimensions of integration led to a symbolic form of ethnic identity for
European-origin groups, the Mexican Americans I interviewed had a more
salient connection to their ethnic identity. Mexicans' immigrant replenishment allowed for greater access to the Mexican ethnic culture—the symbols
and practices emblematic of Mexican ancestry in the United States. Although

the use of Spanish language declined with each passing generation, a trend in my interview sample, as well as nationally representative samples (Rumbaut, Massey, and Bean 2006), shows that the presence of Mexican immigrants provided opportunities for those who spoke Spanish (generally among the older respondents) to maintain their Spanish-language use. For respondents with even a modest foundation of Spanish, the large immigrant presence allowed for improvement in their ability to communicate in Spanish. In some instances, the demand for bilingual employees was a labor-market incentive for respondents to continue to speak Spanish. A growing ideology of multiculturalism and the value of diversity ushered on public celebrations of Mexican ethnicity offered easy access to aspects of Mexican ethnic culture. Interpersonal connection—in marriages, neighborhoods, schools, and places of work—to Mexican immigrants and second-generation Mexican Americans also provided opportunities for later-generation Mexican Americans to access a form of ethnic culture that might have been lost through the generations without a continued influx of immigrants from Mexico.

Mexican Americans also experienced a more salient form of ethnic identity because the dynamics of replenishment created pronounced *inter-* and *intra-*group boundaries (Jiménez 2008). The Mexican Americans I interviewed said that they frequently encountered intergroup social boundaries: "patterns of social interaction that give rise to, and subsequently reinforce, in-group members' self-definition and outsiders' confirmation of group distinctions" (Sanders 2002, 327). Interpersonal interactions in which non-Mexicans, usually whites, associated Mexicanness with foreignness, and occasionally with illegality, animated these boundaries. Comments from friends, coworkers, strangers, or neighbors alluding to a notion of Mexicans as foreigners figured in this respect. But these interactions could also include encounters with law enforcement, and even immigration-enforcement agents, who made assumptions about the legal status of later-generation Mexican Americans. Equally potent in reinforcing intergroup boundaries were public denouncements of Mexican immigrants, usually by local elected officials. Both cities had a history of political backlash against Mexican immigrants, with the elected officials making stinging comments about how "Mexicans" have had a negative impact on local life. Though Mexican Americans were not the targets, the attacks resonated because immigration was a defining event in their family narratives and the larger Mexican-origin narrative in the United States. Together, the more everyday interactions and the public comments associating Mexican ethnic identity with foreignness increased the salience of ethnic identity for Mexican Americans.

The presence of a large Mexican-immigrant population was also a source of boundaries that sliced through the Mexican-origin population along generational lines. These intragroup boundaries were animated by a belief that Mexican-descent individuals closer to the immigrant generation were purveyors of a more "authentic" version the Mexican ethnicity. Encounters with Mexican immigrants or second-generation Mexican Americans gave credence to that notion in the eyes of the people I interviewed. The latter were often challenged about their Mexican ancestry if they did not speak fluent Spanish (most did not, and it was extremely rare for younger respondents to speak any Spanish), if they had a thin knowledge of life in Mexico, if they did not consume a style of Mexican food more likely to be found in contemporary Mexico, or if they did not display musical and artistic taste more commonly found among immigrants and the second generation. In essence, Mexican Americans were squeezed between inter- and intragroup boundaries.

The interactive component of immigrant replenishment took place against a backdrop of multiculturalism and the accompanying value of diversity that had become institutionalized in the United States (Alba and Nee 2003). Respondents viewed an ideology of multiculturalism and a value of diversity, in concert with the immigration-driven growth of the Mexican-origin population, as an opportunity. They noted that the immigration-driven growth of the Mexican-origin population made later-generation Mexican Americans well positioned to benefit from demand for ethnic representation in government and industry, and from retailers, churches, and politicians who hoped to garner attention and attract membership. Their views of these benefits were not purely economic. As younger respondents in particular noted, the celebration of Mexican culture in US popular culture gave them a cultural cachet that had been absent in previous time periods.

In sum, Mexican-immigrant replenishment was a double-edged sword for the people I interviewed. On the one hand, it came with significant boundaries associated with their ethnic identity. On the other hand, immigrant replenishment allowed respondents to enjoy a thicker form of their ethnic identity and benefit from the demand for representation and the greater cultural visibility of people of Mexican descent.

The End of Replenishment and the Beginning of Trumpism

Since the publication of *Replenished Ethnicity*, the two key factors explaining the thicker sense of ethnic identity among later-generation Mexican Americans—the replenishment of an immigrant population and the ideology of multiculturalism—have changed dramatically. What do these changes mean for the contemporary scene? Before tackling that question, it is important to elaborate on what has changed.

Perhaps the most important change is that the nearly one-hundred-year period of continuous Mexican-immigrant replenishment appears to have ended. Beginning with the great recession in 2008, Mexican immigration and settlement declined rapidly, and then turned net negative; the United States is now a net exporter of Mexican immigrants (Pew Hispanic Center 2015).[2] It is difficult to know for certain what accounts for the shift. It is likely a combination of the Great Recession, demographic changes in Mexico that negate the need for a labor-surplus outlet, a stricter immigration-enforcement regime in the United States, and greater economic opportunity in Mexico (Villarreal 2014). It is also unclear whether there will eventually be a return of mass Mexican migration. For now, no such return appears imminent.

The second major change has to do with the valence of Mexican ethnicity in the United States. The positive side of the double-edged sword stemming from multiculturalism may be much duller because of the hyper-politicization of Mexican immigration, led principally by President Trump, and the greater visibility of white nationalism. Both predated Trump's presidency. Hysteria about Mexican immigration and its perceived threat date to the colonization of the Southwest and the waves of Mexican immigration that followed (Gonzales 2016; Minian 2018). When Donald Trump descended Trump Tower on an escalator on June 16, 2015, to announce his candidacy for president, he breathed new life into white nationalism. Then candidate Trump laid out what would be a focal point of his candidacy and eventually his presidency when he disparaged Mexican immigrants as rapists, drug smugglers, and criminals. Some of his policies, policy proposals, and rhetoric were directed at immigrants in general, such as the following: the so-called Muslim ban, a new policy guidance guide for Immigration and Customs Enforcement that made every unauthorized immigrant a priority for deportation, the rescindment of the Deferred Action for Childhood Arrivals (DACA),[3] the zero-tolerance policy at the border that included separating children from their families, the push to build a wall along the southern border, the establishment of the Victims of Immigration Crime Engagement Office within the Department of Homeland Security, and the implementation of a "public charge rule." In pushing for these policies, Trump has often cited crimes committed by unauthorized immigrants and the harmful economic impacts of undocumented immigration (see Gonzales, this volume). Though not always explicit, Mexican immigration is a focus of these policies and the rhetoric that accompany them. At other times, Trump directly pointed toward Mexicans even when a policy had very little to do with immigration. During his run for the president, Trump was being sued by former students from Trump University. Trump attacked Gonzalo Curiel, presiding judge for the United States Court of Appeals for the Ninth Circuit, claiming that Judge Curiel could not be objective because of his Mexican ancestry. No other president in modern US history has so vocally targeted Mexicans (Gonzales, this volume).

No other modern president has stoked white nationalism like Trump. It means that white nationalism is now a more forceful ideological competitor to the multiculturalism that prevailed when I conducted my research on Mexican Americans nearly twenty years ago.

Being Mexican American under Trump

The politics and policies of the Trump presidency fall hardest on Mexican immigrants, especially those who are legally unauthorized. As journalistic reporting and an emerging academic literature have shown, the policies and rhetoric of the president have had a chilling effect on just about every aspect of life (Foer 2018). Increased enforcement has led immigrants to avoid churches, their children's school, interactions with anyone connected to the government, and cooperating with police. There are also likely harmful effects on immigrant integration. Social science research has already shown that unauthorized status is negatively associated with intergenerational integration (Bean, Brown, and Bachmeier 2015), and that this negative association is causal (Hainmueller et al. 2017). When the condition of illegality became acute during the Obama administration, the government broke records for the number of individuals it deported. The political rhetoric of Trump has stoked an intense anti-immigrant sentiment among many white Americans. Combined with aggressive enforcement policies, this rhetoric means that unauthorized immigrants, and the communities in which they live, feel the effects of legal status more than ever. Even immigrants with legal documentation are experiencing negative repercussions as the immigration bureaucracy appears to be churning at an even slower pace under Trump (Maganinni 2017).

The effects are also likely to be significant for later-generation Mexican Americans demographically, politically, socially, and economically.

Changing Demography

The key ingredients in the replenishment argument have disappeared or will likely disappear soon. The demography is already changing. It is important to reiterate, there is no more Mexican-immigrant replenishment; Mexican immigration is net negative (González-Barrera and Krogstad 2018). Because of changing fertility patterns and greater economic opportunities in Mexico, a resurgence of mass Mexican immigration does not appear to be on the horizon. If there is indeed an end to the nearly one-hundred-year replenishment of a Mexican-immigrant population, there will be a radical change in the makeup of the Mexican-origin population that will shape economic, political, and social life for people of Mexican descent for generations to come.

The waning immigration is already altering the composition of the Mexican-origin population. In spite of lower levels of immigration, the Mexican-descent population remains impressively large, accounting for 36 million people in the United States and more than 10 percent of the total US population. The growth of the Mexican-origin population has flattened, but it is not shrinking, in spite of a lack of new immigration. The steady size of the Mexican-origin population is maintained entirely by the birth of US-born individuals, creating a Mexican-origin population that is now more demographically dominated by the US population than at any point in the last three decades. According to the US Census Bureau's American Community Survey and decennial data, Mexican immigrants fell to 30 percent of the total Mexican-origin population in 2018, from 44 percent in 2000 (see figure 8.2).

My analysis of American Community Survey data, along with estimates provided by the Migration Policy Institute (n.d.), reveal that in 2007, 24 percent of the total Mexican-origin population (that is, all people of Mexican descent) were unauthorized immigrants. Among Mexican immigrants, 59 percent were unauthorized in 2007. Just nine years later, in 2016, 15 percent of the total Mexican-origin population was made up of unauthorized immigrants; 47 percent of the

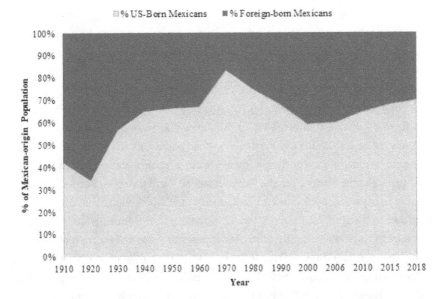

FIGURE 8.2. Ratio of foreign- to US-born Mexican-descent population, 1900–2018. *Sources: US Decennial Census and American Community Survey*

total Mexican-immigrant population was unauthorized. That change is due to a slowing influx of immigrants and some naturalization. Indeed, the composition of the Mexican-origin population is now far more defined by US-born people, and far less by immigrants, including unauthorized immigrants.

CHANGING POLITICS

These changes in the composition of the Mexican-descent population will register politically. Perhaps most fundamentally, the proportion of Mexican-descent individuals who are citizens by birth, not to mention those who have naturalized, will continue to inch up. That will mean an increasing share of the people of Mexican-descent individuals will be eligible to vote and run for office. It is important to note that Mexican immigrants are still much slower to naturalize than other immigrant groups. But the share who are naturalized is growing. According to the Pew Research Center, 42 percent of eligible Mexican immigrants had naturalized in 2015, up from 38 percent in 2005, and from just 20 percent in 1995 (González-Barrera 2017).

The question is whether eligibility will translate into actual participation. If history is any guide, then the Trump presidency appears to be a prod (see Gonzales, this volume). Latinxs, including Mexicans, see today's Trump-era Republican party as anti-immigrant and anti-Latinx (López, González-Barrera, and Krogstad 2019). That sentiment is reminiscent of the way Latinxs in California viewed the Republican Party in the 1990s, when Republicans led the charge in favor of several California ballot initiatives that were unwelcoming toward immigrants, and Latinxs in particular. Those ballot initiatives pushed Latinxs toward formal political participation in greater numbers, and pushed those participating further away from the Republican Party and the state (Bowler, Nicholson, and Segura 2006; Pantoja and Segura 2003). As the Republican Party moved further to the right on immigration, culminating in the nomination of Trump, one of the two major political parties appears to have given up on attracting the Latinx vote (Abrajano and Hajnal 2015). As Republicans repel Latinxs by demonizing immigrants, and Mexicans in particular, the negative edge of the double-edge sword that had been Mexican-immigrant replenishment becomes sharper. If the immigrant experience remains a salient part of the Mexican-origin narrative, and if, as *Replenished Ethnicity* (Jiménez 2010b) showed, Mexican Americans internalize that narrative, then the spate of negative attention directed at the immigrant population is an attack on the entire Mexican-origin population. Given the lack of data, I can only speculate about whether this is true in the current context. But there are indicators suggesting that this is informed speculation. The Pew Research Center examined the views of Latinxs in the United States, showing that nearly half say that the situation of Latinxs has gotten worse compared to the year before; it was the largest share reporting that response since the Great Recession (López, González-Barrera, and Krogstad 2018). It is not just Latinx immigrants expressing more dire views. According to the same report, 44 percent of US-born Latinxs said that in recent years it has become more difficult to live in the United States as a Latinx. Roughly the same share of US-born Latinxs said that "regardless of their own immigration or citizens status, they worry a lot/some that day, I, a family member, or a close friend could be to deported." It would not be a stretch to surmise that the views were as negative among the later generation (the Pew report does not break down the data by generation). But it is also likely the case that even the later generation among Latinxs, including Mexican Americans, see things as having gotten worse under Trump.

As more US-born Latinxs become eligible to vote every day, their political socialization is taking place in an era of Trump. Immigration policies may not directly affect these voters. But the prominence of immigration in the Mexican-origin narrative will shape their political behavior regardless of generation in the United States. Later-generation, US-born individuals among the Mexican-origin population can act as surrogates for ethnic brethren ineligible to participate, as has been the case in California's recent history (Bloemraad and Trost 2008). The 2018 midterm elections suggest that Trump could very well be providing a national version of 1990s California. According to a Latino Decisions (2018) post-election data, three-quarters of Latinx voters said that Donald Trump had said something that made them feel disrespected. That sense of disrespect appears to have translated into turnout rates among Latino voters that outpaced non-Latinos. The Latino Decisions poll shows that Latinx turnout in Latinx-dominant precincts in key states — Arizona, Texas, Nevada, Florida, New Jersey, New York, and New Mexico — nearly doubled, while it was up by just more than a third in non-Latinx precincts. If we are in the midst of a national Proposition 187 moment, the full effect will not likely appear for a decade or more, as it did in California.

The long-term political impact of the changing composition of the Mexican-origin population and the Trump presidency is murky. As the Mexican-origin population has a heavier representation of later-generation individuals, its political leanings will shift, likely becoming more conservative on some issues. And while anti-immigrant and anti-minority politics on the Right appear to rally Latinxs, including Mexicans in the short term (see Barreto, this volume), these same politics could also spur later-generation Mexican Americans to divest in a Mexican ethnic identity as it becomes more stigmatized on the Right. Recall that there is now a substantial Mexican population, including an adult second generation and young third generation, in southern and midwestern states, where Republican politics prevail (Tran and Valdez 2015). Members of stigmatized groups who have an opportunity to disassociate themselves may take the opportunity to do so, avoiding the negative reproductions of that group identity (Hobbs 2014; Huddy 2015). This is not to say that the issues that motivate the Latinx population, including immigration, will also change. As that topic appears further away in the rearview mirror, the motivating issues for Mexican Americans will likely change to emphasize more bread-and-butter issues about which other Americans express concern.

SHIFTING SOCIOECONOMIC FORTUNES?

The ability of people of Mexican descent to fully participate in US society will hinge on their socioeconomic fortunes. Overall, people of Mexican origin tend to be poorer than members of other ethnoracial groups in the United States. But already it appears that declining levels of immigration and a more settled immigrant population are affecting poverty rates for the entire population. According to the US Census Bureau (2019), poverty rates for Hispanics reached a historic low in 2017. There are a number of factors that could contribute to declining poverty. But likely among them is a decade without Mexican-immigrant replenishment, as well as the continued integration of long-settled immigrants and subsequent generations. These aggregate rates hide important variation within the population, especially along generational lines: individuals closer to the immigrant generation exhibit lower levels educational attainment and income, and individuals further from the immigrant generation fare better than their parents (Alba, Jiménez, and Marrow 2014; Bean, Brown, and Bachmeier 2015). There is also some economic advancement across generations that is hidden in statistical analyses because people with Mexican ancestry do not identify themselves as Mexican on surveys. Individuals who have Mexican ancestry, but who do not report it, tend to have higher levels of education and income than the Mexican-origin population in general (Alba, Jiménez, and Marrow 2014; Duncan and Trejo 2018). Even with socioeconomic advancement across the generations, Mexican Americans in the later generations still do not reach parity with native-born whites. In sum, there is a strong tendency toward assimilation, but the trajectory appears to be much flatter than other groups because of historic and present-day discrimination (Telles and Ortiz 2008).

As the Mexican-origin population as a whole marches temporally further away from its immigrant roots, the circumstances under which the immigrant generation arrived will have an imprint on intergenerational socioeconomic advancements well into the future. The central distinguishing factor between those who "make it" and those who do not could very well be whether their immigrant ancestors obtained legal status. There is mounting evidence that not having legal status is a detriment to multiple forms of integration for the immigrant who carries that status, but also for subsequent generations (Bean, Brown, and Bachmeier 2015; González 2015; Hainmueller et al. 2017). When the immigrant generation arrives with documentation or is able to subsequently update their legal status, future generations have much more favorable socioeconomic and health indicators (Bean, Brown, and Bachmeier 2015; Hainmueller et al. 2017).

The reverberation of the condition of legal status into future generations is likely exacerbated by the Trump presidency and the infusion of Trumpism in the Republican Party. For there to be a mass legalization program, which would no doubt speed up the integration of people of Mexican descent, there would need to be a change in the Oval Office, a democratic majority in the House, and bipartisan support in the Senate. Given the shift of the Republican Party from a centrist to restrictionist position on immigration (Abrajano and Hajnal 2015) and the political geography of the United States, it is difficult to foresee that scenario in the near future. It could very well mean that even as unauthorized Mexican immigration fades, the legacy of immigrant generations' legal-status origins will continue to stifle socioeconomic integration.

Geography will inflect the degree of advancement as well. Mexicans historically settled in the Southwest and Chicago, and there is good evidence that states like California offered a context where intergenerational mobility was more likely (Park, Myers, and Jiménez 2014; Telles and Ortiz 2008). With substantial Mexican populations throughout the United States, including in the South and Midwest, the intergenerational socioeconomic fortunes of Mexicans will bear the imprint of the educational and economic opportunities of the regions in which they live (Chetty et al. 2014; Tran and Valdez 2015).

Becoming Mexican American after Replenishment and Trump

The end of Mexican-immigrant replenishment will also have a significant impact on Mexican identity in the United States. Even during a time of heavy immigrant replenishment, there was tremendous social diversity among people of Mexican descent, marked by language, observance of Mexican traditions, connections to Mexico, and geography. Without future waves of Mexican immigrants, Mexican American identity will take on greater influence from experiences inside the United States. As *Replenished Ethnicity* (Jiménez 2010b) documents, the continual influx of Mexican immigrants meant that later-generation Mexican Americans had access to the symbols and practices—the "ethnic stuff" inside of an ethnic boundary—that immigrants bring with them to the United States. In the near term, the large immigrant presence will still offer access to the symbols and practices that sustain a strong sense of ethnic identity among US-born Mexican Americans. But in less than a generation, some of that influence will fade, perhaps most notably in the use of the Spanish language. Language is not dichotomous, where individuals either speak one language or another. There is a spectrum of language expression that includes use of English and Spanish, not to mention the mainstream of Spanish words in the English language and English words in the Spanish language. Still, across the generations, Spanish-language use already declines, a pattern that is likely to accelerate without an influx of Mexican immigrants to provide opportunities and incentives for the continued use of the language (Linton and Jiménez 2009; National Academies of Science, Engineering, and Medicine 2015). A lack of immigrant replenishment will also change how people of Mexican descent form cliques and romantic partnerships. People of Mexican origin already have relatively high intermarriage rates, and those rates increase in each new generation of the United States (Lichter, Carmalt, and Qian 2011). Inter-ethnoracial romantic partnering matters not only because it indicates whether the social boundaries between groups are diminishing, but also because the children that potentially result from those partnerships often have a weak attachment to their ethnic heritage, including when parts of that heritage are from Mexico (Duncan and Trejo 2018; Lee and Bean 2010). Inter-ethnoracial partnering does not necessarily lead to the fading of ethnic identity. Indeed, the non-Mexican partner in a romantic couple can take on something of an affiliative ethnic identity, identifying with the narrative and aspects of the culture of their Mexican-descent partner (Jiménez 2010a; Vasquez 2014). But with a growing population of individuals for whom Mexican ancestry is one among many ancestries, Mexican ethnic identity could take the same symbolic form so prevalent among later-generation descendants of European immigrants (Jiménez 2004; Waters 1990).

The geographic diversity of the Mexican-origin population will also have bearing on identity. As people of Mexican descent "become Mexican American," what becomes of Mexican American identity will have regional overtones. If Texas, New Mexico, and California have historically anchored the three major varieties of Mexican American identity, distinct midwestern, southern, and northeastern variations of Mexican American are already emerging, and will become even more pronounced (Hernández-León and Lakhani 2013; Smith 2005; Zúñiga and Hernández-León 2005). Of course, there are large swaths of the Mexican-origin population along the US-Mexico border for whom flows of immigration are much less relevant. Border regions have a rhythm of back-and-forth movement of people, goods, and culture that will continue regardless of larger immigration patterns (Martínez 1994).

If there will almost certainly be a decline on ready access to Mexican ethnic symbols and practices that come from an immigrant population, less clear is what will become of the boundaries that distinguish people of Mexican descent from non-Mexicans. Boundaries between different subpopulations of the Latinx population are likely to fade. Indeed, many Mexicans do and will continue to identify with a pan-ethnic category fashioned around linkages to individuals with ancestry in Latin American countries, parts of the Caribbean, and Spain. That pan-ethnic identity can emerge from a sense of political but also social solidarity. Nonetheless, a study conducted by the Pew Research Center shows that the pan-ethnic label is less popular than the national origin label, and it fades in its popularity across the generations: whereas 25 percent of the foreign-born generation and 24 percent of the second generation most often describe themselves using a pan-ethnic label, only 14 percent of the third or later generation most often describe themselves in pan-ethnic terms (López, González-Barrera, and López 2017). A pan-ethnic identity is a viable ethnic option now and into the future, it is unlikely to be the default category across the generations.

Another important kind of boundary to consider is that which exists between people of Mexican descent and non-Hispanic whites. Rising intermarriage rates would suggest a decline of these boundaries, though history has shown that intermarriage can coexist with salient intergroup boundaries. As I argued in *Replenished Ethnicity* (2010b), the negative response to the large presence of Mexican immigrants leads to the replenishment of the boundaries that define ethnic difference. Later-generation Mexican Americans experienced these boundaries in everyday encounters, but also through more visible articulations of anti-Mexican rhetoric spouted by politicians. At no time in US history has there been such a persistent and visible denunciation of people of Mexican descent by a politician as there has been under Trump. Even if there is no large-scale Mexican immigration, the politicization of Central American immigration as part of a larger depiction of a "Latin-American invasion" (Chávez 2008) could replenish intergroup boundaries. The data I report earlier from the Pew Research Center suggests that Trump's policies and rhetoric are indeed having a powerful effect on Latinxs regardless of nativity. So long as he is president, and so long as he continues to make immigration a centerpiece of his politics and policy, the boundaries that enclose the Mexican-origin population are likely to become thicker even as the access to the ethnic symbols and practices that enclose it slowly diminish.

Conclusion

The Mexican-origin population is experiencing changes in its composition that should lend to perceptions of the group as less foreign. And yet the politics and policies of Donald Trump portray people of Mexican origin not only as foreigners, but also a threat to the United States. After one hundred years of virtually uninterrupted Mexican immigration, the massive influx of Mexican immigration appears at its end. Just as that demographic fact emerged clearly, Donald Trump built an entire political movement on walling off the US-Mexico border and expunging unauthorized Mexican immigrants, while finding fuel for his wall campaign in the arrival of refugees from Central America. In doing so, he has painted people of Mexican descent in the worst light possible. But just as Mexican immigration appears to have ended, so too has the presidency of Donald Trump. What is clear is that both will have a lasting impact on the Mexican-origin population, shaping not only its composition, but also how the population engages politically and how it integrates socioeconomically and socially. If the past is indicative, the twin forces of demographic change and the spur to political action that is the Trump administration have the potential to put people of Mexican descent in a position to not just become more American, but also to define what is becoming of America.

Notes

1. According to the terms of the treaty, Mexican citizens had to opt out of the becoming US citizens. Otherwise, they automatically became US citizens one year from the signing of the treaty.

2. There is still migration from Mexico to the United States and back, especially near the border. There is also new Mexican immigration. However, Mexican out-migration from the United States outpaces new Mexican immigrant settlement.

3. DACA's rescindment was denied by the US Supreme Court.

CHAPTER NINE

Decolonizing Citizenship

The Movement for Ethnic Studies in Texas

ÁNGELA VALENZUELA

Introduction

It is stunning to consider that, after the founding of the Texas State Board of Education (SBOE) in 1949, it took sixty-five years for the advocacy community to request a separate Mexican American Studies (MAS) course for the state's public schools, in 2014. It took another four years of political, legal, and legislative battles to win, on June 12, 2018, a decisive and historic victory. The SBOE unanimously approved a course elective in MAS as part of the state's secondary school curriculum. This triumph followed an earlier April 11, 2018, victory for African American Studies, Asian American Studies, Native American Studies, and Latino Studies (not to be confused with Mexican American Studies) courses.[1] The message is powerful. Even under Trumpism—and to an extent because of it, as demonstrated herein—major victories are possible.

The June 2018 SBOE decision for MAS was made possible by the tireless work of the National Association of Chicana and Chicano Studies' (NACCS) Tejas Foco conference, particularly the PreK–12 Committee and its allies (Valenzuela 2019). These groups monitored and coordinated the work of Mexican American scholars to advance MAS and ethnic studies, generally, at the high school level before the SBOE. It was my privilege to be an active participant in this effort. Our success was an artifact of generational commitments, particularly among MAS scholars, across time and space. With respect to time, noteworthy is the maturity of a field in higher education born out of civil rights that has progressive, social justice roots with a large, and growing, constituency evident in well-developed MAS programs, centers, departments, and initiatives in US higher education (Macias 2005). Simultaneously, our shared experience of oppression in the geopolitical context of the southwestern United States renders meaningful a borderlands consciousness and epistemology; thus, the contemporaneous and influential ethnic studies battle that took place in the Tucson Independent School District (TUSD) in Arizona was, in many ways, inseparable from our own (Valenzuela 2019). Hence, while this is largely a narrative about Texas, referring Arizona's struggle helps develop the thesis that the struggle for ethnic studies is the work of decolonizing citizenship. While challenging the white nationalist mythologies that Trumpism promotes and that ethnic studies confronts, our legacy struggle for curricular inclusion illuminates how the election of Donald Trump into office was simply a continuing, if hyperbolic, manifestation of how the ideology and politics of white supremacy are an everyday affair under settler colonialism (Tuck and Yang 2012; Calderón 2014).

Indeed, many of the rationales for opposing ethnic studies by white critics fell squarely within the tradition of ideological Trumpism described in other chapters of this collection, particularly hostility toward Latinx. In Arizona, for example, a federal judge ruled that school officials who attempted to shut down a MAS program in Tucson were motivated by "racial animus." The court declared its conviction that "decisions regarding the MAS program were motivated by a desire to advance a political agenda by capitalizing on race-based fears" (quoted in Astor 2017). To wit, in his blog, former Arizona school superintendent John Huppenthal, a principal opponent of MAS, posted calls for "no Spanish radio stations, no Spanish billboards, no Spanish TV stations, no Spanish newspapers. This is America, speak English." He posted his own false claim that the Tucson MAS involved the "rejection of American values and embracement of the values of Mexico in La Raza classrooms," which he asserted "is the rejection of success and embracement of failure" (quoted in Astor 2017).

To unpack and confront these claims, this essay incorporates theories from Chicana feminism (e.g., Anzaldúa 1999; Delgado Bernal 1998; Delgado Bernal et al. 2006), critical Indigenous studies (Vizenor 2008; Tuck and Yang 2012; Calderón 2014), postcolonial scholarship (Quijano 1992, 2007; Valenzuela 2019), and the "border thinking" epistemology that Mignolo (2011) derives principally from Anzaldúa (1999). Border thinking refers to a specific geopolitical locus of enunciation situated in the US borderlands (see also Alcoff 2007). It is distinct from Harding's (1998) concept of "standpoint theory," in which an interchangeability among knowers is not possible. Rather, border thinkers are not only interchangeable, but their ways of knowing bring with them epistemic resources that illuminate the "coloniality of power" (Quijano 2007)—and in so doing, guide political action (Mignolo 2000, 2011; de Sousa Santos 2018).

This chapter also draws on González-López's (2006) concept of the "epistemology of the wound," that proved useful in her research on adult incest survivors. Specifically, for healing to occur, survivors must directly face their deep, painful narratives of abuse at the hands of those who perpetrated violence against them. For NACCS Tejas Foco scholar-activists, this translates into directly confronting the SBOE for its symbolic harm against our community via its state-sanctioned, culturally chauvinist, injurious curriculum that systematically fails to find anything worthy in our history, language, culture, or identities. Hence, the epistemology of the wound is a place of knowing and healing that connects us to a shared experience of oppression in the US borderlands.

The Debunking of a Flawed, Racist Textbook

The first Mexican American history book to ever be considered for adoption by Texas public schools was published by Cynthia Dunbar, a former Texas SBOE member and conservative who once called public education "tyrannical" and a "tool of perversion," and whose ideological leanings are evident in her previously authored text titled *One Nation Under God: How the Left Is Trying to Erase What Made Us Great* (Ayala 2016). Her highly contested, as yet unpublished textbook on Mexican American history, titled *Mexican American Heritage*, was found to be filled with "flaws and racial undertones," including stereotypes about Mexicans being "lazy" as compared to hard working "Europeans or American workers" (Ayala 2016). Mexican American scholars, teachers, legislators, and community leaders—one of whom declared that Dunbar undertook to publish a text in the tradition of Samuel Huntington's divisive *Clash of Civilizations and the Remaking of World Order*—bristled at her racist characterizations in the text and formed a committee to review and critique the book (Oyeniyi 2017).

University of Texas at Austin history professor Emilio Zamora spearheaded this committee, coordinating the critique by numerous MAS historians, citing not only "factual errors," as dictated by the SBOE's rules of the game, but also errors of interpretation and omission, totaling 407 errors. While interpretation and omission errors went against the board's policy and practice of only documenting factual errors, the committee had few options for an omitted history in state curriculum. This undertaking found its way into Zamora's testimony at the momentous September 13, 2016, SBOE textbook hearing:

> The authors are factually incorrect when they say that Latino activists
> joined a counterculture and that they sought to use the university

curriculum to wage a revolution against society. That is untrue. They commit another error when they claim that the Chicano movement basically sought to create a community that resided within but what was untouched by white American society. They're making a separatist argument, which is untrue. I'll be honest with you. There are some people in the '60s and '70s that were making separatists arguments, but the great majority were not. (Texas Education Agency 2016)

Following Professor Zamora was South Texas College history professor Trinidad González, who also spoke to the need to challenge the rules of the game:

The omission errors are so extensive, particularly in every part of the textbook that — you have for instance 49 pages of text and only I think 5 pages are devoted to any way resembling what would be needed in a Mexican American history textbook. In particular and what I find really offensive being from the state of Texas, is they're putting forward a Mexican American history textbook and in no way talk[ing] about Spanish Texas. They mention the California missions, like a paragraph or two and that's it. . . . In order to get to the claims of utilizing the lazy Mexican sort of sources and stuff like that they wanna' make and the radicals and all that, you have to admit the rich, long, Spanish presence in the Southwest, indeed from Florida all the way to California and the history that was developed as a result there. They talk about cowboys, they don't mention Mexican cowboys. So how do you talk about cowboys and the cowboy culture and . . . the history of being cowboys and not mention the fact that the Spanish were the ones that bring that tradition to this area but that is because it fits an agenda they have, I believe, which is to make this argument that Mexican American heritage, Mexican American culture, Mexican American history is some kind of fundamental threat to the U.S. . . . [It] is a polemic masquerading as a textbook and that's why I couch this not just simply as an academic question, but it becomes a moral question of should we accept that kind of presentation that's racist within our educational system? (Texas Education Agency 2016)

It is provocative to consider Professor González's argument that even racist claims need support, which only makes sense if such errors are deemed to be factual, as opposed to racist. By bending the rules to address not just factual errors, but also errors of omission and interpretation, the NACCS Tejas Foco campaign succeeded on November 18, 2016, in having the textbook removed from consideration for Texas public schools. These political victories signaled a new Zeitgeist that has since found expression in Black Lives Matter and other liberation and antifascist movements of our time (Kroichick, 2020).

A New Epochal Zeitgeist

Ethnic studies decolonizes precisely by challenging "settler futurity" that constructs Indigenous people as artifacts of the past while envisioning the future through a false sense of nationhood in the myth of the immigrant nation (Vizenor 2008; Tuck and Yang 2012; Calderón 2014). In Texas, this decolonization of citizenship, it must be noted, is taking place *in the context of a Mexican American community that overwhelmingly holds citizenship.* As Calderón (2014) demonstrates, settler futurity is embodied in the standard Eurocentric, white supremacist social studies curriculum.

The PreK–12 Committee of the NACCS Tejas Foco confronted and ultimately sidestepped this "colonial matrix of power" (Mignolo 2007) that protects settler futurity through the gaps in knowledge that it actively produces (Vizenor 2008; Tuck and Yang 2012; Calderón 2014; Valenzuela 2019). This colonial matrix of power consists of the capacious, multilayered, and intersecting politics, institutions, values, discourses, texts, and curricula that, together with the prescribed "rules of the game," advantage the majority in power in order to ensure the continuance of white supremacy in state-level curriculum and policy processes (Mignolo 2007; Valenzuela 2019). The above-mentioned rule that textbook critics present solely on factual errors, as opposed to errors due either to omission or bias in interpretation, is a good example of how the very process for textbook adoption is profoundly flawed.

To sidestep this matrix of power equates to a breakthrough out of the dark tunnel of what Quijano (1992, 2007) has called "the coloniality of being," toward what de Sousa Santos (2018) calls a new "epochal Zeitgeist." De Sousa Santos characterizes the challenge this way: "First, we don't need alternatives; we need rather an alternative thinking of alternatives. Second, the constant reinterpretation of the world can only be possible in the context of struggle and, therefore, cannot be conducted as a separate task disengaged from struggle" (viii. De Sousa

Santos's concept of an epochal Zeitgeist suggests the intellectual and theoretical dimensions of the decolonizing struggle. Our success in Texas was an artifact of generational commitments across time, decades of work by fellow thinkers and scholars, and a borderlands epistemology born out of a shared experience of oppression.

The Coloniality of Citizenship

In her pathbreaking work on settler colonialism and social studies curricula, Calderón (2014) argues that the very concept of "citizenship" is premised on the modern nation-state that maintains colonial ideologies, values, discourses, and ways of knowing and being that are intertwined with the political project of white supremacy. Within this project, colonial subjects can only get incorporated as minoritized, racialized subjects positioned at the bottom of our nation's race, class, and gendered hierarchy. Notwithstanding decades of research, knowledge production, and theoretical improvements related to asset-based pedagogies such as those advanced in ethnic studies courses, K–12 textbooks and curricula are inexorably "subtractive"; that is, they work to take away knowledge and self-knowledge that students bring with them or that lives in their communities. They carry out a process of ideological, historical, and epistemic erasure through a schooling process that I term "subtractive schooling" (Valenzuela 1999). Relatedly, the concept of "subtractive citizenship" refers to hostile, governmental actions that put "second-class citizens" like ourselves at risk through harmful policies and practices (Valenzuela and Brewer 2010). As Calderón (2014) states, settler societies, meaning colonizers who have no intention of returning to their countries of origin, devise "settler grammars" consisting of values, beliefs, knowledge systems, discourses, and school curricula that undercut full citizenship and democratic participation for colonized peoples (Calderón 2014).

In the policy arena, settler grammars take the form of a capacious array of rules, protocols, timelines, and epistemic norms that delineate the rational, the acceptable, the polite, and the consistent within the extant "regime of truth" (Byrd and Rothberg 2011). As García observes in this volume, the time-honored response has been to advocate for inclusion within the existing framework of state standards and textbook adoption processes. Yet, as the Texas narrative indicates, these processes always default to a Eurocentric curriculum intended to reinscribe subtractive schooling for all of Texas's 5,431,910 students (Texas

Education Agency 2019), albeit particularly for children of color, whose numbers — should they translate into the electoral power that full citizenship implies — could at some point upset the incumbencies of those in power.

On the Texas SBOE, the machinery of the colonial matrix of power is most evident in the seemingly perpetual supermajority of white, conservative Republicans who jealously occupy and hold on to their seats. Out of a total of fifteen seats on the board, only four to five tend to invariably be both minority, specifically Latinx or African American, as well as Democrat. These seats serve districts that are not only exceedingly large, but also partisan and gerrymandered, explaining the lack of diversity on the board. While typically constituting a voting bloc, the minority votes have been perpetually insufficient to obtain even a modicum of curricular inclusion for our community (Valenzuela 1999; Zamora 2012). In a struggle that runs parallel historically to an equally arduous and lengthy one for political rights (Flores 2015), the record shows the Mexican American advocacy community's fight for the inclusion of Mexican American Studies in Texas's state K–12 curriculum squarely about the quest for cultural citizenship as a vehicle for full political rights and representation (Rosaldo 1994, 1997; Rosaldo and Flores 1997; Flores 1997).

In the educational arena, the concept of cultural citizenship calls for education that achieves a profound sense of belonging and an equitable representation in school curricula. In the area of policy, this imperative translates into advocacy for inclusion and substantive representation in the official curriculum. Throughout our four-year battle in Texas, this is exactly what we sought before the ignominious SBOE, albeit through conventional, predetermined processes that structure parameters for thought and agency as predicated by the "rules of the game" for citizen involvement. It is ironic that the very processes established for curricular deliberation, debate, and inclusion are the same ones that have prolonged the struggle, and postponed and denied respectful and equitable inclusion, engineering instead the intentional gap of settler colonialism in Texas, as addressed in the following section.

Defining Ethnic Studies: The Intentional Gap of Settler Colonialism

Ethnic studies, as we know it today, traces back institutionally to the late 1960s, when the first ethnic studies departments and centers were established in higher education with support from the Ford and Rockefeller Foundations (MacDonald and Hoffman 2012). Such developments were made possible by movements on the ground, as in the combined struggles for Mexican American Studies and bilingual education in Crystal City, Texas, in the late 1960s and early 1970s (Trujillo 2014; see also Delgado Bernal 1999). As a casualty either of our nation's so-called culture wars (see Zimmerman 2005 for a critical review) and of the reductive culture of high-stakes testing (see Cashman and McDermott 2013; Valenzuela 2005; McNeil and Valenzuela 2001) and the neoliberal agenda to monetize everything related to education (Altwerger and Strauss 2002), ethnic studies has generally faced an uphill climb despite its demonstrably rich history in the United States (see Hu-DeHart 1993; San Miguel 2005; Au, Brown, and Calderón 2016).

In higher education, *ethnic studies* is an umbrella term that encapsulates African American studies, Asian American studies, Native American studies, and Mexican American studies. Because of its focus on marginal groups, it shares a close affinity with Latins studies and women, gender, and sexuality Studies. In this vein, and as first expressed by Crenshaw (1989), the interconnected aspects of race/ethnicity, class, gender, and sexuality—either for groups or individuals—requires an intersectional look for a complete rendering of how systems of oppression and advantage work within and across categories of difference. Even if not all courses are themselves intersectional, a good example of how this frequently manifests are through courses like those titled La Chicana, often taught in Mexican American studies programs and departments on college campuses (Delgado Bernal 1999).

According to MacDonald and Hoffman (2012) and Macías (2005), ethnic studies is linked to the history of civil rights that has also played out in K–12 and higher education during the late 1960s and early 1970s. At the college or university level, ethnic studies consists of interdisciplinary units of study, lesson plans, courses, concentrations, majors, minors, portfolios (at the graduate student level), or programs that are centered on the knowledge, perspectives, and theoretical frameworks that speak to the lived experiences of an ethnic or racial group. As a field, ethnic studies is largely about knowledge production through research and scholarship, as well as through curriculum and pedagogy, with social justice and community empowerment at its core. Sociocultural thematic content is common. Mexican American studies includes focus on language, history, literature, culture, and social identity. Also common is sociopolitical, thematic content that considers structural relations and systemic inequality, as well as policy, politics, and knowledge of governmental processes and institutions that help prepare both majority and minority youth alike for civic engagement in society (Valenzuela 2016a). Taken together, both perspectives work to empower young people to raise their voices, make their opinions known, and to participate fully in electoral and democratic processes (Sleeter 2011; Romero, Arce, and Cammarota 2009; Cammarota et al. 2018; Zamora and Valenzuela 2018; Valenzuela 2016).

At the K–12 level, there are roughly three approaches to ethnic studies (Zamora and Valenzuela 2018). These consist of infusion approaches where, for example, ethnic studies gets embedded in a social studies, literature, or fine arts course. There are also thematic approaches that incorporate the major racial/ethnic groups sequentially throughout the course in a sole academic semester or year. Important themes are social identity, local history, race, class, gender, sexual oppression, and intersectionalities. These themes may be guided by critical frameworks like critical race theory (Solórzano and Delgado Bernal 2001); settler colonialism; conceptions of whiteness, white privilege, and white supremacy; prejudice; stereotypes; implicit bias; institutionalized forms of discrimination; and so on that might span an entire school year, conceivably corresponding in meaningful ways to Hispanic, Asian American, African American, and Native American heritage months. Lastly, there are single-group approaches such as Mexican American studies, African American studies, Asian American studies, Native American studies, and, occasionally, women and gender studies. For many ethnic studies scholars, the thematic and single-group approaches may be preferable to infusion approaches because of the significant status and standing in the academy that each subgroup has achieved as respected fields of study (Macías 2005; Sleeter 2011). Regardless of approach, ethnic studies arguably occupies one of the intentional knowledge gaps established by the colonial matrix of power (Mignolo 2007; Calderón 2014).

Commenting on the emergence of ethnic studies—often referred to as "multicultural education" at the K–12 level—Sleeter (2016) notes its first official appearance in a 1973 publication of the American Association of Colleges of Teacher Education titled *No One Model American: A Statement on Multicultural Education* (Commission on Multicultural Education). Sleeter adds that, primarily through the work and contributions of scholars of color situated within ethnic studies centers, programs, and departments in higher education institutions, it has been historically connected to K–12 through the content that it provides as new knowledge is created. However, the connection historically, at best, has been through social studies and US and world History courses taught by predominantly white teachers (US Department of Education 2016) who serve as the "curriculum gatekeepers" to historical knowledge (Noboa 2003).

Sleeter's (2016) thorough review of K–12 multicultural education in the United States reveals a continuum of "weak" to "strong" versions—even if, in contrast, only strong ones exist at the higher education level (Valenzuela 2016b). The former consists of a "heroes and holidays" approach, with the latter consisting of those that are critical of Western civilizational hegemony, as more fully addressed below. Ladson-Billings (2009) expresses as much with the concepts of "assimilationist" and "culturally relevant" pedagogy.

As articulated by many scholars (e.g., Au, Brown, and Calderón 2016), culturally relevant pedagogy is philosophically guided by a range of overlapping concerns that include cultural and linguistic preservation, critical and antiracist perspectives, colonization/decolonization, Indigeneity, intersectionalities, power, privilege, whiteness, white supremacy, and inequality. The collective aim of this type of pedagogy is to disrupt imperialist discourses and dispositions, policies, practices, and ideologies in classrooms where youth themselves are encouraged to be transformational. To this, we might add the importance of critical pedagogies for all students if they are to function competently in an increasingly diverse society where more than one out of every two students is a person of color (Krogstad and Fry 2014).

Ethnic studies is not without its pitfalls, however, including the possibility of falling prey to conservative or corporate interests (Sleeter 2016). Even critical approaches can perpetuate what Calderón (2011) terms "colonial blindness," characteristic of weak, normative versions of multicultural education that create knowledge gaps outside the frames established by settler colonialism. Calderón argues that Native Americans' concerns with land rights and struggles for self-determination, including "the importance of native cultures and knowledge in maintaining native sovereignty" (54) can, ironically, be eclipsed in conventional treatments of US minorities (see also Tuck and Yang 2012).[2]

At its best, ethnic studies challenges official knowledge (Apple 2014) and Westernized ways of knowing that objectify children, turning them into objects who "get schooled," rather than truly educated in empowering, life- and culture-affirming ways of knowing and being, positively oriented to others and the natural world (Valenzuela 1999). At the level of community and society, Van Heertum and Torres (2011) refer to this as "el buen vivir" (the good life), in the sense used in contemporary Indigenous thought. However, even as we hold on to this decolonial imaginary, untoward politics, policies, and campaigns never seem far behind, perpetually reopening the wounds of early and ongoing battles against our community.

Epistemology of the Wound: The Decolonial Struggle
for Mexican American Studies

The extended struggle for curricular inclusion positioned members of the PreK–12 Committee of the NACCS Tejas Foco and their allies at the very "core of resistance to empire," carrying out the granular, painstaking work of dismantling the "Eurocentric colonial imaginary" (Mignolo 2000; Alcoff 2012; de Sousa Santos 2018). On the one hand, this has involved expressly cultivating the master's tools to dismantle the master's house (Lorde 2003), as life and career in the academy affords. One the other hand, our commitment tasked us with not only speaking from, but also living in and with the "colonial wound" (Mignolo 2000; Alcoff 2007). To say this as Mexican Americans is not to equate our experience with that of Native Americans (Calderón and Urrieta 2019), but rather to acknowledge the oppression that originates with a shared history of genocide, colonization, and violence, including the pervasive and chronic drumbeat of forced assimilation to which Mexican Americans and Native Americans alike are perpetually subjected.

While colonial matrices of power and settler grammars are durable, the power of an "epistemology of the wound"—meaning *knowing from* the place of injury—cannot be underestimated (González-López 2006). It helps explain both the legacy and durability of struggle. For those in the ethnic studies movement, generally, and the NACCS Tejas Foco specifically, our work has involved a sustained critique of capitalism, patriarchy, and colonialism so that new forms of citizenship can be imagined. In short, it has become a way of living our lives and careers as minoritized faculty, students, and graduate students in the academy.

As university-based scholar-activists, we command the accoutrements of cultural and symbolic capital to effectively challenge colonial symbolic orders, positing the idea that knowledge is either subtractive or additive (Valenzuela 1999), colonial or decolonial (Quijano 1992, 2007), in the face of an established regime of truth embodied in K–12 curricula (Byrd and Rothberg 2011) that itself never requires justification or rationalization for its existence. In contrast, our struggle for inclusion enjoys no such luxury. It serves as a constant reminder that our knowledges, histories, languages, dialects, and cultures are not only subjugated, but also essential to understanding the wounds in our communities that are specific to our experience as Mexican Americans situated in the US borderlands (Anzaldúa 1990). Despite this, to the degree that we are armed with knowledge of our own history, a kind of unifying epistemic exists.

The demand for curricular inclusion in Texas tracks back to World War II and legendary University of Texas professor George I. Sánchez, who decried anti-Mexican segregation and discrimination in US society. This discrimination redounded to the negative and alienating classroom experiences of Mexican American children, which Thomas Carter painfully chronicled in his impactful 1970 publication titled *Mexican Americans in School: A History of Educational Neglect*. According to Zamora (2009), Sánchez was critical of state and federal officials' greater concern with Latin Americans than with Mexican Americans. In a speech delivered before parents and teachers in his hometown of Albuquerque, New Mexico, titled "Pan-Americanism Must Begin at Home" and published in the local newspaper, Sánchez passionately exuded the colonial wound. "It was simply unjust and downright un-American to be interested in the Mexican across the border," he exclaimed, "but not in the one across the tracks." (quoted in Zamora 2009, 101). Zamora, along with the PreK–12 Committee of the NACCS Tejas Foco (myself included), have taken up this legacy agenda to which Sánchez gave voice (Valenzuela 2019).

In 1970, Sánchez and fellow University of Texas professor Américo Paredes, together with a community-based group that included Martha Cotera, Maria Elena Martinez, Modesta Treviño, Emilio Zamora, and others, cofounded the Center for Mexican American Studies (CMAS) (Hinojosa and Rodríguez 2015). By 1971, the University of Texas at Austin began offering an interdisciplinary bachelor of arts degree in Chicano studies. In hearings on K–12 social studies and history standards before the Texas SBOE in 1974, historians Emilio Zamora and Roberto Villarreal testified in favor of the full incorporation of the historical and linguistic heritage of Mexicans in Texas and the United States (Zamora 2019). By 1983, the University of Texas San Antonio offered a bachelor of arts degree in Mexican American studies (Juan Tejeda, personal communication 2018).

The mid-1980s in Texas education policy was the time of the "standards movement," meaning the establishment of the Texas Essential Knowledge and Skills (TEKS) standards for major subject areas like social studies. According to Noboa (2003), this was the first curriculum revision undertaken by the SBOE and the Texas Education Agency in over ten years. This led to the development of new curriculum, pertinent standardized tests, and teacher professional development while affecting texts that the SBOE might adopt in concordance with these educational standards; Noboa cites various studies on curriculum to demonstrate the standards' lack of inclusivity with respect to the Mexican American or Chicana and Chicano experience. Collectively, Garcia (1993) and Glazer and Ueda (1983) conducted in-depth analyses of textbooks over a twenty-year time period between 1970 and 1990, with both studies drawing the same conclusion that the representation of minorities in them had not improved significantly in the social sciences (Garcia 1993, 7). Even when increases in mentions occurred, treatments were so superficial as to make any so-called gains negligible. Noboa concludes: "Thus, the treatment of Latinos in U.S. history textbooks occurs within a general context of omission, distortion and/or underrepresentation regarding the wider Hispanic history and heritage in the Americas as a whole" (2003, 32). A historic court battle for Mexican American Studies similarly took place in the Tucson Unified School District from 2010 to 2017, culminating in *Arce v. Douglas et al.* (2015). As one of three expert witnesses who testified in this court case, I can truthfully say that for the two and a- half years that I was involved in this court battle, the animus of the state against the successful high school MAS program was not only hurtful and personal, but also worrisome for the field to which I and so many others have dedicated our lives and careers. As border thinkers with a borderlands epistemology marked by a shared epistemology of the wound (González-López 2006), everyone knew in their bones that what happened to MAS in Arizona could also happen in Texas (Valenzuela 2019).

Activism in the Borderlands: Arizona and Texas

As a counterweight to the crushing burden of policy streams in educational contexts, abetted by a neoliberal cottage industry that profits from children's failure (Altwerger and Strauss 2002), Macías (2005) documents the expansion of Mexican American studies research and scholarship throughout the 1980s and 1990s in colleges and universities. It resulted in the emergence of a significant force for change over the decades. Notwithstanding their marginal and frequently vexed statuses in their own institutions, these scholars are an academic constituency that is ever attuned to the ongoing colonial, epistemic projects that seek to subjugate either by misrepresenting or erasing the knowledge, cultures, and histories of a people that are not only US citizens, but descendants of the original inhabitants of this continent (Forbes 2005).

It therefore comes as no surprise that many of the same Mexican American studies activists involved in today's K–12 ethnic studies movement also pressured the Texas legislature in 2003 to allow MAS to become an official course of study at community colleges. By 2005, Palo Alto College in San Antonio was among the first community colleges in Texas to offer an associate of arts degree in the field (Juan Tejeda, personal communication 2018).

To achieve this victory, state representative Roberto Alonzo amended Senate Bill 286, requiring public, community colleges located in communities with large numbers of resident Mexican-origin families to evaluate the demand for, and feasibility of, establishing a MAS concentration of studies, upon securing approval from the Texas Higher Education Coordinating Board (THECB) (Texas Legislature Online 2003). A pertinent generational detail here is that Representative Alonzo, a native of Crystal City, Texas, is himself a product of both the Mexican American struggle for civil rights and Mexican American studies itself (Alonzo 1996).

Without champions like Alonzo in the legislature, bills on curriculum like MAS, which are minoritarian in nature, are difficult to pass, primarily because curriculum is supposed to be the domain of the elected SBOE at the K–12 level and the THECB at the college and university level. Although it is legal to circumvent such governing bodies, this strategy can be perceived as unfriendly. Because these bodies do not like to be strong-armed when curriculum bills fail in the legislature, and are later reintroduced before these boards, they risk rejection. Although rejection did not occur in the Texas case, it was definitely possible. On the one hand, the scenario illuminates the "colonial matrix of power" (Mignolo 2007) and how the rules of the game work to disadvantage progressive causes like MAS. On the other, it helps to establish that there are ways to sidestep the colonial matrix of power even while maneuvering within it (Valenzuela 2019).

Extending MAS to the community colleges in Texas in 2003 resulted in the establishment and strengthening of many programs throughout the state. A new, more youthful constituency for change emerged at the community college level; however, as the 2010 SBOE hearings demonstrated, the presence and activism of the civil rights generation continues.

On April 28, 2010, a highly contentious and publicized set of hearings took place in the context of revisions to the 1998 secondary social studies standards. A progressive coalition of individuals and organizations, involving university faculty and organizations (League of United Latin American Citizens, the GI Forum, the Tejano Genealogy Society, and the Comecrudo Native American tribe), fought to reduce the prominence of white males in Texas history curricula by denouncing the glaring omissions of women, African Americans, Mexican Americans, and civil rights history; Despite this effort, the coalition ultimately failed (see Zamora 2012). World history was poorly conceptualized, reifying a Western civilizational perspective.

A few weeks later on May 4, 2010, Dr. Devon Peña, who then served as chair of NACCS, responded strongly, in a letter addressed to Arizona governor Jan Brewer and the people of Arizona, to the wrong-headedness of Senate Bill 1070. SB 1070 was a racial-profiling, show-me-your papers law that targeted for arrest and potential deportation anyone who "looked Mexican."[3] While on its surface, this law was unrelated to Mexican American studies, the anti-immigrant drumbeat picked up noticeably, ushering in full force what we recognize today as the Trumpian, anti-Mexican moment; this was not lost among NACCS's members.[4]

On May 11, 2010, the Arizona state legislature passed House Bill 2281, targeting the TUSD's highly successful K–12 Mexican American Studies program and situating it in the crosshairs of state superintendent Tom Horne. Before the end of the year, on October 18, 2010, TUSD student Maya Arce filed a lawsuit against Horne, alleging a violation of the First and Fourteenth Amendments to the US Constitution (*Arce v. Douglas* 2015; formerly *Arce et al. v. Huppenthal, Arizona Superintendent of Public Instruction et al.*). During his last days in office and before assuming his position as attorney general for the State of Arizona in January 2011, Horne issued a finding that TUSD was in violation of more than one of Arizona Revised Statutes (ARS), rendering the MAS curriculum illegal. Another vehement MAS opponent, John Huppenthal, then replaced Horne as state superintendent of public instruction.

On January 4, 2011, Huppenthal issued a press release supporting Horne's findings that the TUSD MAS program was in violation of ARS 15-11 and 15-112. Instead of enforcing the ruling, however, Huppenthal retained Cambium Inc. as an independent auditor of the MAS program. On May 2, 2011, Cambium released its report, finding no evidence of any violations. Huppenthal rejected the Cambium report and called for the Arizona Department of Education to conduct its own separate investigation. This second investigation gave him the result he wanted: Huppenthal reaffirmed that TUSD's MAS program was in violation of ARS 15-111 and 15-112. In a series of gestures that sent shock waves across the country, books used in TUSD MAS courses were banned and the program was summarily dismantled (see Palos 2011).

As expected, the toxic, high-profile 2010 SBOE debates in Arizona that, for the most part, reinscribed Western European hegemony (Erekson 2016), resonated in Texas. The 2011 session of the Texas state legislature featured the antics of state representative Wayne Christian, a member of the legislature's Texas Conservative Coalition (*Texas Tribune* 2011). Specifically, Christian attempted to amend House Bill 1 to require that 10 percent of all university courses be devoted to teaching Western civilization. His amendment animated Latinx and African American Democrats, who crowded around the microphone to ask whether African American studies or Mexican American studies themes would get incorporated into these courses. Christian responded that we should "teach the truth, not the made up, not the separated," implying that ethnic studies fostered ethnic separatism (*Texas Tribune* 2011).

Although Christian's Amendment 144 was killed on the House Floor, in the following session of the Texas state legislature, Senator—now Lieutenant Governor—Dan Patrick filed Senate Bill 1128 that sought to limit the six-hour undergraduate US history requirement to the US survey and to Texas history (Planas 2013). MAS advocates readily noticed that the bill graphically mirrored the bill passed by the Arizona state legislature that resulted in the dismantling of the MAS program in TUSD. On behalf of the PreK–12 Committee of the NACCS Tejas Foco, University of Texas History professor Emilio Zamora testified in committee against the bill, arguing that this narrowing of the undergraduate history curriculum was unwarranted (Zamora 2018; see also Valenzuela 2019, who elaborates on this pivotal moment).

These reactionary attempts to maintain official knowledge (Apple 2014) embody "settler grammars" that seek primarily "to teach an almost predestined sense of citizenship and democratic participation, at least for some populations." (Calderón 2014, 315) They maintain a "Eurocentric colonial imaginary" that conceives of US history and culture as part of a natural progression of sustained human progress in the Western tradition (Mignolo 2000; Alcoff 2007). Even when thin on detail, like the Christian amendment, or written in arcane legalese, the party affiliations, ideological tendencies, and hubris of these champions of the Western tradition make them easy to spot. That is, whether by busy professors like Zamora, or busy legislators of color consumed by the din of addressing thousands of bills in house and senate chambers, an aching epistemology of the wound equates to strategic, if visceral, resources for action.

In light of the various right-wing developments in Texas and Arizona in the early 2000s, the NACCS Tejas Foco convened at Northwest Vista College in San Antonio on February 20, 2014. At the conference, the MAS PreK–12 Committee sought ways to integrate MAS in Texas public schools while addressing, generally, the state of MAS in Texas public schools. Several members of the PreK–12 Committee had ties to SBOE member Ruben Cortez, a Democrat from Brownsville, meeting regularly with him in the months leading up to the November 21, 2014, hearing in Austin where he first proposed a MAS course and asked the Texas Education Agency to develop attendant state standards. As I have discussed elsewhere (Valenzuela 2019), for members of the Foco, this political decision was a direct outgrowth of a deep sense of solidarity with those who struggled for MAS in Tucson.

Cortez's 2014 proposal, as mentioned, represented the very first time that any SBOE member ever proposed a stand-alone MAS course. At this hearing, a set of scholar-activists—including history professor Emilio Zamora (University of Texas at Austin), music professor Juan Tejeda (Palo Alto College), and history professor Roberto Calderón (University of North Texas Denton)—testified in support. Despite these efforts, the SBOE voted against the proposal 11–3. Cortez salvaged the agenda by getting the board to agree to having publishers submit Mexican American, Asian American, African American, and Native American studies textbooks for mapping onto a special topics MAS course in social studies being taught in the Houston Independent School District. Worthy of note is that special topics courses are allowable by law, but must always meet SBOE approval on a case-by-case basis. They are typically idiosyncratic to specific needs in specific school districts.

Without a doubt, these early steps in 2014 represent the first breaths of what ultimately became our political victory in spring of 2018 that resulted in the passage of MAS, African American Studies, Asian American Studies, and Native American Studies as elective courses in the state of Texas. Most importantly and in contrast to the 2010 debate, in 2014, Ruben Cortez and his voting bloc of three minoritized board members—Marissa Pérez, Erica Beltrán, and Lawrence Allen Jr.—and his large, statewide constituency of NACCS Tejas Foco scholars, succeeded in circumventing the colonial matrix of power by calling for separate, stand-alone, ethnic studies courses. On December 12, 2016, our local community-based organization, Nuestro Grupo (Valenzuela, Zamora, and Rubio, 2015), also successfully advocated for the teaching of ethnic studies in the Austin Independent School District (AISD). After a year of planning (2016–2017) with AISD staff, we devised a comparative-thematic ethnics course for high school students, launched in fall 2017 (Zamora and Valenzuela 2018). Hence, anticipating the Black Lives Matter Movement and the teaching of ethnic studies that young activists are calling for (Kroichick 2020), the course came to be taught in nearly every high school, serving approximately six hundred students districtwide. AISD is one of less than a handful of districts in the state that is currently teaching ethnic studies to scale. This may change soon, however, should House Bill 1504, proposed by Texas state representative Christina Morales (a Democrat representing Houston), become Texas law in the 2021 session. Regardless of the outcome, HB 1504 is historic in that it is the first to link ethnic studies — as a one-unit, yearlong course — to high school graduation, by allowing it to substitute either for world geography or world history in a way that is inclusive of the four major groups named: Mexican Americans, Asian Americans, African Americans, and Native Americans.

Conclusion: Lessons Learned

This essay argues that change is less an artifact of accidental convergences in the Foucauldian (1984) sense, and more an extended, intentional, multisite agenda to liberate subjugated knowledge. As Alcoff (2007) reminds, we must be constantly vigilant of epistemic norms predicated in state curricula, including such notions as "objectivity" and "universal claims," embellished by inference with legitimating procedures and processes like standards development, textbook adoption, teacher professional education, and test development (Noboa 2003). When we are able to recognize that this knowledge amounts to idealized constructions of truth that sacrifice "actually existing knowledges" of the kind that ethnic studies provides, we are better able to potentially reclaim our Indigenous identities while unmasking the Eurocentric fantasy that portrays New England, Protestant, white men as agents and heroes, and the remainder of humanity as non-agents and villains (Noboa 2003, 80; García 1993).

Ethnic studies bears the potential of decolonizing citizenship in its ability to interrupt the official, time-honored, culturally chauvinist curricula through which school districts, schools, and classrooms give meaning to citizenship. The struggle for ethnic studies equates to a decolonial fight for cultural citizenship in the context of official public school curriculum. I refer here specifically to the way the Mexican American community in Texas has struggled consistently to build institutions, claim rights, and right wrongs (see, for example, Zamora 2009).

Trumpism, the ethnic studies movement, and the renewed Black Lives Matter Movement in the wake of the George Floyd murder on May 25, 2020, by a Minneapolis police officer reveal a convergence of forces. What this narrative assures is that what we know as "Trumpism" today was already manifest in

Arizona long before Donald Trump became president. His presidency is less a motivator for ethnic studies than a response to it in a state that he considered his base. Hence, while curriculum that is inclusive of the historical oppression of minoritized communities in the United States bears the potential to constitute a bulwark against racism (Kroichick 2020), the historical record is abundantly clear that our rights to this knowledge is inescapably political.

The larger goal of liberation takes to heart Anzaldúa's (1990) injunction for *nuevas teorías* (new theories) that honor the vexed statuses held by inhabitants of the US borderlands. Such *teorías* engage Indigenous knowledge and identity, lived experience, cosmologies, and philosophies born out of what Mignolo (2011) terms the "colonial difference." With this concept, he converges with Anzaldúa (1999), de Sousa Santos (2018), and González-López (2006), for whom speaking from the perspective of difference, or the "colonial wound," guides our sense of how and when to act in political struggle. Similarly, Foucault, in his conceptualization of power and social change, refers less to constitutions, sovereignty, or the state apparatus, and more to definitions that emerge from daily struggles at the grass-roots level, among those whose fight [was] located in the fine meshes of the web of power" (1984, 58).

Foucault's analysis foregrounds not the "constituent subject" portrayed in most historical treatments, but rather the "constitution of the subject within a historical framework"—that is, "genealogy" or "archaeology." Both offer ways to study knowledge as discourse practices that construct specific forms of the human subject (e.g., "low achiever," "deviant," "high achiever," "activist," etc.) (1984, 58). While the human subject is a product of schooling, ethnic studies holds possible new ways of knowing and being that bring with them the knowledge, skills, and dispositions to challenge the "official future" embedded within settler colonial futurity that is otherwise embedded in our states' K–12 curricula (Vizenor 2008; Tuck and Yang 2012; Calderón 2014).

As the paradigm shift in Texas attests, significant change comes not as a technical fix or a theoretical intervention, but rather through the messiness and meaningfulness of actual struggle led, in the present case, by a mature cadre of scholar-activists with roots dating back to the late 1960s and early 1970s. Only when working intimately in concert with others in a social movement do we know how and when to act, freshly haunted—and thusly motivated—by the epistemology of the wound (González-López 2006). We might even construe this deep sense of obligation either as ancestral memory or a "generational haunting"—as constituent components to this wound. It is profoundly spiritual.

When a loss of dignity is deeply felt, including by those who came before us, this mobilizes us toward a decolonial imaginary. Here, the journey is as important as the "arriving," embodying what the Reverend Martin Luther King Jr. once extolled as the "beloved community" in pursuit of a just and caring world devoid of bigotry and hatred (Jain 2017). What these wounds portend for our children and unborn generations is not an abstraction. Instead, for us activist border thinkers in the movement, the psychic, emotional, and spiritual need to enunciate a new reality for the kind of world that we seek motivates and compels. . For ethnic studies teachers, professors, researchers, and students, our task is therefore to continue to speak from the wound, as individuals and collectivities, as the only reliable counterpoint to the forces of ignorance, violence, and hatred that threaten to consume the world and the planet.

Much is therefore owed in our past and present to the many who have produced knowledge, who have developed nuevas teorías, and who have stood up, in ways big and small, to the ghastly and systematic erasure of our histories, languages, cultures, values, and ways of knowing and being in the world. All of this work is for the benefit of humanity in a deeply troubled world.

Notes

1. Elsewhere, I explain how on April 12, 2016, in the process of a successful campaign to get ethnic studies courses passed by the SBOE, meaning African American Studies, Asian American Studies, Native American Studies, and Latino Studies, a right-wing member of the board, David Bradley, proposed a course name titled Ethnic Studies: An Overview of Americans of Mexican Descent, thusly muting advocates' victory with this objectionable name (Valenzuela 2019; see also Pulte 2018). Beyond member Bradley, responsible for these twists and turns was a Latina member of the board, Georgina Pérez, who not only seconded the motion that was thereafter accepted by the board, but also called for—against advocates' wishes—"Latino Studies," instead of "Mexican American Studies." In a personal communication to me on January 31, 2018, she said that she preferred "Latino Studies" because "Mexican American Studies" would never get past this board. Fortunately, we proved her wrong upon securing board approval on June 12, 2018, for a course named Ethnic Studies: Mexican American Studies.

2. In a similar vein, Walsh (2012) expresses concern with a lack of focus in South American, postcolonial scholarship on the construction of the Afro-Caribbean, colonial experience in racialized terms.

3. This prompted Alabama and Georgia to pass similar legislation (Peña 2010; Duara 2016).

4. For three legislative sessions, in 2011, 2015, and 2017, Texas Republicans filed bills outlawing "sanctuary cities"; operationally, this meant that sheriffs could hand over detained immigrants to federal law enforcement authorities. A 2015 article in the *Texas Tribune* mentions "No Arizona Hate in Texas," a much-heard mantra that directly referenced Arizona's SB 1070 (Aguilar 2015).

Epilogue

MARY LOUISE PRATT, RENATO ROSALDO,
AND PHILLIP B. GONZALES

The Trump playbook was seriously challenged by the two crises that befell the final year of his term: the COVID-19 pandemic and the global antiracist uprising triggered by the murder of George Floyd by police in Minneapolis. In many respects, the virus was the wrong kind of enemy for Trumpian theatrics. It was invisible and indifferent; it did not recognize conflict. It could not be shamed, silenced, or fired. It was blindly egalitarian—all humans were potential hosts, though the harm it caused was dramatically unequal. While Trump succeeded in politicizing responses to the virus, his inability to address it as a public health problem was a chief reason for his electoral loss.

The pandemic brought an untimely end to Trump's favorite political "showbiz" (Brooks 2019) spectacle, indoor mass rallies in large spaces like stadiums and airplane hangars. For a while, daily briefings at the White House became the new presidential stage, but these did not serve him well, for they highlighted his inability to offer guidance, empathy, and moral vision called for from civic leaders during a national crisis (these falling instead to New York governor Cuomo). Performing his adversarial mode like a broken record, the president sought opportunities to dispute with medical experts, contradicting the scientists with his own ungrounded views: the virus would disappear; it would be over by Easter; we should try treating it with bleach, disinfectant, or hydroxychloroquine. This time, however, his disputations and lies cost lives.

Following his playbook, Trump fomented populist libertarian resistance to government-ordered shutdowns and mask mandates. The result was an escalation of violence. In Michigan, white nationalist militia members, rifles in hand, occupied the state capitol building to protest shutdown orders and intimidate elected legislators, even as plans to kidnap and murder the governor were revealed.

Over the summer of 2020, the base followed his lead, holding church services, beach parties, barbecues, car rallies, and protests in the name of the freedom both to risk infection and to spread it to others. Spread it did, exploding across the West and the South, particularly in states where Republican governors had refused shutdown measures. Favoring chaos, the White House openly withheld leadership. It refused to confirm that the virus was real, refused to mandate face masks, and demanded that schools reopen. Mayors and governors were left to lead; many did so brilliantly, while the Trump machine set up a new and, for them, more suitable object for its displays of aggression: the demonstrators responding to the George Floyd murder, demonized as the "radical left."

The COVID-19 pandemic had dramatic consequences for Mexican Americans, Latinxs, and all people of color. Concentrated in the rank and file of health care and other service workers, people of color were hyperexposed to the virus. Underpaid in these jobs, many lived in crowded housing where contagion was impossible to avoid. Many had family responsibilities that made self-isolation impossible. Sick leave was nonexistent and access to medical care minimal, especially for undocumented people, who often had no choice but to work even when ill. Health vulnerabilities made them, along with other poor people, far more likely to die once they were infected. Daily life-and-death dramas laid bare the racialized inequalities of US society and the mass impoverishment resulting from four decades of neoliberal economic policies. The government's category of "essential workers" came to mean "disposable people." According to the APM Research Lab, adjusting for age, the COVID-19 death rate for Hispanics was 2.5 times that of White Americans by early July 2020. For African Americans the rate was 3.8 times higher, and for Native Americans it was 3.2 times higher (APM Research Lab Staff 2020).

The daily display of these inequities formed the background for the second watershed episode in which the Trump playbook faltered: the national, and international, uprising against racism triggered by the video-recorded murder of George Floyd on May 25, 2020. The images of George Floyd's murder by a Minneapolis police officer traveled much faster than COVID-19. If the virus sent people into their homes on a mass scale, Floyd's death brought them out into the streets en masse in nearly every town and city in the country. It was a powerful repudiation of Trumpism's bedrock creed, white nationalism.

The Trumpian playbook thought it saw a politically viable adversary, and a path to a theatrical win: violent state repression displayed in public spaces, accompanied by calls for law and order. In a notorious phone call with governors on June 1, 2020, the president excoriated them for appearing weak in the face of the demonstrators. "You have to dominate," he barked, "or you're wasting your time. They're going to run over you. . . . You've got to arrest people, you have to track people, you have to put them in jail for 10 years." Secretary of Defense Mike Esper agreed with the inherent authoritarian rage: "I think the sooner that you mass and dominate the battlespace, the quicker this dissipates and we can get back to the right normal." Attorney General William Barr parroted the rhetoric: "Law enforcement response is not gonna work unless we dominate the streets; as the president said, we have to control the streets" (Balsamo 2020). Team Trump set an example for events to come after the 2020 presidential election by turning Washington, DC, into a theater of war.

In response to peaceful demonstrations outside, the president's office called in US Army and National Guard units and erected eight-foot barriers around the White House ("Build the wall!"). Armed agents, unidentified and in riot gear, violently attacked peaceful protestors to clear space for a presidential photo-op in front of a church. But the play backfired. High-ranking military officials spoke out, rejecting the commander in chief's attempt to use the armed forces against civilians. It was a humiliating defeat for the president. Even the Bible he waved in his hand was upside down.

Day after day, the George Floyd demonstrations displayed the emergence of a new political community. Not only did people of color demand an end to white supremacist society, so did many, if not most, white people. Alongside people of color, white Americans in huge numbers marched as members of the new mobilization, repudiating racism as a founding principle of the society. As the 2020 election approached and in the face of falling poll numbers, the Trump regime (now acting as a regime) opted for escalation, extending and transgressing the limits on presidential power, challenging anyone to try to stop him. Fear of the mob became the theme of his reelection campaign. The strategy did not work.

What did work, however, was Trump's long-standing claim that if he lost the election, this fact in and of itself would be proof of massive fraud. He created a powerful myth for his aggrieved followers to inhabit. Watch the polling sites, he predicted—you'll see it happening. Militias and militants, mobilized to fight against racial justice protests, began preparing for civil war. Americans and the world witnessed an unimaginable spectacle of delusion: over 40 percent of the electorate apparently convinced that the election was illegitimate, despite overwhelming evidence to the contrary, including over fifty judicial rulings. That intensely meaningful, morally galvanizing myth of fraud culminated (we hope) in the storming of the Capitol on January 6, 2021, an event without precedent in the history of the United States. That moment of Trumpism's triumph may also mark the beginning of its decline.

This volume appears at a moment many see as a political crossroads, in which the United States will choose between racial democracy and white supremacy, between majority or minority rule. Inclusive democracy, we have learned, cannot be taken for granted; it must be constantly defended and perfected, as both a reality and an ideal. White supremacy, we have learned, will never go away in the United States. It must be delegitimized and held in abeyance through constant effort. Whatever possibilities emerge in our near future, none of them will make the others go away. Latinx people are not going to go away either. Their complex and growing presence will remain a key factor in the making of America, and it must remain the object of vital research efforts across the disciplines. Many lines of inquiry have shaped this volume. A few in particular stand out.

1. Demographics count. In the United States, White racial panic is fed by the undeniable fact that whites will soon be less than a majority, whether or not they like it. Many—too many, evidently—rage at the thought. Many others, however, maintain the goal of a just, multiracial, multiethnic society.

2. Electoral politics matter. Trumpism's most powerful unintended consequence may be the revindication of electoral politics among people who had acquired the habit of thinking their politics beyond the electoral. As the unprecedented turnout in 2020 affirms, Trumpism made it overwhelmingly clear that citizens must act both in the streets and at the ballot box.

3. The Latinx vote matters. The Latinx electorate plays an increasingly decisive role in US democracy at all levels. According to the UCLA Latino Policy and Politics Initiative, this sector, 16.6 million strong, increased its voting rate in the 2020 presidential election by nearly 40 percent over the 2016 presidential election, far greater than the 15.9 percent increase among voters of all races. It played central roles in the swinging of elections in thirteen states—including the battlegrounds of Arizona (where Latinxs comprise 25.2 percent of registered voters), Wisconsin, Pennsylvania, and Georgia—toward Joe Biden for president.

In twelve of those states, Latinxs supported Biden by a margin of at least two to one; in nine states, by at least three to one (Mendez 2021).

These rates suggest that the Latinx vote did its part to foment what Gonzales in this volume calls anti-Trumpism. Whether or not these results will be sustained in the future elections remains to be seen. To what extent, for example, will Latinx people group according to their distinct histories and to what extent will they be guided by a sense of shared interests? By what paths do they become candidates for office? How will they continue to alter the national conversation?

4. Racist, anti-immigrant, and anti-Latinx sentiment are not going to simply dissolve. What tools will social institutions and Latinx people develop to counter them? This question arises particularly with respect to young people. Their political lives and imperatives will continue to diverge from those of their parents, as the challenges of climate change, declining educational opportunity, and economic insecurity become more acute. They will construct their identities differently as well, especially if their communities and families are less often replenished by new arrivals. What role will language play for them? What kinds of educational programs will best empower them? In what creative forms will they express themselves?

5. Immigration policy and the activities of enforcement agencies demand continued critical analysis. The long-standing ideal of a "comprehensive immigration policy" may be set aside to open up other possibilities. The status of undocumented people, their families, and DACA candidates must be resolved, and it appears that President Biden is committed to redressing Trump's regressive policies and ending his politics of dehumanization and cruelty. The roots of crisis in Central America must also be addressed, a powerful role that has been assigned to Vice President Kamala Harris.

This book has demonstrated how the exclusion and marginalization of Mexican Americans, as well as Central Americans, were part of the foundational narrative of the United States, and that these carried over to other Latinx peoples incorporated into the union. The struggle for Latinx citizenship and belonging is thus not a side effect that is going to dissipate. This struggle will continue to be part of the experience of Mexican Americans and all Latinx people. But, of course, this will not be the whole story. It remains essential that scholars continue to capture Latinx experience in all its depth and complexity, as it unfolds. The question of how the ubiquitous Latinx presence is shaping mainstream culture in the United States remains particularly rich and important. Literature, media, the arts, and expressive culture have little presence in this volume, whose center of gravity lies more in the social sciences, but their value as a source of insight into Latinx experience should not be underestimated. They will have much to reveal as we seek to grasp the Trumpian era and engage the politics of change to come.

AAUP. 2016. "The Atmosphere on Campus in the Wake of the Elections." November 22, 2016. https://www.aaup.org/news/atmosphere-campus-wake-elections#. YCxEFxNKhn6.

ABC7. 2020. "Racist Tirade: Woman Exercising in Park near Los Angeles Told to Go Back to Asia." Streamed on June 11, 2020. YouTube video, 2:27. https://www .youtube.com/watch?v=_w4J9XRMhpE.

ABC News. 2019. "Trump Asks Steve Cortes: 'Who Do You Like More, the Country or the Hispanics?'" September 16, 2019. https://abcnews.go.com/Politics/video /trump-asks-steve-cortes-country-hispanics-65693814.

Abrajano, Marisa, and Zoltan L. Hajnal. 2015. *White Backlash: Immigration, Race, and American Politics*. Princeton, NJ: Princeton University Press.

Acevedo, Nicole. 2019. "Why Are Migrant Children Dying in U.S. Custody?" *NBC News*, May 29, 2019. https://www.nbcnews.com/news/latino/why-are -migrant-children-dying-u-s-custody-n1010316?fbclid=IwAR38n79Vu1jBLe jqEPL8NCeCJ7qaGinN2TJOuTfEkVI1BKJDyISX3Jee7Rs.

ADL. n.d. "Hate Slogans/Slang Terms." Anti-Defamation League. https://www.adl.org /education/references/hate-symbols/diversity-white-genocide. Accessed March 9, 2021.

Aguilar, Julián. 2015. "Six Years Later, Fight over Anti-sanctuary Cities Bill Has Changed." *Texas Tribune*, January 15, 2015. https://www.texastribune.org /2017/01/15/sanctuary-city-legislation-then-and-now/.

Ahmed, Sara. 2014. *The Cultural Politics of Emotion*. Edinburgh: Edinburgh University Press.

Alba, Davey. 2021. "Anti-Asian Online Posts Helped Set the Stage for Real-World Violence." *New York Times*, March 20, 2021. https://www.nytimes. com/2021/03/19/technology/how-anti-asian-activity-online-set-the-stage- for-real-world-violence.html.

Alba, Richard D. 1990. *Ethnic Identity: The Transformation of White America*. New Haven, CT: Yale University Press.

Alba, Richard, Tomás R. Jiménez, and Helen B. Marrow. 2014. "Mexican Americans as a Paradigm for Contemporary Intra-Group Heterogeneity." *Ethnic and Racial Studies* 37, no. 3 (January): 446–66. http://dx.doi.org/10.1080/01419870.2013 .786111.

Alba, Richard, and Victor Nee. 2003. *Remaking the American Mainstream: Assimilation and Contemporary Immigration*. Cambridge, MA: Harvard University Press.

Alcoff, Linda Martín. 2005. *Visible identities: Race, Gender, and the Self*. New York and London: Oxford University Press.

———. 2007. "Mignolo's Epistemology of Coloniality." *CR: The New Centennial Review* 7, no. 3 (Winter): 79–101. https://doi.org/10.1353/ncr.0.0008.

Alexandrov, Nick. 2019. "Trump on the Border: More of the Same." *CounterPunch*, April 29, 2019. https://www.counterpunch.org/2019/04/29/trump-on-the -border-more-of-the-same/.

Ali, Wajahat. 2018. "Deradicalizing White People." *New York Review of Books*, August 16, 2018. https://www.nybooks.com/daily/2018/08/16/deradicalizing -white-people/.

Alonzo, Roberto R. 1996. "Oral History Interview with Roberto R. Alonzo, 1996." Interview by José Angel Gutiérrez. December 16, 1996. https://library.uta.edu /tejanovoices/xml/CMAS_001.xml.

Altwerger, Bess, and Steven L. Strauss. 2002. "The Business behind Testing." *Language Arts* 79, no. 3 (January): 256–62. https://www.jstor.org/stable/i40072302.

American Association of Colleges of Teacher Education. 1973. *No One Model American: Statement on Multicultural Education*. Washington, DC: Commission on Multicultural Education.

American GI Forum of Texas and Texas State Federation of Labor. 1953. *What Price Wetbacks?* Austin, TX: Allied Printing Trades Council.

Amnesty International. 2018. *USA: 'You Don't Have Any Rights Here': Illegal Pushbacks, Arbitrary Detention & Ill-Treatment of Asylum-Seekers in the United States*. London: Amnesty International Ltd. Peter Benenson House. https://www .amnesty.org/download/Documents/AMR5191012018ENGLISH.PDF.

Anderson, Benedict. 1983. *Imagined Communities: Reflections on the Origin and Spread of Nationalism*. London: Verso.

Anderson, Carol. 2016. *White Rage: The Unspoken Truth of our Racial Divide*. New York: Bloomsbury Publishing USA.

Anker, Elisabeth. 2014. *Orgies of Feeling: Melodrama and the Politics of Freedom*. Durham, NC: Duke University Press.

Anzaldúa, Gloria. 1990. *Making Face, Making Soul / Haciendo Caras: Creative and Critical Perspectives by Feminists of Color*. San Francisco: Aunt Lute Foundation Books.

———. 1999. *Borderlands / La Frontera*. 2nd ed. San Francisco: Aunt Lute Books.

APM Research Lab. 2020. "The Color of Coronavirus: Covid-19 Deaths by Race and Ethnicity in the U.S." *APM Research Lab*, July 22, 2020. https://www.apmre searchlab.org/covid/deaths-by-race.

Apple, Michael W. 2014. *Official Knowledge: Democratic Education in a Conservative Age*. New York: Routledge.

Applebaum, Anne. 2018. "A Warning from Europe: The Worst Is Yet to Come." *Atlantic* October 2018. https://www.theatlantic.com/magazine/archive/2018/10/poland-polarization/568324/.

———. 2020a. "History Will Judge the Complicit." *Atlantic*, July–August, 2020. https://www.theatlantic.com/magazine/archive/2020/07/trumps-collaborators/612250/.

———. 2020b. *Twilight of Democracy: The Seductive Allures of Authoritarianism*. New York: Penguin Random House.

Arce, Carlos, Cristin Tzintzun Ramírez, and Adrienne Pulido. 2018. *We Are Texas: An Analysis of Young Latino Voters in the Lone Star State*. Austin, TX: Jolt Initiative. http://www.joltinitiative.org/wp-content/uploads/2018/10/Jolt-We-Are-Texas.pdf.

Arce v. Douglas. 2015. 793 F.3d 968, 986. 9th Cir. 2015.

Arendt, Hannah. 1973. *The Origins of Totalitarianism*. New York: Houghton Mifflin Harcourt.

Astor, Maggie. 2017. "Tucson's Mexican Studies Program Was a Victim of 'Racial Animus,' Judge Says." *New York Times*, August 23, 2017. https://www.nytimes.com/2017/08/23/us/arizona-mexican-american-ruling.html.

AV Press Releases. 2018. "David Leopold: Stephen Miller Is a White Nationalist." America's Voice. June 25, 2018. https://americasvoice.org/press_releases/david-leopold-stephen-miller-is-a-white-nationalist/.

Arpaio, Joe, and Len Sherman. 2008. *Joe's Law: America's Toughest Sheriff Takes on Illegal Immigration, Drugs, and Everything Else that Threatens America*. New York: AMACOM.

Au, Wayne, Anthony L. Brown, and Dolores Calderón. 2016. *Reclaiming the Multicultural Roots of U.S. Curriculum: Communities of Color and Official Knowledge in Education*. New York and London: Teachers College Press.

Averbuch, Maya, and Elisabeth Malkin. 2018. "Migrants in Tijuana Run to U.S. Border, but Fall Back in Face of Tear Gas." *New York Times*, November 25, 2018. https://www.nytimes.com/2018/11/25/world/americas/tijuana-mexico-border.html.

Axelrod, Tal. 2020. "Trump Threatens to Withhold Visas for Countries That Don't Quickly Repatriate Citizens." *Hill*, April 10, 2020. https://thehill.com/homenews/administration/492321-trump-threatens-to-withhold-visas-for-countries-that-dont-quickly.

Ayala, Eva-Marie. 2016. "Textbook Depicts Mexican-Americans as 'Lazy,' Some out to 'Destroy This Society,' Historians Say." *Dallas Morning News*, September 6, 2016. https://www.dallasnews.com/news/education/2016/09/06/textbook-depicts-mexican-americans-as-lazy-some-out-to-destroy-this-society-historians-say/.

Baker, Mike, Thomas Fuller, and Sergio Olmos. 2020. "Federal Agents Push into Portland Streets, Stretching Limits of Their Authority." *New York Times*, July 25, 2020. https://www.nytimes.com/2020/07/25/us/portland-federal-legal-jurisdiction-courts.html.

Baker, Peter, and Michael D. Shear. 2019. "El Paso Shooting Suspect's Manifesto Echoes Trump's Language." *New York Times*, August 4, 2019. https://www.nytimes.com/2019/08/04/us/politics/trump-mass-shootings.html.

Balderrama, Francisco E., and Raymond Rodríguez. 2006. *Decade of Betrayal: Mexican Repatriation in the 1930s*. Albuquerque: University of New Mexico Press.

Baldwin, James. (1955) 2012. *Notes of a Native Son*. Reprint, Boston: Beacon Press. Citations refer to the Beacon edition.

———. (1963) 1992. *The Fire Next Time*. Reprint, New York: Vintage. Citations refer to the Vintage edition.

Balsamo, Michael. 2016. "Trump Puts New Spotlight on Long Island Gang Killings." *BBC News*, December 8, 2016. https://www.bbc.com/news/world-us-canada-39149712.

———. 2020. "Barr: Law Enforcement Must 'Dominate' Streets amid Protests." *Spokesman-Review*, June 2, 2020. https://www.spokesman.com/stories/2020/jun/02/barr-law-enforcement-must-dominate-streets-amid-pr/.

Barajas, Michael. 2018. "Redistricting Guru Michael Li on Texas' Gerrymandered Maps." *Texas Observer*, April 23, 2018. https://www.texasobserver.org/meet-michael-li-redistricting-guru/.

Barker, Aaron. 2020. "'This Is Not Hollywood': Acevedo Tells Trump 'It's Time to Be Presidential.'" *Click2Houston*, June 2, 2020. https://www.click2houston.com/news/local/2020/06/02/this-is-not-hollywood-acevedo-tells-trump-its-time-to-be-presidential/.

Bean, Frank D., Susan K. Brown, and James D. Bachmeier. 2015. *Parents Without Papers: The Progress and Pitfalls of Mexican American Integration*. New York: Russell Sage Foundation.

Beauchamp, Zack. 2019. "The New Reactionaries." *Vox*, February 26, 2019. https://www.vox.com/policy-and-politics/2019/2/26/18196429/trump-news-white-nationalism-hazony-kaufmann.

Bebout, Lee. 2016. *Whiteness on the Border: Mapping the U.S. Racial Imagination in Brown and White*. New York: New York University Press.

Behrens, Susan Fitzpatrick. 2009. "Plan Mexico and Central American Migration." North American Congress on Latin America. January 12, 2009. http://nacla .org/node/5406.

Beinart, Peter. 2016. "The Republican Party's White Strategy." *Atlantic*, July/August 2016. https://www.theatlantic.com/magazine/archive/2016/07/the-white -strategy/485612/.

———. 2018. "There Is No Immigration Crisis." *Atlantic*. June 27, 2018.

Beirch, Heidi. 2008. "John Tanton's Private Papers Expose More Than 20 Years of Hate." Southern Poverty Law Center. November 30, 2018. https://www .splcenter.org/fighting-hate/intelligence-report/2008/john-tanton%E2%80 %99s-private-papers-expose-more-20-years-hate.

Beltrán, Cristina. 2010. *The Trouble with Unity: Latino Politics and the Creation of Identity*. New York and London: Oxford University Press.

———. 2020. *Cruelty as Citizenship: How Migrant Suffering Sustains White Democracy*. Minneapolis: University of Minnesota Press.

Benkler, Yochai, Robert Faris, and Hal Roberts. 2018. *Network Propaganda: Manipulation, Disinformation, and Radicalization in American Politics*. New York: Oxford University Press.

Berlant, Lauren. 2011. *Cruel Optimism*. Durham, NC: Duke University Press.

Bernard, Diane. 2018. "The Time a President Deported 1 Million Mexican Americans for Supposedly Stealing U.S. Jobs." *Washington Post*, August 13, 2018. https:// www.washingtonpost.com/news/retropolis/wp/2018/08/13/the-time-a -president-deported-1-million-mexican-americans-for-stealing-u-s-jobs/.

Berry, Lynn, and Aamer Madhani. 2020. "For Nation's Birthday, Trump Stokes the Divisions within US." *AP News*, July 6. https://apnews.com/article/95698f178 a15e56a0f4e286708d06668.

Bertrand, Natasha. 2018. "Paul Manafort and Trump's Pardon Pattern." *Atlantic*, August 24, 2018. https://www.theatlantic.com/politics/archive/2018/08/paul -manafort-and-trumps-pardon-pattern/568438/.

Bishop, Sarah C. 2018. *Undocumented Storytellers: Narrating the Immigrant Rights Movement*. New York and London: Oxford University Press.

Blanchard, Sarah, Erin R. Hamilton, Nestor Rodríguez, and Hirotoshi Yoshioka. 2011. "Shifting Trends in Central American Migration: A Demographic Examination of Increasing Honduran-U.S. Immigration and Deportation." *Latin Americanist* 55, no. 4: 61–84. https://doi.org/10.1111/j.1557-203X.2011.01128.x.

Blitzer, Jonathan. 2019. "How Trump's Tariff Threat Could Outsource the Asylum Crisis to Mexico." *New Yorker*, June 19, 2019. https://www.newyorker .com/news/news-desk/how-trumps-tariff-threat-could-outsource- the-asylum-crisis-to-mexico.

Bloemraad, Irene, and Christine Trost. 2008. "It's a Family Affair: Intergenerational Mobilization in the Spring 2006 Protests." *American Behavioral Scientist* 52, no. 4 (December): 507–32. https://doi.org/10.1177/0002764208324604.

Borger, Gloria. 2019. "Trump Sees the Wall as a Monument to Himself." *CNN*, January 22, 2019. https://www.cnn.com/2019/01/22/politics/president -trump-border-wall-symbol-monument-legacy.

Bort, Ryan. 2018. "The Trump Administration Will Stop at Nothing to Keep America White." *Rolling Stone*, August 7, 2018. https://www.rollingstone.com/politics /politics-news/stephen-miller-immigration-707424/.

Bouie, Jamelle. 2019. "Stephen Miller's Sinister Syllabus." *New York Times*, November 15, 2019. https://www.nytimes.com/2019/11/15/opinion/stephen-miller-emails .html?fbclid=IwAR1am_roZCADYu2LXE07AmN504MTkR1-yaPz3bdxKH q8XRPXcBen-zLyGY4.

Bowler, Shaun, Stephen P. Nicholson, and Gary M. Segura. 2006. "Earthquakes and Aftershocks: Race, Direct Democracy, and Partisan Change." *American Journal of Political Science* 50, no. 1 (January): 146–59. https://www.jstor.org /stable/3694262.

Bradner, Eric, and Fredreka Schouten. 2018. "Trump's Racist Video Is Part of a Broader GOP Midterm Strategy Aimed at the Conservative Base." *CNN*, November 1, 2018. https://www.cnn.com/2018/11/01/politics/trump-ad-republicans -immigration-scare-tactics.

Brimelow, Peter. 1992. "Time to Rethink Immigration?" *National Review*, June 22, 1992.

Brooks, Brad. 2019. "Victims of Anti-Latino Hate Crimes Soar in U.S.: FBI Report." *Reuters*, November 20, 2019. https://www.reuters.com/article/us-hatecrimes -report/victims-of-anti-latino-hate-crimes-soar-in-us-fbi-report-idUSKB N1XM2OQ.

Brooks, David. 2006. "Immigrants to Be Proud of." *New York Times*, March 30, 2006. https://www.nytimes.com/2006/03/30/opinion/immigrants-to-be-proud-of .html.

———. 2019. "Our Disgrace at the Border." *New York Times*, April 11, 2019. https:// www.nytimes.com/2019/04/11/opinion/border-crisis-immigration.html.

Brown, Wendy. 2017. *Undoing the Demos: Neoliberalism's Stealth Revolution*. Near Futures Series. New York: Zone Books.

Buchanan, Patrick J. 1991. "America First Means Chopping Foreign Aid." *San Antonio Express-News*, October 26, 1991.

———. 2002. *The Death of the West: How Dying Populations and Immigrant Invasions Imperil Our Country and Civilization*. New York: St. Martin's Press.

———. 2007. *State of Emergency: The Third World Invasion and Conquest of America.* New York: St. Martin's Press.

Budiman, Abby. 2020. "Key Findings about U.S. Immigrants. Pew Research Center. August 20. 2020. https://www.pewresearch.org/fact-tank/2020/08/20/key -findings-about-u-s-immigrants/.

Byrd, Jodi A., and Michael Rothberg. 2011. "Between Subalternity and Indigeneity: Critical Categories for Postcolonial Studies. *Interventions* 13, no. 1 (February): 1–12. https://doi.org/10.1080/1369801X.2011.545574.

Calavita, Kitty. 1989. "The Contradictions of Immigration Lawmaking: The Immigration Reform and Control Act of 1986." *Law & Policy* 11, no. 1 (January): 17–47. https://doi.org/10.1111/j.1467-9930.1989.tb00019.x.

Calderón, Dolores. 2011. "Locating the Foundations of Epistemologies of Ignorance in Education Ideology and Practice." In *Epistemologies of Ignorance in Education,* edited by Erik Malewski and Nathalia Jaramillo, 105–27. Charlotte, NC: Information Age Publishing.

———. 2014. "Uncovering Settler Grammars in Curriculum." *Educational Studies* 50, no. 4 (February): 313–38. https://doi.org/10.1080/00131946.2014.926904.

Calderón, Dolores, and Luis Urrieta Jr. 2019. "Studying in Relation: Critical Latinx Indigeneities and Education." *Equity & Excellence in Education* 52, no. 2–3 (November): 219–38. https://doi.org/10.1080/10665684.2019.1672591.

Calderón, Roberto R. 2000. *Coal Mining Labor in Texas and Coahuila, 1880–1930.* College Station: Texas A&M University Press.

Campisi, Jessica, and Jaquetta White. 2018. "Finally, 11 months after Maria, Power Is Restored in Puerto Rico—Except for 25 Customers." *CNN,* August 7 2018. https://www.cnn.com/2018/08/07/us/puerto-rico-maria-power-restored -wxc-trnd/index.html.

Cappellari, Caterina. 2019. "TPS Extensions for El Salvador, Haiti, Honduras, Nicaragua, and Sudan." *National Law Review.* November 4, 2019. https:// www.natlawreview.com/article/tps-extensions-el-salvador-haiti-honduras -nicaragua-and-sudan.

Cashman, Timothy G., and Benjamin R. McDermott. 2013. "International Issues, High-Stakes Testing, and Border Pedagogy: Social Studies at Border High School." *Issues in Teacher Education* 22, no. 2 (November): 55–68. https:// eric.ed.gov/?id=EJ1014013.

Castro, Joaquín (@JoaquinCastrotx). 2019. Twitter, January 27, 2019. https://twitter .com/JoaquinCastrotx/status/1089649776474447874?s=20.

Chait, Jonathan. 2017. "Donald Trump's Race War." *New York Magazine,* April 3, 2017. https://nymag.com/intelligencer/2017/04/trump-is-failing-at-policy-but -winning-his-race-wars.html.

Chapman, Leonard. 1976. "Illegal Aliens: Time to Call a Halt!" *Reader's Digest* 109: 188–92.

———. 1992. "A Vast and Silent Invasion." *Atlantic Monthly*. May 1992.

Chávez, Leo R. 2008. "Spectacle in the Desert: The Minuteman Project on the US-Mexico Border." In *Global Vigilantes*, edited by David Pratten and Atreyee Sen, 25–46. New York: Columbia University Press.

———. 2013. *The Latino Threat: Constructing Immigrants, Citizens, and the Nation*. 2nd ed. Stanford, CA: Stanford University Press.

———. 2017. *Anchor Babies and the Challenge of Birthright Citizenship*. Stanford, CA: Stanford University Press.

Chávez, Lydia. 1998. *The Color Bind: California's Battle to End Affirmative Action*. Berkeley: University of California Press.

Chávez, Nicole. 2018. "Lawmakers Say Speech Proves Trump Doesn't Care about Puerto Rico Crisis." *CNN*, January 31, 2018. https://www.cnn.com/2018/01/31/politics/puerto-rico-sotu-reaction/index.html?sr=twCNNp013118puerto-rico-sotu-reaction0626AMVODtop&CNNPolitics=Tw.

Chetty, Raj, Nathaniel Hendren, Patrick Kline, and Emmanuel Saez. 2014. "Where Is the Land of Opportunity? The Geography of Intergenerational Mobility in the United States." *Quarterly Journal of Economics* 129, no. 4 (September): 1553–1623. https://doi.org/10.1093/qje/qju022.

Childress, Sonia. 2017. "Beyond Empathy." Medium. March 20, 2017. https://medium.com/@firelightmedia/beyond-empathy-ad6b5ad8a1d8.

Chishti, Muzaffar, Sarah Pierce, and Jessica Bolter. 2017. "The Obama Record on Deportations: Deporter in Chief or Not?" Migration Policy Insitute. January 26, 2017. https://www.migrationpolicy.org/article/obama-record-deportations-deporter-chief-or-not.

Choiniere, Alyssa. 2019. "Patrick Crusius: 5 Fast Facts You Need to Know." Heavy. August 8, 2019. https://heavy.com/news/2019/08/patrick-crusius/.

Citrin, Jack, and Benjamin Highton. 2002. *How Race, Ethnicity, and Immigration Shape the California Electorate*. San Francisco: Public Policy Institute of California.

Cloud, David S., and Molly O'Toole. 2019. "Pentagon Eases Rules to Expand Military's Role with Migrants on Border." *Los Angeles Times*, April 26, 2019. https://www.latimes.com/politics/la-na-pol-20190426-trump-loosens-rules-on-military-interaction-with-migrants-at-border-20190426-story.html.

Coffino, Eli. 2006. "A Long Road to Residency: The Legal History of Salvadoran and Guatemalan Immigration to the United States with a Focus on Nacara." *Cardozo Journal of International and Comparative Law*. 14, no. 177: 176–208.

Cohn, Nate, and Alicia Palapiano. 2018. "How Broad, and How Happy, Is the Trump

Coalition?" *New York Times*, August 9, 2018. https://www.nytimes.com /interactive/2018/08/09/upshot/trump-voters-how-theyve-changed.html ?searchResultPosition=1.

Cohn, D'Vera, Jeffrey S. Passel, and Ana González-Barrera. 2017. "Rise in U.S. Immigrants from El Salvador, Guatemala and Honduras Outpaces Growth from Elsewhere." Pew Research Center. December 7, 2017. https://www .pewhispanic.org/2017/12/07/rise-in-u-s-immigrants-from-el-salvador -guatemala-and-honduras-outpaces-growth-from-elsewhere/.

Coll, Kathleen M. 2010. *Remaking Citizenship: Latina Immigrants and New American Politics*. Stanford, CA: Stanford University Press.

Collinson, Stephen. 2018. "Trump Shocks with Racist New Ad Days before Midterms." *CNN*, October 31, 2018. https://www.cnn.com/2018/10/31/politics/donald -trump-immigration-paul-ryan-midterms/index.html.

Contreras, Guillermo. 2019. "DPS Emails Show Texas Governor Pressed for Voter Purge That Used Flawed Data." *San Antonio Express-News*, June 5, 2019. https://www.expressnews.com/news/local/article/DPS-emails-show-Texas -governor-pressed-for-voter-13936493.php.

Coutin, Susan Bibler. 1993. *The Culture of Protest: Religious Activism in the US Sanctuary Movement*. Boulder, CO: Westview Press.

———. 2003. "Cultural Logics of Belonging and Movement: Transnationalism, Naturalization, and US Immigration Politics." *American Ethnologist* 30, no. 4 (November): 508–26. https://doi.org/10.1525/ae.2003.30.4.508.

Crenshaw, Kimberley. 1989. "Demarginalizing the Intersection of Race and Sex: A Black Feminist Critique of Antidiscrimination Doctrine, Feminist Theory and Antiracist Politics." *University of Chicago Legal Forum* 1989, no. 1: 139–67. http://chicagounbound.uchicago.edu/uclf/vol1989/iss1/8.

Crowley, Michael. 2019. "At Rally, President Accuses Liberal Critics of Seeking the Nation's 'Destruction.'" *New York Times*, July 17, 2019. https://www.nytimes .com/2019/07/17/us/politics/trump-send-her-back-ilhan-omar.html.

Cummings, William. 2018. "'I Am a Nationalist': Trump's Embrace of Controversial Label Sparks Uproar." *USA Today*, October 24, 2018. https://www.usatoday .com/story/news/politics/2018/10/24/trump-says-hes-nationalist-what -means-why-its-controversial/1748521002/.

Crusius, Patrick. 2019. "The Inconvenient Truth." Drudge Report. August 3, 2019. https://drudgereport.com/flashtx.htm.

Davidson, Chandler. 1990. *Race and Class in Texas Politics*. Princeton, NJ: Princeton University Press.

Dávila, Arlene. 2008. *Latino Spin: Public Image and the Whitewashing of Race*. New York: New York University Press.

Davis, Julie Hirschfeld, and Michael D. Shear. 2019. *Border Wars: Inside Trump's Assault on Immigration*. New York: Simon & Schuster.

Davy, Megan. 2006. "The Central American Foreign Born in the United States." Migration Policy Institute. April 1, 2006. https://www.migrationpolicy.org/article /central-american-foreign-born-united-states-2004.

De Genova, Nicholas. 2004. "The Legal Production of Mexican/Migrant 'Illegality.'" *Latino Studies* 2, no. 2 (August):160–85. https://doi.org/10.1057/palgrave.lst .8600085.

De León, Arnoldo. 1983. *They Called Them Greasers: Anglo Attitudes Toward Mexicans in Texas, 1821–1900*. Austin: University of Texas Press.

———. 1997. *The Tejano Community, 1836–1900*. Dallas: Southern Methodist University Press.

Delgado Bernal, Dolores. 1998. "Using a Chicana Feminist Epistemology in Educational Research." *Harvard Educational Review* 68, no. 4: 555–83. https://doi.org /10.17763/haer.68.4.5wv1034973g22q48.

———. 1999. "Chicana/o Education from the Civil Rights Era to the Present." In *The Elusive Quest for Equality: 150 Years of Chicano/Chicana Education*, edited by José F. Moreno, 77–108. Cambridge, MA: Harvard Education Press.

Delgado Bernal, Dolores, C. Alejandra Elenes, Francisca E. Godinez, and Sofia Villenas, eds. 2006. *Chicana/Latina Education in Everyday Life: Feminist Perspectives on Pedagogy and Epistemology*. Albany: State University of New York Press.

Denvir, Daniel. 2020. *All-American Nativism: How the Bipartisan War on Immigrants Explains Politics as We Know It*. New York: Verso.

DeParle, Jason. 2019. "How Stephen Miller Seized the Moment to Battle Immigration." *New York Times*, August 17, 2019. https://www.nytimes.com/2019/08/17/us /politics/stephen-miller-immigration-trump.html.

de Sousa Santos, Boaventura. 2018. *The End of the Cognitive Empire*. Durham, NC: Duke University Press.

de Vogue, Ariane, Devan Cole, and Jamie Ehrlich. 2020. "Supreme Court Blocks Trump from Ending DACA." *CNN*, June 18, 2020. https://www.cnn. com/2020/06/18/politics/daca-immigration-supreme-court/index.html.

Dickey, Jeff D. 2019. *American Demagogue: The Great Awakening and the Rise and Fall of Populism*. New York: Pegasus.

Dictionary.com. n.d. "President Trump's Favorite Words." Accessed March 11, 2021. https://www.yourdictionary.com/slideshow/donald-trump-20-most -frequently-used-words.html.

Domínguez Zamorano, Neidi, Jonathan Perez, Jorge Guitierrez, and Nancy Meza.

2010. "DREAM Activists: Rejecting the Passivity of the Nonprofit, Industrial Complex." Truthout. September 21, 2010. https://truthout.org/articles/dream-activists-rejecting-the-passivity-of-the-nonprofit-industrial-complex/.

Dorschner, John. 2017. "Controversial Mariel Study Puts Cuban-American Professor in Middle of Storm." *Miami Herald*, July 20, 2017. https://www.miamiherald.com/news/local/community/miami-dade/article162682623.html.

Douthat, Ross. 2018a. "The White Strategy." *New York Times*, August 11, 2018. https://www.nytimes.com/2018/08/11/opinion/sunday/the-white-strategy.html.

———. 2018b. "A Defeat for White Identity." *New York Times*, November 10, 2018. https://www.nytimes.com/2018/11/10/opinion/sunday/racism-economics-trump-midterms.html.

Doyle, Pat. 2008. "Thursday: Bachmann, Tinklenberg Air it Out." *Star Tribune*, October 18, 2008. http://www.startribune.com/thursday-bachmann-tinklenberg-air-it-out/31145584/?refresh=true.

Du Bois, W. E. Burghardt. 1897. "Strivings of the Negro People." *Atlantic*, August 1897. https://www.theatlantic.com/magazine/archive/1897/08/strivings-of-the-negro-people/305446/.

———. (1903) 1995. *The Souls of Black Folk*. Reprint, New York: Penguin Books. Citations refer to the Penguin edition.

———. (1935) 1998. *Black Reconstruction in America, 1869–1880*. Reprint, Florence, MA: Free Press. Citations refer to the Free Press edition.

———. 1915. "The African Roots of War." *Atlantic*, May 1915. https://www.theatlantic.com/magazine/archive/1915/05/the-african-roots-of-war/528897/.

Dunbar-Ortiz, Roxanne. 2014. *An Indigenous Peoples' History of the United States*. New York: Beacon Press.

———. 2018. "Settler-Colonialism, Immigration, and White Nationalism in the US." Lecture presented at the New School, New York City, November 26, 2018.

Duncan, Brian, and Stephen J. Trejo. 2018. "Identifying the Later-Generation Descendants of U.S. Immigrants: Issues Arising from Selective Ethnic Attrition." *ANNALS of the American Academy of Political and Social Science* 677, no. 1 (April): 131–38. https://doi.org/10.1177/0002716218763293.

Duncan, Joe. 2019. "Trump's Wall Is a Monument to White Nationalism." Medium. March 17, 2019. https://medium.com/moments-of-passion/trumps-wall-is-a-monument-to-white-nationalism-82c8d30b1a58.

Dunn, Timothy J. 1996. *The Militarization of the U.S.- Mexico Border, 1978–1992: Low-Intensity Conflict Doctrine Comes Home*. Austin, TX: Center for Mexican American Studies.

Editorial Board. 2016. "A Chance to Reset the Republican Race." *New York Times*,

January 31, 2016. https://www.nytimes.com/2016/01/31/opinion/sunday/a-chance-to-reset-the-republican-race.html.

Edwards, Julia. 2016. "U.S. Deportation Raids Target Central American Families: Lawyers." *Reuters*, May 27, 2016. https://www.reuters.com/article/us-usa-immigration-deportation-idUSKCN0YI2LO.

Elfrink, Tim. 2019. "The Chairman of the Far-Right Proud Boys Sat Behind Trump at His Latest Speech." *Washington Post*, February 19, 2019. https://www.washingtonpost.com/nation/2019/02/19/far-right-proud-boys-chairman-sat-behind-trump-his-latest-speech/?noredirect=on&utm_term=.42a9b68f6092.

Emory, William H. 1857. *Report on the United States and Mexican Boundary Survey*. Washington, DC: Cornelius Wendell.

England, Sarah. 2009. "Afro-Hondurans in the Chocolate cCty: Garifuna, Katrina, and the Advantages of Racial Invisibility in the Nuevo New Orleans." *Journal of Latino/Latin American Studies* 3, no. 4 (September): 31–55. https://doi.org/10.18085/llas.3.4.g77818x261q80158.

Epstein, Reid J. 2016. "Trump Attacks Federal Judge in Trump U Case." *Wall Street Journal*, May 27, 2016. http://libproxy.unm.edu/login?url=https://search.proquest.com/docview/2014526492?accountid=14613.

Epstein, Reid J., Jennifer Medina, and Nick Corasaniti. 2020. "Historic Wins for Women of Color as Nation Protests Systemic Racism." *New York Times*, June 3, 2020. https://www.nytimes.com/2020/06/03/us/politics/june-primary-elections-results.html.

Erekson, Keith A, ed. 2016. *Politics and the History Curriculum: The Struggle over Standards in Texas and the Nation*. New York: Palgrave Macmillan.

Esquivel, Paloma, Esmeralda Bermúdez, Giulia McDonnell Nieto del Rio, Louis Sahagún, and Cindy Cárcamo. 2019. "For Latinos, El Paso is a Devastating New Low in a Trump Era." *Los Angeles Times*, August 5, 2019. https://www.latimes.com/california/story/2019-08-05/mood-in-latino-community-in-wake-of-shootings-in-el-paso-and-gilroy.

Exum, Andrew. 2018. "America's Gun-Culture Problem." *Atlantic*, March 5, 2018. https://www.theatlantic.com/politics/archive/2018/03/american-gun-culture/554870/.

Fagen, Richard R. 1979. "Mexican Petroleum and U.S. National Security." *International Security* 4, no. 1 (1979): 39–53.

Falla, Ricardo. 1994. *Massacres in the Jungle: Ixcán, Guatemala, 1975–1982*. Boulder, CO: Westview Press.

Fanon, Franz. (1952) 2008. *Black Skin, White Masks*. Reprint, New York: Grove Press. Citations refer to Grove edition.

Fernandes, Sujatha. 2017. *Curated Stories: The Uses and Misuses of Storytelling.* New York and London: Oxford University Press.

Flores, Henry. 2015. *Latinos and the Voting Rights Act: The Search for Racial Purpose.* New York: Lexington Books.

Flores, Richard R. 2002. *Remembering the Alamo: Memory, Modernity, and the Master Symbol.* Austin: University of Texas Press.

Flores, William Vincent. 1997. "Citizens vs. Citizenry: Undocumented Immigrants and Latino Cultural Citizenship." In *Latino Cultural Citizenship: Claiming Identity, Space, and Rights,* edited by William V. Flores and Rina Benmayor, 255–77. Boston: Beacon Press.

Flores, William Vincent, and Rina Benmayor. 1997. *Latino Cultural Citizenship: Claiming Identity, Space, and Rights.* Boston: Beacon Press.

Flynn, Meagan. 2019. "'Malignant, Dangerous, Violent': Trump Rally's 'Send Her Back!' Chant Raises New Concerns of Intolerance." *Washington Post,* July 18, 2019. https://www.washingtonpost.com/nation/2019/07/18/malignant -dangerous-violent-trump-rallys-send-her-back-chant-raises-new-concerns -intolerance/.

Foer, Franklin. 2018. "How Trump Radicalized ICE." *Atlantic,* September 2018. https:// www.theatlantic.com/magazine/archive/2018/09/trump-ice/565772/.

Fredericks, Bob. 2018. "Trump Administration Seeks to Limit Legal Immigrants Becoming Citizens." *New York Post,* August 7, 2018. https://nypost.com/2018 /08/07/trump-administration-seeks-to-limit-legal-immigrants-becoming -citizens/.

Foley, Neil. 2014. *Mexicans in the Making of America.* Cambridge, MA: Harvard University Press.

Foley, Ryan. 2019. "Meet the Press Panel Melts Down over Trump's 'Performative Narcissism.'" *NewsBusters,* April 15, 2019. https://www.newsbusters.org /blogs/nb/ryan-foley/2019/04/15/mtp-panel-melts-down-over-trumps -performative-narcissism-warns.

Foner, Eric. 2019. *The Second Founding: How the Civil War and Reconstruction Remade the Constitution.* New York: W. W. Norton & Company.

Forbes, Jack D. 2005. "The Mestizo Concept: A Product of European Imperialism." Unpublished manuscript.

Ford, Matt. 2016. "Trump Attacks a 'Mexican' U.S. Federal Judge." *Atlantic,* May 28, 2016. https://www.theatlantic.com/politics/archive/2016/05/trump-judge -gonzalo-curiel/484790/.

Foster, John Bellamy. 2017. *Trump in the White House: Tragedy and Farce.* New York: Monthly Review Press.

Foucault, Michel. 1983. "The Subject and Power." In *Beyond Structuralism and Herme-neutics*, edited by H. Dreyfus and P. Rabinow, 208–26. Chicago: University of Chicago Press.

———. 1984. *The Foucault Reader*. New York: Pantheon.

Fox, Cybelle, and Thomas A. Guglielmo. 2012. "Defining America's Racial Boundaries: Blacks, Mexicans, and European Immigrants, 1890–1945." *American Journal of Sociology* 118, no. 2 (September): 327–79. https://www.journals.uchicago.edu/doi/10.1086/666383.

Friedman, Uri. 2017. "What Is a Nativist?" *Atlantic*, April 11, 2017. https://www.theatlantic.com/international/archive/2017/04/what-is-nativist-trump/521355/.

Fritze, John, and David Jackson. 2019. "Donald Trump to Visit Grief-Stricken El Paso and Dayton Even Though Some Want Him to Stay Away." *USA Today*, August 7, 2019. https://www.usatoday.com/story/news/politics/2019/08/07/trump-visits-dayton-el-paso-grief-mass-shootings/1920474001/.

Funes, Yessenia. 2017. "Puerto Rico's Humanitarian Crisis Takes on New Urgency with Alarming Death Counts." *Earther*, December 8, 2017. https://earther.com/puerto-ricos-humanitarian-crisis-takes-on-new-urgency-w-1821135423.

Gabriel, Trip. 2019a. "Before Trump, Steve King Set the Agenda for the Wall and Anti-Immigrant Politics." *New York Times*, January 10, 2019. https://www.nytimes.com/2019/01/10/us/politics/steve-king-trump-immigration-wall.html.

———. 2019b. "A Timeline of Steve King's Racist Remarks and Divisive Actions." *New York Times*, January 15, 2019. https://www.nytimes.com/2019/01/15/us/politics/steve-king-offensive-quotes.html.

Gálvez, Alyshia. 2013. "Immigrant Citizenship: Neoliberalism, Immobility and the Vernacular Meanings of Citizenship." *Identities* 20, no. 6 (October): 720–37. https://doi.org/10.1080/1070289X.2013.842475.

Gamboa, Suzanne. 2017. "Latinos Are in D.C. to Celebrate, Protest Trump's Inauguration." *NBC News*, January 20, 2017. https://www.nbcnews.com/storyline/inauguration-2017/latinos-are-d-c-celebrate-protest-trump-s-inauguration-n709216.

———. 2019. "Some El Paso Residents Outraged by Trump's Speech That 'Failed to Mention Latinos.'" *NBC News*, August 5, 2019. https://www.nbcnews.com/news/latino/he-failed-mention-latinos-el-paso-residents-respond-trump-s-n1039436.

Gans, Herbert J. 1979. "Symbolic Ethnicity: The Future of Ethnic Groups and Cultures in America." *Ethnic and Racial Studies* 2, no. 1 (January): 1–20. https://doi.org/10.1080/01419870.1979.9993248.

Ganz, John. 2018. "Trump's New Target in the Politics of Fear: Citizenship." *New York*

Times, July 23, 2018. https://www.nytimes.com/2018/07/23/opinion/trump-birthright-citizenship-mccarthy.html.

Garcilazo, Jeffrey Marcos. 2012. *Traqueros: Mexican Railroad Workers in the United States, 1870–1930*. Denton: University of North Texas State Press.

García, Jesus. 1993. "The Changing Image of Ethnic Groups in Textbooks." *Phi Delta Kappan 75*, no. 1 (September): 29–35. https://www.jstor.org/stable/20405020?seq=1.

García, Sandra. 2019. "Brokaw Apologizes for Comments About Hispanics." *New York Times*, January 29, 2019. https://www.nytimes.com/2019/01/28/business/media/tom-brokaw-hispanics-assimilation.html.

Gellner, Ernest. 1964. *Thought and Change*. Chicago: University of Chicago Press.

Genovese, Michael. 2017. *How Trump Governs*. Amherst, NY: Cambria Press.

Gessen, Masha. 2020. *Surviving Autocracy*. New York: Riverhead Books.

Geyer, Georgie Ann. 1983. "States Conduct Own Foreign Policy." *Houston Post*, November 10, 1983.

Gjelten, Tom. 2015. "The Immigration Act That Inadvertently Changed America." *Atlantic*, October 2, 2015. https://www.theatlantic.com/politics/archive/2015/10/immigration-act-1965/408409/.

Glazer, Nathan, and Reed Ueda. 1983. *Ethnic Groups in History Textbooks*. Washington, DC: Ethics and Public Policy Center.

Glissant, Édouard. 1997. *Poetics of Relation*. Ann Arbor: University of Michigan Press.

Golash-Boza, Tanya. 2012. *Immigration Nation: Raids, Detentions, and Deportations in Post-9/11 America*. Boulder, CO: Paradigm Publishers.

Goldberg, Jonah. 2018. "The Border Wall Is a Symbol of Our Symbolic Politics." *National Review*, December 28, 2018. https://www.nationalreview.com/2018/12/border-wall-immigration-debate-political-symbol/.

Goldmacher, Shane. 2016. "Trump's English-Only Campaign." *Politico*, September 23, 2016. https://www.politico.com/story/2016/09/donald-trumps-english-only-campaign-228559.

Gómez, Laura. 2018. *Manifest Destinies: The Making of the Mexican American Race*. New York: New York University Press.

Gonzales, Alfonso. 2013. *Reform without Justice: Latino Migrant Politics and the Homeland Security State*. New York: Oxford University Press.

Gonzales, Phillip B. 2016. *Política: Nuevomexicanos and American Political Incorporation, 1821–1910*. Lincoln: University of Nebraska Press.

González, John Morán. 2009. *Border Renaissance: The Texas Centennial and the Emergence of Mexican American Literature*. Austin: University of Texas Press.

González, Roberto G. 2015. *Lives in Limbo: Undocumented and Coming of Age in America*. Oakland: University of California Press.

González-Barrera, Ana. 2015. *More Mexicans Leaving Than Coming to the U.S.* Washington, DC: Pew Research Center. November 19, 2015. https://www .pewresearch.org/hispanic/2015/11/19/more-mexicans-leaving-than -coming-to-the-u-s/.

———. 2017. *Mexicans among Least Likely Immigrants to Become American Citizens*. Washington, DC: Pew Research Center. January 29, 2017. https://www .pewresearch.org/hispanic/2017/06/29/mexican-lawful-immigrants-among -least-likely-to-become-u-s-citizens/.

González-Barrera, Ana, and Jens Manuel Krogstad. 2018. "Naturalization Rate among U.S. Immigrants up since 2005, with India among the Biggest Gainers." Pew Research Center. January 8, 2018. https://www.pewresearch.org/fact-tank /2018/01/18/naturalization-rate-among-u-s-immigrants-up-since-2005-with -india-among-the-biggest-gainers/.

———. 2019. "What We Know about Illegal Immigration from Mexico." Pew Research Center. January 28, 2019. https://www.pewresearch.org/fact-tank /2019/06/28/what-we-know-about-illegal-immigration-from-mexico/.

González-López, Gloria. 2006. "Epistemologies of the Wound: Anzaldúan Theories and Sociological Research on Incest in Mexican Society." *Human Architecture: Journal of the Sociology of Self-Knowledge* 4, no. 3 (Summer): 17–24. https://www.okcir.com/product/journal-article-epistemologies-of-the -wound-anzalduan-theories-and-sociological-research-on-incest-in -mexican-society-by-gloria-gonzalez-López/.

Gooding-Williams, Robert. 2019. "Membership, Citizens, and Democracy." *Public Books*, September 24, 2019. https://www.publicbooks.org/membership -citizenship-and-democracy/.

Goodman, Carly. 2018. "Angry That ICE Is Ripping Families Apart? Don't Just Blame Trump. Blame Clinton, Bush and Obama, Too." *Washington Post*, June 11, 2018. https://www.washingtonpost.com/news/made-by-history/ wp/2018/06/11/angry-that-ice-is-ripping-families-apart-dont-just-blame -trump-blame-clinton-bush-and-obama-too/.

Grandin, Greg. 2019. *The End of Myth: From the Frontier to the Border Wall in the Mind of America*. New Yok: Metropolitan Books.

Gratton, Brian, and Emily Merchant. 2013. "Immigration, Repatriation, and Deportation: The Mexican-Origin Population in the United States, 1920–1950." *International Migration Review* 47, no. 4 (December): 944–75. https://doi .org/10.1111/imre.12054.

Green, Joshua. 2018a. *Devil's Bargain: Steve Bannon, Donald Trump, and the Nationalist Uprising*. New York: Penguin Books.

———. 2018b. "The Guy Who Thought Up 'the Wall' Says Trump Should Shut Government to Fund It." *Bloomberg Businessweek*, December 20, 2018. https://www.bloomberg.com/news/articles/2018–12–20/the-guy-who -thought-up-the-wall-says-trump-should-shut-government-to-fund-it.

Greenberg, Stanley B. 2018. "Trump Is Beginning to Lose His Grip." *New York Times*, November 17, 2018. https://www.nytimes.com/2018/11/17/opinion/sunday /trump-is-beginning-to-lose-his-grip.html.

Greenberg, Zoe, and Christina Prignano. 2019. "Despite Condemnation of Hate, Trump Has Ramped Up His Use of 'Invasion' Rhetoric in Recent Months." *Boston Globe*, August 5, 2019. https://www.bostonglobe.com/news/politics /2019/08/05/despite-condemnation-hate-trump-has-ramped-his-use -invasion-rhetoric-recent-months/4tDIwWiWdbYawAS7vjhAoK/story.html.

Guerrero, Jean. 2020. *Hate Monger: Stephen Miller, Donald Trump, and the White Nationalist Agenda.* New York: HarperCollins.

Guidotti-Hernández, Nicole M. 2011. *Unspeakable Violence: Remapping U.S. and Mexican National Imaginaries.* Durham, NC: Duke University Press.

Guinier, Lanier, and Gerald Torres. 2003. *The Miner's Canary: Enlisting Race, Resisting Power, Transforming Democracy.* Cambridge, MA: Harvard University Press.

Guttentag, Lucas, and Stefano M. Bertozzi. 2020. "Trump Is Using the Pandemic to Flout Immigration Laws." *New York Times*, May 12, 2020. https://www .nytimes.com/2020/05/11/opinion/trump-coronavirus-immigration.html.

Gutiérrez, David. 1995. *Walls and Mirrors: Mexican Americans, Mexican Immigrants, and the Politics of Ethnicity.* Berkeley: University of California Press.

Gzesh, Susan. 2006. "Central Americans and Asylum Policy in the Reagan Era." Migration Policy Institute. April 1, 2006. https://www.migrationpolicy.org /article/central-americans-and-asylum-policy-reagan-era.

Hagan, Jacqueline Maria. 1994. *Deciding to Be Legal: A Maya Community in Houston.* Philadelphia: Temple University Press.

Hanchard, Michael George. 2018. *The Spectre of Race: How Discrimination Haunts Western Democracy.* Princeton, NJ: Princeton University Press.

Hartman, Saidiya V. 1997. *Scenes of Subjection: Terror, Slavery, and Self-Making in Nineteenth-Century America.* London and New York: Oxford University Press.

Hainmueller, Jens, Duncan Lawrence, Linna Martén, Bernard Black, Lucila Figueroa, Michael Hotard, Tomás R. Jiménez, Fernando Mendoza, Maria I. Rodríguez, Jonas J. Swartz, and David D. Laitin. 2017. "Protecting Unauthorized Immigrant Mothers Improves Their Children's Mental Health." *Science* 357, no. 6355 (September): 1041–44. https://doi.org/10.1126/science.aan5893.

Haltinner, Kristin. 2018. "Right-Wing Ideologies and Ideological Diversity in the Tea Party." *Sociological Quarterly* 59, no. 3 (August): 449–70. https://doi.org /10.1080/00380253.2018.1479196.

Hall, Stuart, and David Held. 1990. "Citizens and Citizenship." In *New Times: The Changing Face of Politics in the 1990s*, edited by Stuart Hall and Martin Jacques, 173–88. New York: Verso.

Haney López, Ian. 2004. *Racism on Trial: The Chicano Fight for Justice.* Cambridge, MA: Harvard University Press.

———. 2006. *White by Law: The Legal Construction of Race.* New York: New York University Press.

Haney López, Ian, and Michael Olivas. 2008. "Jim Crow, Mexican Americans, and the Anti-Subordination Constitution: The Story of Hernandez v. Texas." In *Race Law Stories*, edited by Rachel F. Moran and Devon Wayne Carbado, 273–310. New York: Foundation Press.

Hanson, Victor Davis. 2019. *The Case for Trump.* New York: Basic Books.

Harding, Sandra. 1998. *Is Science Multicultural? Postcolonialisms, Feminisms, and Epistemologies.* Bloomington: Indiana University Press.

Hattam, Victoria. 2007. *In the Shadow of Race: Jews, Latinos, and Immigrant Politics in the United States.* Chicago: University of Chicago Press.

Hayes-Bautista, David E., Werner O. Schink, and Jorge Chapa. 1988. *The Burden of Support: Young Latinos in an Aging Society.* Stanford, CA: Stanford University Press.

Heer, Jeet. 2016. "Republic of Fear." *New Republic*, March 31, 2016. https://newrepublic .com/article/132114/republic-fear.

Held, Joseph, ed. 1996. *Populism in Eastern Europe: Racism, Nationalism, and Society.* New York: Columbia University Press.

Hellmann, Jessie. 2016. "Trump Vows to Deport Millions Immediately." *Hill*, November 13, 2016. https://thehill.com/blogs/ballot-box/presidential-races/305774 -trump-vows-to-deport-millions-of-criminal-undocumented.

Henderson, Timothy J. 2007. *A Glorious Defeat: Mexico and Its War with the United States.* New York: Hill and Wang.

Herman, Ken. 2019. "Texas Lawmakers Reminded of Declining White Population." *Austin American Statesman*, February 22, 2019. https://www.statesman .com/news/20190222/herman-texas-lawmakers-reminded-of-declining -white-population.

Hernández Álvarez, José. 1966. "A Demographic Profile of the Mexican Immigration to the United States, 1910–1950." *Journal of Inter-American Studies* 8, no. 3 (July): 471–96. https://doi.org/10.2307/165263.

Hernández, Kelly Lytle. 2017. "Largest Deportation Campaign in U.S. History Is No Match for Trump's Plan." *Conversation*, March 8, 2017. http://theconversa tion.com/largest-deportation-campaign-in-us-history-is-no-match-for -trumps-plan-73651.

Hernández-León, Rubén, and Sarah Morando Lakhani. 2013. "Gender, Bilingualism, and the Early Occupational Careers of Second-Generation Mexicans in the South." *Social Forces* 92, no. 1 (September): 59–80. http://www.jstor.org /stable/43287517.

Higham, John. (1955) 2002. *Strangers in the Land: Patterns of American Nativism, 1860–1925*. Reprint, Ann Arbor: University of Michigan Press.

Hildreth, Matt. 2018. "Is Stephen Miller a White Nationalist?" America's Voice. June 25, 2018. https://americasvoice.org/blog/stephen-miller-white-nationalist/.

Hinojosa, Clarissa E., and Juan Carlos Rodríguez. 2015. "Américo Paredes." Texas State Historical Association Online. https://tshaonline.org/handbook/online /articles/fpa94.

Hobbs, Allyson Vanessa. 2014. *A Chosen Exile: A History of Racial Passing in American Life*. Cambridge, MA: Harvard University Press.

Hoffman, Abraham. 1974. *Unwanted Mexican Americans in the Great Depression: Repatriation Pressures, 1929–1939*. Tucson: University of Arizona Press.

Hohmann, James. 2018. "Trump's True Priorities Revealed in Holiday News Dumps." *Washington Post*, January 2, 2018. https://www.washingtonpost.com/news /powerpost/paloma/daily-202/2018/01/02/daily-202-trump-s-true-priorities -revealed-in-holiday-news-dumps/5a4af37830fb0469e883fe50/?noredirect =on&utm_term=.13ab30ccc61d.

Hong, Nicole, Juliana Kim, Ali Watkins, and Ashley Southall. 2021. "Brutal Attack on Filipino Woman Sparks Outrage: 'Everybody Is on Edge." *New York Times*, March 30, 2021. https://www.nytimes.com/2021/03/30/nyregion/asian-attack -nyc.html.

hooks, bell. 1989. "Choosing the Margin as a Space of Radical Openness." *Framework: The Journal of Cinema and Media*, no. 36: 15–23. https://www.jstor.org/stable /44111660.

Hoover, Herbert. 1930. "Annual Message to the Congress on the State of the Union." The American Presidency Project. December 2, 1930. https://www. presidency.ucsb.edu/documents/annual-message-the-congress -the-state-the-union-22.

Horsman, Reginald. 1986. *Race and Manifest Destiny: The Origins of American Racial Anglo-Saxonism*. Cambridge, MA: Harvard University Press.

Horton, Sarah, and Angela Stuesse. 2016. "Criminalizing Immigrants Hurts All Workers as IRCA Turns 30." *Daily Kos*. November 3, 2016. https://www.dailykos

.com/stories/2016/11/3/1590562/-Criminalizing-Immigrants
-Hurts-All-Workers-as-IRCA-Turns-30.

HoSang, Daniel, and Joseph E. Lowndes. 2019. *Producers, Parasites, Patriots: Race and the New Right-Wing Politics of Precarity*. Minneapolis: University of Minnesota Press.

Houston Chronicle Editorial Board. 2019. "SB9 Another Desperate Attempt at Voter Suppression in Texas." *Houston Chronicle*, April 16, 2019. https://www
.houstonchronicle.com/opinion/editorials/article/SB9-another-desperate
-attempt-at-voter-13769725.php/.

Huddy, Leonie. 2015. "Group Identity and Political Cohesion." In *Emerging Trends in the Social and Behavioral Sciences*, edited by Robert A. Scott, Stephen Michael Kosslyn, and Marlis Buchmann, 1–14. Hoboken, NJ: John Wiley & Sons.

Hu-DeHart, Evelyn. 1993. "The History, Development, and Future of Ethnic Studies." *Phi Delta Kappan*, 75, no. 1 (September): 50–54. http://www.jstor.org/stable
/20405023.

Human Rights Alliance .n.d. Human Rights Alliance for Child Refugees & Families. Accessed March 12, 2021. http://www.refugeerightsnow.com/about.

Huntington, Samuel. 1996. *The Clash of Civilizations and the Remaking of the World Order*. New York: Simon & Schuster.

———. 2004a. "The Hispanic Challenge." *Foreign Policy*, no. 141 (March–April): 30–45. https://doi.org/10.2307/4147547.

———. 2004b. *Who Are We? The Challenges to America's National Identity*. New York: Simon & Schuster.

Ibe, Peniel. 2019. "Trump's Attacks on the Legal Immigration System Explained." American Friends Service Committee (AFSC). July 29, 2019. https://www
.afsc.org/blogs/news-and-commentary/trumps-attacks-legal-immigration
-system-explained.

———. 2020. "The Dangers of Trump's 'Safe Third Country" Agreements in Central America." American Friends Service Committee (AFSC). July 28, 2020.
https://www.afsc.org/blogs/news-and-commentary/dangers-trumps
-safe-third-country-agreements-central-america.

Ignatiev, Noel. 2008. *How the Irish Became White*. New York: Routledge.

Irby, Kate. 2019. "'Trump Effect:' California Latino Voters Showed Up in Force in 2018." *McClatchy DC Bureau*, January 29, 2019. https://www.mcclatchydc
.com/news/politics-government/election/article225181845.html.

Jiménez, Tomás R. 2004. "Negotiating Ethnic Boundaries: Multiethnic Mexican Americans and Ethnic Identity in the United States." *Ethnicities* 4, no. 1 (March): 75–97. https://doi.org/10.1177/1468796804040329.

———. 2008. "Mexican-Immigrant Replenishment and the Continuing Significance of Ethnicity and Race." *American Journal of Sociology* 113, no. 6 (May): 1527–67. https://doi.org/ 10.1086/587151.

———. 2010a. "Affiliative Ethnic Identity: A More Elastic Link between Ethnic Ancestry and Culture." *Ethnic and Racial Studies* 33, no. 10 (November): 1756–75. https://doi.org/ 10.1080/01419871003678551.

———. 2010b. *Replenished Ethnicity: Mexican Americans, Immigration, and Identity.* Berkeley: University of California Press.

Johnson, Benjamin Heber. 2005. *Revolution in Texas: How a Forgotten Rebellion and Its Blood Suppression Turned Mexicans Into Americans.* New Haven, CT: Yale University Press.

Jones, Bradley. 2019. "Majority of Americans Continue to Say Immigrants Strengthen the U.S." Pew Research Center. January 21, 2019. https://www.pewresearch .org/fact-tank/2019/01/31/majority-of-americans-continue-to-say -immigrants-strengthen-the-u-s/.

Jordan, Winthrop D. (1968) 2012. *White over Black: American Attitudes toward the Negro, 1550–1812.* Reprint, Chapel Hill: University of North Carolina Press. Citations refer to University of North Carolina edition.

Joseph, Paeiel. 2018. "We're Way Past Willie Horton Now." *CNN,* November 2, 2018. https://www.cnn.com/2018/11/02/opinions/trump-immigration-ad-willie -horton-joseph.

Judis, John, and Ruy A. Teixeira. 2002. *The Emerging Democratic Majority.* New York: Scribner.

Kahn, Robert S. 1996. *Other People's Blood: US Immigration Prisons in the Reagan Decade.* New York: Routledge.

Kamen, Al. 1990. "Central America Is No Longer the Central Issue for Americans." *Austin American Statesman,* October 21, 1990.

Kanno-Youngs, Zolan. 2019. "Homeland Security Dept. Affirms Threat of White Supremacy after Years of Prodding." *New York Times,* October 1, 2019. https://www.nytimes.com/2019/10/01/us/politics/white-supremacy -homeland-security.html.

Kanno-Youngs, Zolan, and Maggie Haberman. 2020. "Trump Administration Moves to Solidify Restrictive Immigration Policies." *New York Times,* June 12, 2020. https://www.nytimes.com/2020/06/12/us/politics/coronavirus-trump -immigration-policies.html.

Karni, Annie, and Sheryl Gay Stolberg. 2019. "Trump Offers Temporary Protections for 'Dreamers' in Exchange for Wall Funding." *New York Times,* January 19, 2019. https://www.nytimes.com/2019/01/19/us/politics/trump-proposal -daca-wall.html.

Kazanjian, David. 2003. *The Colonizing Trick: National Culture and Imperial Citizen-ship in Early America*. Minneapolis: University of Minnesota Press.

Kennedy, Paul. 1987. *The Rise and Fall of Great Powers: Economic Change and Military Conflict from 1500 to 2000*. New York: Random House.

———. 1992. "The Internationalization of Yale." *Yale Alumni Magazine*, February 1992.

———. 1993. *Preparing for the Twenty-First Century*. New York: Random House.

Kerwin, Donald. 2020. *Immigrant Detention and COVID-19: How the US Detention System Became a Vector for the Spread of the Pandemic*. Washington, DC: Center for Migration Studies. https://cmsny.org/publications/immigrant -detention-covid/.

Kerwin, Donald, and Serena Yi-Ying Lin. 2009. *Immigrant Detention: Can ICE Meet Its Legal Imperatives and Case Management Responsibilities?* Washington, DC: Migration Policy Institute. September 2009. https://www.migration policy.org/research/immigrant-detention-can-ice-meet-its-legal-imperatives -and-case-management-responsibilities.

Key, V. O., Jr. 1949. *Southern Politics in State and Nation*. New York: Alfred A. Knopf.

King, Noel. 2019. "Stephen Miller and White Nationalism." *NPR*, November 14, 2019. https://www.npr.org/2019/11/14/779208233/stephen-miller-and-white -nationalism.

Kitroeff, Natalie. 2019. "Bank-Rolling the Anti-Immigration Movement." In *Daily Podcast*, August 19, 2019. https://the-daily.simplecast.com/episodes/ bankrolling-the-anti-immigration-movement-b__BKKOT.

Klein, Ezra. 2018. "White Threat in a Browning America: How Demographic Change Is Fracturing Our Politics." *Vox*, July 30, 2018. https://www.vox.com/policy -and-politics/2018/7/30/17505406/trump-obama-race-politics-immigration.

Krogstad, Jens Manuel, and Ana González-Barrera. 2014. "Number of Latino Chil-dren Caught Trying to Enter U.S. Nearly Doubles in Less Than a Year." Pew Research Center. June 10, 2014. https://www.pewresearch.org/fact-tank /2014/06/10/number-of-latino-children-caught-trying-to-enter-u-s-nearly -doubles-in-less-than-a-year/.

Krogstad, Jens Manuel, and Richard Fry. 2014. "Dept. of Ed. Projects Public Schools Will Be 'Majority-Minority' This Fall." Pew Research Center. August 18, 2014. https://www.pewresearch.org/fact-tank/2014/08/18/u-s-public-schools -expected-to-be-majority-minority-starting-this-fall/.

Krogstad, Jens Manuel, Renee Stepler, and Mark Hugo López. 2015. "English Proficien-cy on the Rise Among Latinos." Pew Research Center. May 12, 2015. https:// www.pewresearch.org/hispanic/2015/05/12/english-proficiency-on-the -rise-among-latinos/.

Kroichick, Ron. 2020. "Black Lives Matter Gives Fresh Urgency to Bay Area Ethnic

Studies Programs." *San Francisco Chronicle*, June 29, 2020. https://www.sf chronicle.com/education/article/Black-Lives-Matter-gives-fresh-urgency-to -Bay-15371747.php.

Krugman, Paul. 2020. "A Plague of Willful Ignorance." *New York Times*, June 22, 2020. https://www.nytimes.com/2020/06/22/opinion/coronavirus-trump.html.

Kulish, Nicholas and Mike McIntire. 2019. "An Heiress Intent on Closing America's Doors." *New York Times*, August 14, 2019. https://www.nytimes.com /2019/08/14/us/anti-immigration-cordelia-scaife-may.html.

Ladson-Billings, Gloria. 2009. *The Dreamkeepers: Successful Teachers of African American Children*. New York: John Wiley & Sons.

Lake, Jennifer E., Kristin M. Finklea, Mark Eddy, Celinda Franco, Chad C. Haddal, William J. Krouse, Mark A. Randol. 2010. *Southwest Border Violence: Issues in Identifying and Measuring Spillover Violence*. Washington, DC: Congressional Research Service. February 16, 2010. https://trac.syr.edu/immigration /library/P4351.pdf.

Lamar, Mirabeau Buonaparte. 1921. *The Papers of Mirabeau Buonaparte Lamar*. Vol. I, edited by Charles Adams Gulick Jr., Katharine Elliott, Winnie Allen, and Harriet Smither. Austin, TX: A. C. Baldwin & Sons.

Lamm, Richard. 1985. "Two Volatile Groups Threaten to Boil Over Melting Pot." *Albuquerque Journal*, September 23, 1985.

Lamm, Richard D., and Gary Imhoff. 1985. *The Immigration Time Bomb: The Fragmenting of America*. New York: Truman Talley Books.

Langewiesche, William. 1992. "The Border." *Atlantic Monthly*, May 1992.

Lapham, Lewis. 2004. "Tentacles of Rage: The Republican Propaganda Mill, a Brief History." *Harper's Magazine*, September 2004, 31–41.

Latino Decisions. 2018. *2018 American Election Eve Poll: Results Latino Voters*. https:// latinodecisions.com/polls-and-research/2018-american-election-eve-poll/.

Lee, Jennifer, and Frank D. Bean. 2010. *The Diversity Paradox: Immigration and the Color Line in Twenty-First Century America*. New York: Russell Sage Foundation Publications.

León, Christina A. 2017. "Forms of Opacity: Roaches, Blood, and Being Stuck in Xandra Ibarra's Corpus." *ASAP/Journal* 2, no. 2: 369–94. https://doi.org /10.1353/asa.2017.0037.

Leonhardt, David. 2017. "Truth, Fiction and Lou Dobbs." *New York Times*, May 30, 2017. https://www.nytimes.com/2007/05/30/business/30leonhardt.html.

LeTourneau, Nancy. 2019. "Donald Trump and Fox News Promote Great Replacement Theory." *Washington Monthly*, August 6, 2019. https://washingtonmonthly .com/2019/08/06/donald-trump-and-fox-news-promote-the-great -replacement-theory/.

Levin, Jonathan, and Yalixa Cruz. 2018. "For Puerto Rico, Dream of Financial Recovery Masks Grim Reality." *Yahoo! Finance*, August 10, 2018. https://finance.yahoo .com/news/puerto-rico-dream-financial-recovery-100000579.html.

Lichter, Daniel T., Julie H. Carmalt, and Zhenchao Qian. 2011. "Immigration and Intermarriage among Hispanics: Crossing Racial and Generational Boundaries." *Sociological Forum* 26, no. 2 (May): 241–64. https://doi.org/10.1111/j.1573 -7861.2011.01239.x.

Limón, José E. 1994. *Dancing with the Devil: Society and Cultural Poetics in Mexican-American South Texas*. Madison: University of Wisconsin Press.

Lind, Dara. 2018. "Judge Blocks Trump's Efforts to End Temporary Protected Status for 300,000 Immigrants." *Vox*, October 4, 2018. https://www.vox.com /policy-and-politics/2018/10/4/17935926/tps-injunction-chen-news.

———. 2019. "'Immigrants Are Coming over the Border to Kill You' Is the Only Speech Trump Knows How to Give." *Vox*, January 9, 2019. https://www.vox .com/2019/1/8/18174782/trump-speech-immigration-border.

Linton, April, and Tomás R. Jiménez. 2009. "Contexts for Bilingualism among US-Born Latinos." *Ethnic and Racial Studies* 32, no. 6 (June): 967–95. https:// doi.org/10.1080/01419870802337351.

Lipsitz, George. 2006. *The Possessive Investment in Whiteness: How White People Profit from Identity Politics*. Philadelphia: Temple University Press.

Liptak, Adam. 2016. "Donald Trump Could Threaten U.S. Rule of Law, Scholars Say." *New York Times*, June 3, 2016. https://www.nytimes.com/2016/06/04/us /politics/donald-trump-constitution-power.html.

Livingston, Alexander. 2016. *Damn Great Empires! William James and the Politics of Pragmatism*. New York: Oxford University Press.

Long, Colleen. 2019. "Trump Moves to Effectively End Asylum at Southern Border." *AP News*, July 15, 2019. https://apnews.com/article/6bef9ed6c48b4c2ea 203cbbea3ccacad.

López, Gustavo, and Jens Manuel Krogstad. 2017. "Key Facts about Unauthorized Immigrants Enrolled in DACA." Pew Research Center. September 25, 2017. https://www.pewresearch.org/fact-tank/2017/09/25/key-facts-about -unauthorized-immigrants-enrolled-in-daca/.

López, Mark Hugo, Ana González-Barrera, and Jens Manuel Krogstad. 2018. *Many Latinos Blame Trump Administration for Worsening Situation of Hispanics*. Washington, DC: Pew Research Center. October 25, 2018. https://www .pewresearch.org/hispanic/2018/10/25/more-latinos-have-serious-concerns -about-their-place-in-america-under-trump/.

López, Mark Hugo, Ana González-Barrera, and Gustavo López. 2017. *Hispanic Identity Fades across Generation as Immigrant Connections Fall Away*. Washington,

DC: Pew Research Center, December 20, 2017. https://www.pewresearch
.org/hispanic/2017/12/20/hispanic-identity-fades-across-generations-as
-immigrant-connections-fall-away/.

Lorde, Audre. 2003. "The Master's Tools Will Never Dismantle the Master's House." In
Feminist Postcolonial Theory: A Reader, edited by Reina Lewis and Sara Mills,
25–29. New York: Routledge.

Los Angeles Times. 1978. "Fragments from an Interview with Ex-CIA Director, William
Colby." June 6, 1978.

Lowe, Lisa. 2015. *The Intimacies of Four Continents.* Durham, NC: Duke University Press.

Lowry, Rich. 2019. "Immigration Restriction Is Not Hate." *POLITICO,* August 7, 2019.
https://www.politico.com/magazine/story/2019/08/07/trump-immigration
-restriction-terrorism-227610/.

Lozada, Carlos. 2017. "Samuel Huntington, a Prophet for the Trump Era." *Washington
Post,* July 18, 2017. https://www.washingtonpost.com/news/book-party/wp
/2017/07/18/samuel-huntington-a-prophet-for-the-trump-era/.

Lozano, Rosina. 2018. *An American Language: The History of Spanish in the United
States* Berkeley: University of California Press.

Lukens, Patrick. 2012. *A Quiet Victory for Latino Rights: FDR and the Controversy over
Whiteness.* Tucson: University of Arizona Press.

MacDonald, Victoria-María, and Benjamin Polk Hoffman. 2012. "'Compromising *La
Causa*?' The Ford Foundation and Chicano Intellectual Nationalism in the
Creation of Chicano History, 1963–1977." *History of Education Quarterly* 2,
no. 52 (May): 251–81. https://doi.org/10.1111/j.1748-5959.2011.00390.x.

Macías, Reynaldo F. 2005. "*El Grito en Aztlán*: Voice and Presence in Chicana/o
Studies." *International Journal of Qualitative Studies in Education* 18, no. 2
(August): 165–84. https://doi.org/10.1080/0951839042000333965.

Maganinni, Stephen. 2017. "Immigrants Will Face Additional Scrutiny to Get Permanent Residency, Trump Administration Says." *Sacramento Bee,* August 31,
2017. https://www.sacbee.com/news/politics-government/article170472367
.html.

Markel, Howard, and Alexandra Minna Stern. 2002. "The Foreignness of Germs: The
Persistent Association of Immigrants and Disease in American Society."
Milbank Quarterly 80, no. 4 (December): 757–88. https://doi.org
/10.1111/1468-0009.00030.

Márquez, Benjamin. 2014. *LULAC: The Evolution of a Mexican American Political
Organization.* Austin: University of Texas Press.

Marshall, T. H. 1987. *Citizenship and Social Class: And Other Essays.* London:
Pluto Press.

Martínez, Monica Muñoz, Nicole G. Sintetos, Katie Vogel, and Ricardo Frasso Jara-
     millo. 2017. *Refusing to Forget: The Life of Jovita Idar*. Austin, TX: Refusing to
     Forget. Summer 2017. https://refusingtoforget.org/lesson-plans/.

Martínez, Oscar J. 1975. "On the Size of the Chicano Population: New Estimates,
     1850–1900." *Aztlan: International Journal of Chicano Studies Research* 6, no. 1
     (Spring): 43–67.

————. 1994. *Border People: Life and Society in the U.S.-Mexico Borderlands*. Tucson:
     University of Arizona Press.

Massey, Douglas S., Jorge Durand, and Nolan J. Malone. 2002. *Beyond Smoke and
     Mirrors: Mexican Immigration in an Era of Free Trade*. New York: Russell
     Sage Foundation.

Massey, Douglas S., Jorge Durand, and Karen A. Pren. 2016. "Why Border Enforce-
     ment Backfired." *American Journal of Sociology* 121, no. 5 (March): 1557–600.
     https://doi.org/10.1086/684200.

McClanahan, Annie. 2019. "Life Expectancies: Mortality, Exhaustion, and Economic
     Stagnation." *Theory & Event* 22, no. 2 (April): 360–81. https://muse.jhu.edu
     /article/722829.

McGranahan, Carole. 2016. "Theorizing Refusal: An Introduction." *Cultural Anthropol-
     ogy* 31, no. 3: 319–25. https://doi.org/10.14506/ca31.3.01.

McMahon, Robert. 2006. "Tancredo: Tough Immigration Reform Essential to
     Maintain U.S. Identity." Council on Foreign Relations. July 24, 2006.
     https://www.cfr.org/interview/tancredo-tough-immigration-reform
     -essential-maintain-us-identity.

McNeil, L. and Valenzuela, A. 2001. "The Harmful Impact of the TAAS System of
     Testing in Texas: Beneath the Accountability Rhetoric." In *Raising Standards
     or Raising Barriers? Inequality and High-Stakes Testing in Public Education*,
     edited by Gary Orfield and Mindy L. Korhnhaber, 127–50. New York: The
     Century Foundation.

Menjívar, Cecilia. 2006. "Liminal Legality: Salvadoran and Guatemalan Immigrants'
     Lives in the United States." *American Journal of Sociology* 111, no. 4 (January):
     999–1037. https://doi.org/10.1086/499509.

Menjívar, Cecilia, and Leisy Janet Abrego. 2012. "Legal Violence: Immigration Law and
     the Lives of Central American Immigrants." *American Journal of Sociology*
     117, no. 5 (March): 1380–1421. https://doi.org/10.1086/663575.

Merica, Dan. 2017. "Travel Ban Architect Writing Trump's Speech on Islam." *CNN*,
     May 19, 2017. https://www.cnn.com/2017/05/19/politics/stephen-miller-islam
     -travel-ban-speech-writing/index.html.

Mignolo, Walter D. 2000. *Local Histories/Global Designs: Coloniality, Subaltern Knowl-
     edges, and Border Thinking*. Princeton, NJ: Princeton University Press.

———. 2007. "Introduction: Coloniality of Power and De-colonial Thinking." *Cultural Studies* 21, no. 2–3 (April): 155–67. https://doi.org/10.1080/09502380601162498.

———. 2011. "Epistemic Disobedience and the Decolonial Option: A Manifesto." *Transmodernity: Journal of Peripheral Cultural Production of the Luso-Hispanic World* 1, no. 2 (Fall): 3–23. https://escholarship.org/uc/item/62j3w283.

Migration Policy Institute. n.d. "Comprehensive Immigration Reform." Accessed March 12, 2021. https://www.migrationpolicy.org/topics/comprehensive-immigration-reform.

Miles, Jack. 1992. "Blacks versus Browns: The Struggle for the Bottom Rung." *Atlantic Monthly*, October 1992.

Miller, Hayley. 2018. "Arizona Lawmaker: Immigration a 'Threat' Because 'There Aren't Enough White Kids." *HuffPost*, June 14, 2018. https://www.huffpost.com/entry/david-stringer-arizona-immigration_n_5b226b5fe4b0adfb827185ba.

Mills, Charles. 1999. *The Racial Contract*. Ithaca, NY: Cornell University Press.

Minian, Ana Raquel. 2018. *Undocumented Lives: The Untold Story of Mexican Migration*. Cambridge, MA: Harvard University Press.

Molina, Natalia. 2014. *How Race Is Made in America: Immigration, Citizenship, and the Historical Power of Racial Scripts*. Berkeley: University of California Press.

Montejano, David. 1987. *Anglos and Mexicans in the Making of Texas, 1836–1986*. Austin: University of Texas Press.

———. 1999. "On the Future of Anglo-Mexican Relations in the United States." In *Chicano Politics and Society in the Late Twentieth Century*, edited by David Montejano, 234–257. Austin: University of Texas Press.

———. 2004. "Who Is Samuel P. Huntington? The Intelligence Failure of a Harvard Professor." *Texas Observer*, August 13, 2004. https://www.texasobserver.org/1727-who-is-samuel-p-huntington-the-intelligence-failure-of-a-harvard-professor/.

Mora, Cristina. 2014. *Making Hispanics: How Activists, Bureaucrats, and Media Constructed a New American*. Chicago: University of Chicago Press.

Morgan, Edmund. 1975. *American Slavery, American Freedom: The Ordeal of Colonial Virginia*. New York: W. W. Norton and Company.

Morrison, Toni. 1993. *Playing in the Dark: Whiteness and the Literary Imagination*. Visalia, CA: Vintage.

Moten, Fred. 2009. *B Jenkins*. Durham, NC: Duke University Press.

Mudde, Case. 2017. *The Far Right in America*. New York: Routledge.

Mueller, Zachary. 2019. "Stephen Miller Is Trump's Biggest Loser." America's Voice.

April 18, 2019. https://americasvoice.org/blog/miller-is-trumps
-biggest-loser/.

Murphy, Kevin. 2011. "Kansas Lawmaker Suggests Immigrants Be Shot Like Hogs."
Reuters, March 25, 2011. https://www.reuters.com/article/us-immigration
-kansas/kansas-lawmaker-suggests-immigrants-be-shot-like-hogs-id
USTRE72O71H20110325.

Mutz, Diana C. 2018. "Status Threat, Not Economic Hardship, Explains the 2016
Presidential Race." *Proceedings of the National Academy of Sciences* 115, no. 19
(May 8): E4330–339. https://doi.org/10.1073/pnas.1718155115.

National Academies of Science, Engineering, and Medicine. 2015. *The Integration of
Immigrants into American Society*. Washington, DC: National Academies
Press. https://doi.org/10.17226/21746.

Naughton, Michael. 2017. "Cornel West's 'Prophetic Fightback.'" Harvard Divinity
School. August 30, 2017. https://hds.harvard.edu/news/2017/08/30/cornel
-wests-prophetic-fightback#.

Navarrette, Ruben. 2019a. "El Paso Shooter Puts Mexican Americans in Crosshairs."
West Central Tribune, August 9, 2019. https://www.wctrib.com/opinion
/columns/4602570-Ruben-Navarrette-El-Paso-shooter-puts-Mexican
-Americans-in-the-crosshairs.

———. 2019b. "Let's Not Be in Such a Hurry to Leave El Paso." *Pittsburgh Post-
Gazette*, August 23, 2019. https://www.post-gazette.com/opinion
/Op-Ed/2019/08/23/Ruben-Navarrette-Jr-El-Paso-mass-shooting-reflection
/stories/201908230032.

Neate, Rupert, and Jo Tuckman. 2015. "Donald Trump: Mexican Migrants Bring
'Tremendous Infectious Disease' to US." *Guardian*, July 6, 2015. https://
www.theguardian.com/us-news/2015/jul/06/donald-trump-mexican
-immigrants-tremendous-infectious-disease.

Negroponte, Diana Villiers. 2014. "The Surge in Unaccompanied Children from
Central America: A Humanitarian Crisis at Our Border." *Up Front* (blog),
Brookings Institution. July 2, 2014. https://www.brookings.edu/blog
/up-front/2014/07/02/the-surge-in-unaccompanied-children-from-central
-america-a-humanitarian-crisis-at-our-border/.

Nelson, Michael. 2018. *Trump's First Year*. Charlottesville: University of Virginia Press.

Nehru, Jawaharlal. (1953) 2018. "On the Dangers of Narrow Nationalism" (in "'My
Dear Chief Minister' . . . Three Letters Nehru Wrote That Indians Today
Need to Read"). *Wire*, November 14, 2018. https://thewire.in/government
/three-letters-nehru-wrote-chief-ministers-indians-today-need-read.

Neiwert, David. 2020. "Domestic Terrorism Database of the Trump Years Shows How
the Radical Right Has Gone on a Rampage." *Daily Kos*, July 9, 2020. https://

www.dailykos.com/stories/2020/7/9/1959514/-Domestic-terrorism-database
-of-the-Trump-years-shows-how-the-radical-right-has-gone-on-a-rampage
?detail=emaildksp.

Neuburger, Bruce. 2019. "The Border, Trumpian Madness and the Clash of Demographics." *CounterPunch*, April 15, 2019. https://www.counterpunch.org/2019
/04/15/the-border-trumpian-madness-and-the-clash-of-demographics/.

Ngai, Mae M. 2004. *Impossible Subjects: Illegal Aliens and the Making of Modern America*. Princeton, NJ: Princeton University Press.

Niezen, Ronald. 2010. *Public Justice and the Anthropology of Law*. Cambridge, MA:
Cambridge University Press.

Nolan, Rachel. 2020. "A Translation Crisis at the Border." *New Yorker*, January 6, 2020.
https://www.newyorker.com/magazine/2020/01/06/a-translation-crisis
-at-the-border.

NYSYLC. n.d. "Mission Statement." Accessed February 26, 2021. https://www.nysylc
.org/what-we-do/.

Obama, Barack. 2006. *The Audacity of Hope: Thoughts on Reclaiming the American
Dream*. New York: Crown Publishers.

———. 2008. "Obama's Remarks to La Raza." *RealClear*. July 13, 2008. https://www
.realclearpolitics.com/articles/2008/07/obamas_remarks_to_la_raza.html.

———. 2014. "Letter from the President—Efforts to Address the Humanitarian
Situation in the Rio Grande Valley Areas of Our Nation's Southwest Border."
Office of the Press Secretary, Washington, DC: The White House. June 30,
2014. https://obamawhitehouse.archives.gov/the-press-office/2014/06/30
/letter-president-efforts-address-humanitarian-situation-rio-grande-valle.

Oboler, Suzanne. 2006. "Redefining Citizenship as a Lived Experience." In *Latinos
and Citizenship: The Dilemnas of Belonging*, edited by Suzanne Oboler, 3–30.
New York: Palgrave MacMillan.

Ollstein, Alice. 2018. "Data Clashes with Emotion as CPAC Immigration Panel
Goes off the Rails." *Talking Points Memo*, February 23, 2018. https://
talkingpointsmemo.com/dc/data-clashes-with-emotion-as-cpac
-immigration-panel-goes-off-the-rails.

Olmos, Sergio, Mike Baker, and Zolan Kanno-Youngs. 2020. "Federal Agents Unleash
Militarized Crackdown on Portland." *New York Times*, July 17, 2020. https://
www.nytimes.com/2020/07/17/us/portland-protests.html.

Olson, Joel. 2004. *The Abolition of White Democracy*. Minneapolis: University of
Minnesota Press.

———. 2008. "Whiteness and the Polarization of American Politics." *Political
Research Quarterly* 61, no. 4 (December): 704–18. http://www.jstor.org/
stable/20299771.

Ong, Aihwa. 1996. "Cultural Citizenship as Subject-Making: Immigrants Negotiate Racial and Cultural Boundaries in the United States." *Current Anthropology* 37, no. 5 (December): 737–62. https://www.jstor.org/stable/2744412.

OnTheIssues. n.d. "Tom Tancredo on Immigration." Accessed March 12, 2021. http://www.ontheissues.org/House/Tom_Tancredo_Immigration.htm.

Oppenheimer, Andres. 2005. "My Opinion." *Arizona Daily Star*, June 18, 2005. http://www.azbilingualed.org/News%202005/myopinionandresoppenheimer.htm.

Orr, Gabby, and Andrew Restuccia. 2019. "How Stephen Miller Made Immigration Personal." *POLITICO*, April 22, 2019. https://www.politico.com/story/2019/04/22/stephen-miller-immigration-trump-1284287.

O'Shea, Elena Zamora. 2000. *El Mesquite: A Story of the Early Spanish Settlements Between the Nueces and the Rio Grande*. College Station: Texas A&M Press.

Osnos, Evan. 2018. "Trump vs. the 'Deep State.'" *New Yorker*, May 21, 2018. https://www.newyorker.com/magazine/2018/05/21/trump-vs-the-deep-state.

———. 2020. "The Greenwich Rebellion: How Country-Club Republicans Learned to Ignore Their Neighbors and Love Trump." *New Yorker*, May 11, 2020. https://www.newyorker.com/magazine/2020/05/11/how-greenwich-republicans-learned-to-love-trump.

Oyeniyi, Doyin. 2017. "Proposed Mexican-American Heritage Textbook Is A Continuation of the Problem with U.S. History Classes." *Texas Monthly*, October 6, 2017. https://www.texasmonthly.com/the-daily-post/proposed-mexican-american-heritage-textbook-continuation-problem-u-s-history-classes/.

Painter, Nell Irvin. 2011. *The History of White People*. New York: Norton & Co.

Pallares, Amalia. 2014. *Family Activism: Immigrant Struggles and the Politics of Noncitizenship*. New Brunswick, NJ: Rutgers University Press.

Palos, Ari Luis, dir. 2011. *Precious Knowledge: Arizona's Battle over Ethnic Studies*. Tucson, AZ: Dos Vatos Productions.

Palumbo-Liu, David. 2002. "Multiculturalism Now: Civilization, National Identity, and Difference before and after September 11." *Boundary 2* 29, no. 2 (Summer): 109–28. https://doi.org/10.1057/9781403983398_9.

Pantoja, Adrian D., and Gary M. Segura. 2003. "Fear and Loathing in California: Contextual Threat and Political Sophistication among Latino Voters." *Political Behavior* 25, no. 3 (September): 265–86. http://www.jstor.org/stable/3657321.

Paredes, Américo. 1971. *"With His Pistol in His Hand": A Border Ballad and Its Hero*. Austin: University of Texas Press.

Park, Julie, Dowell Myers, and Tomás R. Jiménez. 2014. "Intergenerational Mobility of the Mexican-Origin Population in California and Texas Relative to a

Changing Regional Mainstream." *International Migration Review* 48, no. 2 (July): 442–81. https://doi.org/10.1111/imre.12086.

Parker, Kathleen. 2019. "The Wall Is a Testament to Trump's Toxic Narcissism." January 11, 2019. https://www.washingtonpost.com/opinions/the-wall-is-a-testament-to-trumps-toxic-narcissism/2019/01/11/f67f33e8-15ea-11e9-90a8-136fa44b80ba_story.html.

Parker, Richard. 2017. "The Military Was Ready in Texas and Florida. What Went Wrong in Puerto Rico?" *POLITICO*, October 2, 2017. https://www.politico.com/magazine/story/2017/10/02/us-military-puerto-rico-215668.

Partlow, Joshua, and David A. Fahrenthold. 2019. "How Two Housekeepers Took On the President—and Revealed That His Company Employed Undocumented Immigrants." *Washington Post*, December 4, 2019. https://www.washingtonpost.com/politics/how-two-undocumented-housekeepers-took-on-the-president--and-revealed-trumps-long-term-reliance-on-illegal-immigrants/2019/12/04/3dff5b5c-0a15-11ea-bd9d-c628fd48b3a0_story.html.

Passel, Jeffrey S., and D'Vera Cohn. 2018. *U.S. Unauthorized Immigrant Total Dips to Lowest Level in a Decade*. Washington, DC: Pew Research Center. November 27, 2018. https://www.pewresearch.org/hispanic/2018/11/27/u-s-unauthorized-immigrant-total-dips-to-lowest-level-in-a-decade/.

Pebley, Anne R, Luis Rosero-Bixby, and Elena Hurtado. 1997. *Demographic Diversity and Change in the Central American Isthmus*. Santa Monica, CA: Rand Corporation.

Peck, Raoul, dir. 2016. *I Am Not Your Negro*. New York: Magnolia Pictures.

Peltier, Elian. 2020. "Jean Raspail, Whose Immigration Novel Drew the Far Right, Dies at 94." *New York Times*, June 24, 2020. https://www.nytimes.com/2020/06/22/books/jean-raspail-author-white-supremacists.html.

Peña, Devon. 2010. Correspondence to Governor Jan Brewer and the People of Arizona. https://www.naccs.org/images/naccs/ltrs/SB_1070.pdf.

Perla, Hector, Jr., and Susan Bibler Coutin. 2012. "Legacies and Origins of the 1980s US–Central American Sanctuary Movement." In *Sanctuary Practices in International Perspectives*, edited by Randy Lippert and Sean Rehaag, 91–109. Routledge.

Peters, Jeremy W. 2019. "Michael Savage Has Doubts about Trump. His Conservative Radio Audience Does Not." *New York Times*, June 18, 2019. https://www.nytimes.com/2019/06/18/us/politics/michael-savage-trump.html?.

Peters, Jeremy, W., Michael M. Grynbaum, Keith Collins, Rich Harris, and Rumsey Taylor. 2019. "How the El Paso Gunman Echoed the Words of Right-Wing Pundits." *New York Times*, August 11, 2019. https://www.nytimes.com/interactive/2019/08/11/business/media/el-paso-killer-conservative-media.html.

Pew Research Center. 2017. "The Partisan Divide on Political Values Grows Wider."
    October 5, 2017. https://www.pewresearch.org/politics/2017/10/05/4-race
    -immigration-and-discrimination/.

Phillips, Fred M. 2019. "Old Rhetoric of Hatred Makes a Chilling Return." *Albuquerque
    Journal*, March 26, 2019.

Phillips, Kevin. 1969. *The Emerging Republican Majority*. New Rochelle, NY: Arlington
    House.

Pitti, Stephen. 2013. "Congressman King, Cantaloupe Calves and Drug Mules."
    Huffington Post, July 25, 2013. https://www.huffpost.com/entry/steve-king
    -immigration_b_3653145.

Pitts, Leonard. 2018. "No Fair Observer Should Be Shocked by Trump's Performance
    in Helsinki." *Albuquerque Journal*, July 20, 2018. https://www.abqjournal
    .com/1198704/no-fair-observer-should-be-shocked-by-trumps-performance
    -in-helsinki.html.

Planas, R. 2013. "Texas Ethnic Studies Bill Protested by Latino Activists." *Huffington
    Post*, March 18, 2013. https://www.huffingtonpost.com/2013/03/18/texas
    -ethnic-studies-bill-protested-latino-activists_n_2902948.html.

Plascencia, Luis F. B. 2012. *Disenchanting Citizenship: Mexican Migrants and the
    Boundaries of Belonging*. New Brunswick, NJ: Rutgers University Press.

Polk, James K. 1846. Occupation of Mexican Territory. Message from the President of
    the United States in Answer to a Resolution of the House of Representatives
    of the 15th Instant Relative to the Occupation of Mexican Territory, Decem-
    ber 22. House Exec. Doc. no. 60, 30th Congress, 1st session.

Polletta, Francesca. 2009. *It Was Like a Fever: Storytelling in Protest and Politics*.
    Chicago: University of Chicago Press.

Portes, Alejandro, and Rubén Rumbaut. 2001 *Legacies: The Story of the Immigrant
    Second Generation*. Berkeley: University of California Press.

———. 2014. *Immigrant America: A Portrait*. Berkeley: University of California Press.

Portillo Villeda, Suyapa G. 2016. "Organizing Resistance in Honduras." *NACLA Report
    on the Americas* 48, no. 3 (September): 213–16. https://doi.org/10.1080/10714
    839.2016.1228165.

Poston, Dudley, and Rogelio Saenz. 2019. "The US White Majority Will Disappear
    Forever." *Conversation*, April 30, 2019. https://theconversation.com/the
    -us-white-majority-will-soon-disappear-forever-115894.

Potts, Monica. 2019. "In the Land of Self-Defeat." *New York Times*, October 4, 2019.
    https://www.nytimes.com/2019/10/04/opinion/sunday/trump-arkansas
    .html.

Pulte, G. 2018. "Too Dangerous to Be Called Mexican American Studies." *Texas Tribune*, April 23, 2018. https://www.tribtalk.org/2018/04/23/too-dangerous-to-be-called-Mexican American-studies/.

Quijano, Aníbal. 1992. "Colonialidad y modernidad/racionalidad." *Perú indígena* 13, no. 29: 11–20. https://www.lavaca.org/wp-content/uploads/2016/04/quijano.pdf.

———. 2007. "Coloniality and Modernity/Rationality." *Cultural studies* 21, no. 2–3 (April), 168–78. https://doi.org/10.1080/09502380601164353.

Ramos, George. 1995. "Angry Words of Ruben Salazar Remain Potent." *Los Angeles Times*, May 15, 1995. https://www.latimes.com/archives/la-xpm-1995-05-15-me-860-story.html.

Ramos, Raúl. 2019. "The Alamo Is a Rupture." *Guernica*, February 19, 2019. https://www.guernicamag.com/the-alamo-is-a-rupture-texas-mexico-imperialism-history/

Rapoport, Ronald B., Alan I. Abramowitz, and Walter J. Stone. 2016. "Why Trump Was Inevitable." *New York Review of Books*, June 23, 2016. https://www.nybooks.com/articles/2016/06/23/why-trump-was-inevitable/.

Reagan, Ronald. 1983. "President Reagan's Address on Central America to Joint Session of Congress." *New York Times*, April 28, 1983. https://www.nytimes.com/1983/04/28/world/president-reagan-s-address-on-central-america-to-joint-session-of-congress.html.

Remnick, David. 2020. "An American Uprising." *New Yorker*, May 31, 2020. https://www.newyorker.com/news/daily-comment/an-american-uprising-george-floyd-minneapolis-protests.

Resto-Montero, Gabriela. 2017. "With the Rise of the Alt-Right, Latino White Supremacy May Not Be a Contradiction in Terms." *Mic*, December 27, 2017. https://mic.com/articles/187062/with-the-rise-of-the-alt-right-latino-white-supremacy-may-not-be-a-contradiction-in-terms#.LaHLSIeYj.

Rich, Adrienne. 1986. *Blood, Bread, and Poetry: Selected Prose, 1979–1985*. New York: Norton.

Rocco, Raymond. 2014. *Transforming Citizenship: Democracy, Membership, and Belonging in Latino Communities*. East Lansing: Michigan State University.

Roedigger, David. 2007. *The Wages of Whiteness: Race and the Making of the American Working Class*. New York: Verso.

Rogers, Adam. 2018. "Calling the Caravan's Migrants 'Diseased' Is a Classic Xenophobic Move." *Wired*, October 31, 2018. https://www.wired.com/story/calling-the-caravans-migrants-diseased-is-a-classic-xenophobic-move/.

Rogers, David. 2014. "Child Migrants a Neglected Challenge." *POLITICO*,

May 28, 2014. https://www.politico.com/story/2014/05/flood-of-child
-migrants-a-neglected-challenge-107198.

Rogers, Katie. 2019a. "Before Joining White House, Stephen Miller Pushed White
Nationalist Theories." *New York Times*, November 13, 2019. https://www
.nytimes.com/2019/11/13/us/politics/stephen-miller-white-nationalism.html.

———. 2019b. "Emails Outline Anti-immigration Group's Connection to Stephen Miller." *New York Times*, November 14, 2019. https://www.nytimes.com/2019
/11/14/us/politics/immigration-trump.html.

Rogin, Michael Paul. 1975. *Fathers and Children: Andrew Jackson and the Subjugation of
the American Indian*. New York: Knopf.

Romero, Augustine, Sean Arce, and Julio Cammarota. 2009. "A Barrio Pedagogy: Identity, Intellectualism, Activism, and Academic Achievement through
the Evolution of Critically Compassionate Intellectualism." *Race Ethnicity
and Education* 12, no. 2 (July): 217–33. https://doi.org/10.1080
/13613320902995483.

Romo, Ricardo. 1977. "The Urbanization of Southwestern Chicanos in Early Twentieth
Century." *New Scholar* 6: 183–207.

Rosaldo, Renato. 1994. "Cultural Citizenship and Educational Democracy." *Cultural
Anthropology* 9, no. 3 (August): 402–11. https://doi.org/10.1525/can.1994
.9.3.02a00110.

———. 1997. "Cultural Citizenship, Inequality, and Multiculturalism." In *Latino
Cultural Citizenship: Claiming Identity, Space, and Rights*, edited by
William V. Flores and Rina Benmayor, 27–38. Boston: Beacon Press.

Rosaldo, Renato, and William V. Flores. 1997. "Identity, Conflict, and Evolving Latino
Communities: Cultural Citizenship in San Jose, California." In *Latino
Cultural Citizenship: Claiming Identity, Space, and Rights*, edited by William
V. Flores and Rina Benmayor, 57–96. Boston: Beacon Press.

Rose, Joel. 2019. "Leaked Emails Fuel Calls for Stephen Miller to Leave White House."
NPR, November 26, 2019. https://www.npr.org/2019/11/26/783047584/leaked
-emails-fuel-calls-for-stephen-miller-to-leave-white-house.

———. 2020. "Immigration Grinds to a Halt as President Trump Shuts Borders."
NPR, March 18, 2020. https://www.npr.org/2020/03/18/817965714
/immigration-grinds-to-a-halt-as-president-trump-shuts-borders.

Roy, Arundhati. 2004. "The NGO-ization of Resistance." Streamed on August 16, 2004.
YouTube video, 5:51. https://www.youtube.com/watch?v=zTFC9OSGL34.

Rubio, Elizabeth Hanna, and Xitlalli Álvarez Almendáriz. 2019. "Refusing 'Undocumented': Imagining Survival Beyond the Gift of Papers." Member Voices,
Fieldsights, January 17, 2019. https://culanth.org/fieldsights/1630-refusing-
undocumented-imagining-survival-beyond-the-gift-of-papers.

Rucker, Philip, and Ellen Nakashima. 2017. "Trump Asked Sessions about Closing Case against Arpaio, an Ally since 'Birtherism.'" *Washington Post*, August 26, 2017. https://www.washingtonpost.com/politics/trump-asked-sessions-about -closing-case-against-arpaio-an-ally-since-birtherism/2017/08/26/15e5d7b2 -8a7f-11e7-a94f-3139abce39f5_story.html.

Ruíz, Vicki L. 1987. *Cannery Women, Cannery Lives: Mexican Women, Unionization, and the California Food Processing Industry, 1930–1950*. Albuquerque: University of New Mexico Press.

Rumbaut, Rubén. 2017. "Immigrant America: From the Great Inclusion to the Great Expulsion?" *El País*, January 17, 2017. https://elpais.com/elpais/2017/01/12 /inenglish/1484243067_373334.html.

Rumbaut, Rubén G., Douglas S. Massey, and Frank D. Bean. 2006. "Linguistic Life Expectancies: Immigrant Language Retention in Southern California." *Population and Development Review* 32, no. 3 (September): 447–60. https:// EconPapers.repec.org/RePEc:bla:popdev:v:32:y:2006:i:3:p:447-460.

Rupar, Aaron. 2019. "Trump Turns Shooting Migrants into a Punchline at Florida Rally." *Vox*, May 9, 2019. https://www.vox.com/2019/5/9/18538124 /trump-panama-city-beach-rally-shooting-migrants.

Russell, John G. 2019. "America's White Problem Revisited." *CounterPunch*, September 2, 2019. https://www.counterpunch.org/2019/09/02/americas -white-problem-revisited/.

Ryan, Charlotte, and William A. Gamson. 2006. "The Art of Reframing Political Debates." *Contexts* 5, no. 1 (February): 13–18. https://doi.org/10.1525/ctx .2006.5.1.13.

Saenz, Rogelio. 2018. "Declining White Population Is Spawning Fear, Bias." *San Antonio Express-News*, July 21, 2018. https://www.mysanantonio.com/opinion /commentary/article/Declining-white-population-is-spawning-fears-bias -13092533.php.

Salazar, Ruben. 1970. "Who Is a Chicano? And What Is It the Chicanos Want?" *Los Angeles Times*. February 6, 1970.

Saldaña-Portillo, María Josefa. 2016. *Indian Given: Racial Geographies Across Mexico and the United States*. Durham, NC: Duke University Press.

Samuels, Brett. 2019. "Trump Rally Crowd Chants 'Send Her Back' about Ilhan Omar." *Hill*, July 17, 2019. https://thehill.com/homenews/administration/453633- trump-rally-crowd-chants-send-her-back-about-omar.

Sánchez, George J. 1993. *Becoming Mexican American: Ethnicity, Culture, and Identity in Chicano Los Angeles, 1900–1945*. New York: Oxford University Press

Sanders, Jimy, M. 2002. "Ethnic Boundaries and Identity in Plural Societies." *Annual*

Review of Sociology 28:327–57. https://doi.org/10.1146/annurev.soc
.28.110601.140741.

San Miguel, Guadalupe, Jr. 2005. *Brown, Not White: School Integration and the Chicano Movement in Houston*. College Station: Texas A&M University Press.

San Miguel, Guadalupe, Jr., and Rubén R. Donato. 2009. "Latino Education in Twentieth-Century America: A Brief History." In *Handbook of Latinos and Education*, edited by Enrique G. Murillo, Sofia A. Villenas, Ruth Trinidad Galván, Juan Sánchez Muñoz, Corinne Martínez, and Margarita Machado-Casas, 53–88. New York: Routledge.

Santa Ana, Otto. 2002. *Brown Tide Rising: Metaphors of Latinos in Contemporary American Public Discourse*. Austin: University of Texas Press.

Saramo, Samira. 2017. "The Meta-violence of Trumpism." *European Journal of American Studies* 12, no. 2 (Summer): 1–17. https://doi.org/10.4000/ejas.12129.

Sassen, Saskia. 2002. "Towards Post-national and Denationalized Citizenship." In *Handbook of Citizenship Studies*, edited by Engin F. Isin and Bryan S. Turner: 277–91. London: SAGE.

Sati, Joel. 2017. "Noncitizenship and the case for illegalized persons." *Berkeley Blog*, University of California, Berkeley. January 24, 2017. https://blogs.berkeley.edu/2017/01/24/noncitizenship-and-the-case-for-illegalized-persons/.

Savage, Michael. 2015. *Government Zero*. New York: Utopia Productions.

Schuyler, George S. 2011. *Black No More*. New York: Modern Library

Schwartz, Emma. 2018. "Quick Facts: Hurricane Maria's Effect on Puerto Rico." ReliefWeb. January 22, 2018. https://reliefweb.int/report/puerto-rico-united-states-america/quick-facts-hurricane-marias-effect-puerto-rico.

Seelke, Clare Ribando, and Kristin Finklea. 2017. *U.S.-Mexican Security Cooperation: The Merida Initiative and Beyond*. Washington DC: Congressional Research Service. June 29, 2017. https://fas.org/sgp/crs/row/R41349.pdf.

Semple, Kirk, and Lara Jakes. 2019. "Mexican Leader Draws Line on Trump Terrorist Plan: 'Interventionism: No.'" *New York Times*, November 29, 2019. https://www.nytimes.com/2019/11/27/world/mexico-trump-terrorist-cartel.html.

Serwer, Adam. 2018. "Cruelty Is the Point." *Atlantic*, October 3, 2018. https://www.theatlantic.com/ideas/archive/2018/10/the-cruelty-is-the-point/572104/.

Shear, Michael D. 2019. "At Rally for India's Modi, Trump Plays Second Fiddle but a Familiar Tune." *New York Times*, September 22, 2019. https://www.nytimes.com/2019/09/22/us/politics/trump-modi-houston-rally.html.

———. 2020. "Trump Amplifies 'White Power' on Twitter." *New York Times*, June 29, 2020. https://www.nytimes.com/2020/06/28/us/politics/trump-white-power-video-racism.html.

Shear, Michael D., and Julie Hirschfeld Davis. 2019. "Shoot Migrants' Legs, Build Alligator Moat: Behind Trump's Ideas for Border." *New York Times*, October 2, 2019. https://www.nytimes.com/2019/10/01/us/politics/trump-border-wars.html.

Shephard, Katie. 2018. "Patriot Prayer Is Recruiting Out-Of-Town Far-Right Activists—and Alex Jones—to Protest in Portland on August 4." *Willamette Week*, July 13, 2018. https://www.wweek.com/news/courts/2018/07/13/patriot-prayer-is-recruiting-out-of-town-far-right-activists-and-alex-jones-to-protest-in-portland-on-august-4/.

Shepherd, Sara. 2017. "Barack Obama's 12 Most Memorable Speeches." *Lawrence Journal-World*, January 9, 2017. https://www2.ljworld.com/news/2017/jan/09/barack-obamas-12-most-memorable-speeches/.

Sherman, Gabriel. 2018. "Stephen Actually Enjoys Seeing Those Pictures at the Border." *Vanity Fair*, June 25, 2018. https://www.vanityfair.com/news/2018/06/stephen-miller-family-separation-white-house.

Shorman, Jonathan. 2017. "Kris Kobach at 20: Keenly Focused on Apartheid South Africa, Not Immigration." *Kansas City Daily Star*, October 13, 2017. https://www.kansascity.com/news/politics-government/article178646656.html.

Sierra, Christine. 1999. "In Search of National Power: Chicanos Working the System on Immigration Reform, 1976–1986." In *Chicano Politics and Society in the Late Twentieth Century*, edited by David Montejano, 131–53. Austin: University of Texas Press.

Simon, Abigail. 2018. "People Are Angry President Trump Used This Word to Describe Undocumented Immigrants." *Time Magazine*, June 19, 2018. https://time.com/5316087/donald-trump-immigration-infest/.

Simón, Yara. 2019. "'This is My Country, Too': Latina Confronts Man Who Harassed Her for Speaking Spanish." *Remezcla*, March 18, 2019. http://remezcla.com/culture/mexican-american-woman-spanish-walmart-confrontation/.

Simpson, Audra. 2007. "On Ethnographic Refusal: Indigeneity, 'Voice' and Colonial Citizenship." *Junctures: The Journal for Thematic Dialogue* 9:67–80. https://junctures.org/index.php/junctures/article/view/66/60.

———. 2014. *Mohawk Interruptus: Political Life across the Borders of Settler States.* Durham, NC: Duke University Press.

Sleeter, Christine E. 2011. "The Academic and Social Value of Ethnic Studies: A Research Review." Washington, DC: National Education Association Research Department. http://www.nea.org/assets/docs/NBI-2010-3-value-of-ethnic-studies.pdf.

———. 2016. "Ethnicity and the curriculum." In *The SAGE Handbook of Curriculum, Pedagogy and Assessment*, edited by Dominic Wyse, Louise Hayward, and Jessica Pandya, 231–46. Los Angeles: SAGE.

Smarsh, Sarah. 2018. "Liberal Blind Spots Are Hiding the Truth about 'Trump Country.'" *New York Times*, July 19, 2018. https://www.nytimes.com/2018/07/19 /opinion/trump-corporations-white-working-class.html.

Smith, Andrea. 2006. "Heteropatriarchy and the Three Pillars of White Supremacy: Rethinking Women of Color Organizing." In *Color of Violence: The INCITE! Anthology*, edited by INCITE! Women of Color Against Violence, 66–73. Boston: South End Press.

Smith, Anthony D. 1991. *National Identity*. London: Penguin.

Smith, James P. 2003. "Assimilation across the Latino Generations." *American Economic Review* 93, no. 2(May): 315–19. https://doi.org/10.1257/000282803321947263.

Smith, Michael M. 1980. *The Mexicans in Oklahoma. Newcomers to a New Land*. Norman: University of Oklahoma Press.

Smith, Robert C. 2005. *Mexican New York: The Transnational Lives of New Immigrants*. Berkeley: University of California Press.

Solórzano, Daniel G., and Dolores Delgado Bernal 2001. "Examining Transformational Resistance through a Critical Race and LatCrit Theory Framework: Chicana and Chicano Students in an Urban Context." *Urban Education* 36, no. 3 (May): 308–42. https://doi.org/10.1177%2F0042085901363002.

Song, Sarah. 2018. *Immigration and Democracy*. New York: Oxford University Press.

Sonmez, Felicia, and Mike DeBonis. 2019. "Trump Tells Four Liberal Congresswomen to 'Go Back' to Their Countries, Prompting Pelosi to Defend Them." *Washington Post*, July 14, 2019. https://www.washingtonpost.com/politics /trump-says-four-liberal-congresswomen-should-go-back-to-the-crime -infested-places-from-which-they-came/2019/07/14/b8bf140e-a638-11e9 -a3a6-ab670962db05_story.html.

Sotomayor, Sonia. 2020. Concurring. *Department of Homeland Security et al. v. Regents of the University of California et al.* 591 U.S., June 18 (2020). https://www .supremecourt.gov/opinions/19pdf/18-587_5ifl.pdf.

Southern Poverty Law Center. 2019. "Hate Groups Reach Record High." February 19, 2019. https://www.splcenter.org/news/2019/02/19/hate-groups-reach -record-high.

Starkman, Dean. 2007. "Of Lepers and Lou Dobbs: Dobbs Has a Leprosy Problem." *Columbia Journalism Review*, May 30, 2007. https://archives.cjr.org/the _audit/of_lepers_and_lou_dobbs.php.

Stephens, Bret. 2019. "Mexico's Fast Track toward a Failed State." *New York Times*, November 7, 2019. https://www.nytimes.com/2019/11/07/opinion/mexico -mormons.html.

Stern, Mark Joseph. 2019. "Texas Republicans Are Lying about Voter Fraud to Justify a

Massive, Racist Voter Purge." *Slate*, February 4, 2019. https://slate.com/news
-and-politics/2019/02/texas-republicans-racist-illegal-voters-purge.html.

Stewart, Emily. 2020. "George Floyd's Killing Has Opened the Wounds of Centuries
of American Racism." *Vox*, June 10, 2020. https://www.vox.com/identities
/2020/5/30/21275694/george-floyd-protests-minneapolis-atlanta-new-
york-brooklyn-cnn.

Stoddard, Lothrop. 1920. *The Rising Tide of Color Against White World-Supremacy*.
New York: Charles Scribner's Sons.

———. 1927. *Re-Forging America: The Story of Our Nationhood*. New York: Charles
Scribner's Sons.

Stumpf, Juliet P. 2006. "The Crimmigration Crisis: Immigrants, Crime, and Sovereign
Power." *American University Law Review* 56, no. 2 (December): 367–419.
https://digitalcommons.wcl.american.edu/aulr/vol56/iss2/3/.

Sullivan, Sean. 2016. "Trump Says Judge's Mexican Heritage Presents 'Absolute
Conflict' in Trump University Cases." *Washington Post*, June 2, 2016. https://
www.washingtonpost.com/news/post-politics/wp/2016/06/02/trump
-says-judges-mexican-heritage-presents-absolute-conflict-in-trump
-university-cases/?utm_term=.51b621239c3b.

Swain, Carol. 2002. *The New White Nationalists in America: Its Challenge to Integration*.
Cambridge, UK: Cambridge University Press.

Ta, Linh. 2019. "Iowa's Steve King Has a History of Controversial Remarks." *Des
Moines Register*, August 14, 2019. https://www.desmoinesregister.com/story
/news/politics/2018/11/01/steve-king-jewish-muslim-republican-racist-poll
-congress-iowa-4th-election-controversial-offensive/1844672002/.

Tancredo, Tom. 2015a. "Is Trump a Highway or a Bridge to Conservative Victory."
Breitbart News, July 31, 2015. https://www.breitbart.com/politics/2015/07/31
/tancredo-is-trump-a-highway-or-a-bridge-to-conservative-victory/.

———. 2015b. "Illegal Alien Crime Accounts for Over 30% of Murders in Many States.
Breitbart News, August 8, 2015. https://www.breitbart.com/politics/2015
/08/08/illegal-alien-crime-accounts-for-over-30-of-murders-in-some-states/.

Tankersley, Jim. 2016. "Donald Trump's New Team of Billionaire Advisers Could
Threaten His Populist Message." *Washington Post*, August 5, 2016. https://
www.washingtonpost.com/news/wonk/wp/2016/08/05/donald-trumps
-economic-team-the-ultra-rich-to-the-rescue/.

Tanton, John, and Wayne Lutton. 1993. "Immigration and Criminality." *Journal of
Social, Political and Economic Studies* 18, (no. 2): 217–34.

Tarrow, Sidney. 2013. *The Language of Contention: Revolutions in Words 1688-2012*. New
York: Cambridge University Press.

Tavernise, Sabrina. 2018. "Fewer Births Than Deaths among Whites in Majority of U.S. States." *New York Times*, June 20, 2018. https://www.nytimes.com/2018/06 /20/us/white-minority-population.html.

Taylor, Paul S. 1930. "Research Note." *Journal of the American Statistical Association* 25, no. 170 (June): 206–7.

Telles, Edward E., and Vilma Ortiz. 2008. *Generations of Exclusion: Mexican Americans, Assimilation, and Race*. New York: Russell Sage Foundation.

Texas Education Agency. 2016. "Committee of the Full Board at 12:25 p.m." Admin-Monitor. September 13, 2016. Video, 5:06:59. http://www.adminmonitor.com /tx/tea/committee_of_the_full_board/201609132/.

———. 2019. *Enrollment in Texas Public Schools, 2018–19*. Document No. GE19 601 13. Austin, TX: Division of Research and Analysis, Office of Governance and Accountability.

Texas Tribune. 2011. "State Rep. Wayne Christian and State Rep. Borris Miles." Streamed on April 2, 2011. YouTube Video, 3:38. https://www.youtube.com /watch?v=ZAB2kDocC_g.

Thompson, Juan. 2015. "Nothing Funny about a Leading Presidential Candidate Spreading Racist Propaganda on Crime." The Intercept. November 24, 2015. https://theintercept.com/2015/11/24/nothing-funny-about-trump-spreading -racist-propaganda-on-crime/.

Thrush, Glenn. 2012. "Rep. King Compares Immigrants to Dogs." *POLITICO*, May 22, 2012. https://www.politico.com/blogs/politico44/2012/05/rep-king -compares-immigrants-to-dogs-124240.

Time. 1990. "What Will the U.S. Be Like When Whites Are No Longer the Majority?" April 1990.

Timmons, Heather. 2018. "Watch: A Furious Tampa Crowd Screams at the Press, Just as Trump Intended." *Quartz*, August 1, 2018. https://qz.com/1345622 /video-of-a-trump-rally-crowd-harassing-the-press-in-tampa/.

Tomasky, Michael. 2018. "The Midterms: So Close, So Far Apart." *New York Review of Books*, December 20, 2018. https://www.nybooks.com/articles/2018/12/20 /the-midterms-so-close-so-far-apart/.

Torres, Verónica. 2004. "The Central American Struggle for Amnesty and Residency: Nicaraguan, Salvadoran and Guatemalan Cases." *Diálogo* 8, no. 1: 4.

TRAC (Transactional Records Access Clearinghouse). 2017. *Immigration Court Dispositions Drop 9.3 Percent under Trump*. Syracuse: TRAC. July 17, 2017. https:// trac.syr.edu/immigration/reports/474/.

Tran, Van C., and Nicol M. Valdez. 2015. "Second-Generation Decline or Advantage?

Latino Assimilation in the Aftermath of the Great Recession." *International Migration Review* 51, no. 1 (August): 1–36. https://doi.org/10.1111/imre.12192.

Trujillo, Armando L. 2014. *Chicano Empowerment and Bilingual Education: Movimiento Politics in Crystal City, Texas.* New York: Routledge.

Trump, Donald. 2013. "Donald Trump Remarks at Conservative Political Action Conference." *C-SPAN,* March 15, 2013. Video, 15:08. https://www.c-span.org /video/?311543-1/donald-trump-remarks-conservative-political-action -conference.

———. 2015. "Donald Trump Presidential Campaign Announcement Full Speech." Trump Tower New York. Streamed on June 16, 2015. YouTube video, uploaded by C-Span, 47:08. https://www.youtube.com/watch?v=apjNfkysjbM.

———. 2016. "Full Text: Donald Trump 2016 RNC Draft Speech Transcript." *POLITICO,* July 21, 2016. https://www.politico.com/story/2016/07/full -transcript-donald-trump-nomination-acceptance-speech-at-rnc-225974.

———. 2017a. Executive Order: Enhancing Public Safety in the Interior of the United States. January 25, 2017. https://www.whitehouse.gov/presidential-actions /executive-order-enhancing-public-safety-interior-united-states/.

———. 2017b. "Transcript of AP Interview with Trump." By Julie Pace. *AP News,* April 23, 2017. https://apnews.com/article/c810d7de280a47e88848b0ac74690c83.

———. (@realDonaldTrump). 2018. Twitter, February 23, 2018..

———. (@realDonaldTrump). 2019a. Twitter, August 4, 2019.

———. 2019b. "Trump Says the US is 'Full' on Visit to US-Mexico Border." Streamed on April 6, 2019. YouTube video, uploaded by the *Guardian,* 0:36. https:// www.youtube.com/watch?v=9Elvmx1mQ3s.

Tuck, Eve, and K. Wayne Yang. 2012. "Decolonization Is Not a Metaphor." *Decolonization: Indigeneity, Education & Society* 1, no. 1 (September): 1–40. https://jps .library.utoronto.ca/index.php/des/article/view/18630/15554.

———. 2014. "R-Words: Refusing Research." In *Humanizing Research: Decolonizing Qualitative Inquiry with Youth and Communities,* edited by Django Paris and Maisha T. Winn, 223–48. London: SAGE.

Turner, Scott. 2020. "NM Delegation: Trump Census Order May Cut State Funding." *Albuquerque Journal,* August 1, 2020. https://www.abqjournal.com/1481688 /nm-delegation-trump-census-order-may-cut-state-funding-ex-some-780m -is-at-stake-if-just-1-of-the-population-is-not-counted.html.

Tyson, Alec, and Shiva Maniam. 2016. "Behind Trump's Victory: Divisions by Race, Gender, Education." Pew Research Center. November 9, 2016. www. pewresearch.org/fact-tank/2016/11/09/behind-trumps-victory-divisions -by-race-gender-education/.

UCLA Latino Policy & Politics Initiative. 2019. "New UCLA Study Finds 96% Growth in Latino Vote Across 8 States." https://latino.ucla.edu/press/new-ucla -study-finds-96-growth-in-latino-vote-across-8-states/.

Uhls, Yalda. 2018. "The Cruel Irony of the Migrant Mom in a 'Frozen' T-Shirt." *CNN*, November 27, 2018. https://www.cnn.com/2018/11/26/opinions/ migrant-mother-frozen-photographs-uhls/index.html.

Ulloa, Jazmine. 2020. "In Courting Latino Voters, Joe Biden Grapples with Obama's History as 'Deporter in Chief.'" *Boston Globe*, January 29, 2020. https://www .bostonglobe.com/2020/01/30/nation/courting-latino-voters-joe-biden -grapples-with-obamas-history-deporter-chief/.

US Census Bureau. 2019. "Hispanic Poverty Rate Hit an All-Time Low in 2017." February, 27, 2019. https://www.census.gov/library/stories/2019/02/hispanic -poverty-rate-hit-an-all-time-low-in-2017.html.

US Congress. 2007. House Joint Resolution 19: Proposing an Amendment to the Constitution of the United States to Establish English as the Official Language of the United States.

US Department of Education. 2016. "The State of Racial Diversity in the Educator Workforce." Washington, DC: Office of Planning Evaluation and Policy Development, Policy and Program Studies. July 16, 2016.

Valenzuela, Ángela. 1999. *Subtractive Schooling: U.S.-Mexican Youth and the Politics of Caring*. New York: State University of New York Press.

———, ed. 2005. *Leaving Children Behind: How "Texas-Style" Accountability Fails Latino Youth*. New York: State University of New York Press.

———. 2016a. No. 10-CV-623 TUC AWT: Expert Report of Ángela Valenzuela, Ph.D. Tucson, AZ: (D. Ariz.).

———, ed. 2016b. *Growing Critically Conscious Teachers: A Social Justice Curriculum for Educators of Latino/a Youth*. New York: Teachers College Press.

———. 2019. "The Struggle to Decolonize Official Knowledge in Texas' State Curriculum: Side-Stepping the Colonial Matrix of Power." *Equity & Excellence in Education*. 52, no. 2–3 (August)): 197–215. https://doi.org/10.1080/10665684 .2019.1649609.

Valenzuela, Ángela, and Curtis Brewer. 2010. "Submerged in a Neoliberal Utopia: Disruption, Community Dislocation and Subtractive Citizenship." In *Educating the Global Citizen in the Shadow of Neoliberalism: Thirty Years of Educational Reform in North America*, edited by Liliana Olmos, Carlos Alberto Torres, and Rich Van Heertum, 28–43. Oak Park, IL: Bentham Science.

Valverde, Miriam. 2017. "Donald Trump's Misleading Claims in the Kate Steinle Case, Fact-Checked." *PolitiFact*, December 18, 2017. https://www.politifact.com/

truth-o-meter/article/2017/dec/18/Donald-Trumps-misleading-claims-in
-Kate-Steinle/.

van den Berge, Pierre L. 1967. *Race and Racism: A Comparative Perspective*. New York: John Wiley & Sons.

Van Heertum, Rich, and Carlos Alberto Torres 2011. "Educational Reform in the U.S, in the Past 30 Years: Great Expectation and the Fading of the American Dream." In *Educating the Global Citizen in the Shadow of Neoliberalism: Thirty Years of Educational Reform in North America*, edited by Liliana Olmos, Carlos Alberto Torres, and Rich Van Heertum, 2–27. Oak Park, IL: Bentham Science.

Varela, Julio Ricardo. 2019. "Kirstjen Nielsen's Resignation Shows Stephen Miller Is Consolidating His Power over Immigration Policy." *NBC News*, April 8, 2019. https://www.nbcnews.com/think/opinion/kirstjen-nielsen-s-resignation
-shows-stephen-miller-consolidating-his-power-ncna992181.

————. 2020. "As He Bungles This Crisis, Trump Turns to a Familiar Scapegoat: Immigration." *Washington Post*, March 23, 2020. https://www.washingtonpost.com/opinions/2020/03/23/
he-bungles-this-crisis-trump-turns-familiar-scapegoat-immigration/.

Vargas, Zaragosa. 2017. *Crucible of Struggle: A History of Mexican Americans from Colonial Times to the Present Era*. New York: Oxford University Press.

Vásquez, Jessica M. 2014. "The Whitening Hypothesis Challenged: Biculturalism in Latino and Non-Hispanic White Intermarriage." *Sociological Forum* 29, no. 2 (June): 386–407. https://doi.org/10.1111/socf.12089

Verza, Maria, and Ben Fox. 2020. "US Expels Thousands to Mexico after Largely Halting Asylum." *AP News*, April 9, 2020. https://apnews.com/
article/7e9426532434bdda47f270a57d091c91.

Villanueva, James. 2011. *Remembering Slaton, Texas: Centennial Stories, 1911–2011*. Cheltenham, UK: The History Press.

Villanueva, Nicholas. 2017. *The Lynching of Mexicans in the Texas Borderlands*. Albuquerque: University of New Mexico Press.

Vinik, Danny. 2018. "How Trump favored Texas over Puerto Rico." *POLITICO*, March 27, 2018. https://www.politico.com/story/2018/03/27/
donald-trump-fema-hurricane-maria-response-480557.

Viramontes, María Helena. 2007. *Their Dogs Came with Them: A Novel*. New York: Atria.

Vizenor, Gerald. 2008. *Survivance: Narratives of Native Presence*. Lincoln: University of Nebraska Press.

Vore, Adrian. 2015. "'Immigrant' vs. 'Migrant': What's the Difference?" *San Diego Union-Tribune*, September 25, 2015. https://www.sandiegouniontribune.com
/opinion/readers-rep/sdut-immigrant-migranr-undocumented-europe-syria
-2015sep25-story.html.

Walsh, Catherine. 2012. "'Other' Knowledges, 'Other' Critiques: Reflections on the Politics and Practices of Philosophy and Decoloniality in the 'Other' America." *Transmodernity: Journal of Peripheral Cultural Production of the Luso-Hispanic World* 1, no. 3 (Spring): 11–27. https://escholarship.org/uc /item/6qd721cp.

Warzel, Charlie. 2019. "Why Trump Tweeted about Civil War." *New York Times*, September 30, 2019. https://www.nytimes.com/2019/09/30/opinion/trump -civil-war.html.

Warren, Robert. 2019. *US Undocumented Population Continued to Fall from 2016 to 2017, and Visa Overstays Significantly Exceeded Illegal Crossings for the Seventh Consecutive Year*. Washington, DC: Center for Migration Studies. January 16, 2019. https://cmsny.org/publications/essay-2017-undocumented -and-overstays/.

Waters, Mary C. 1990. *Ethnic Options: Choosing Identities in America*. Berkeley: University of California Press.

Weber, David J. 1973. *Foreigners in Their Native Land: Historical Roots of the Mexican Americans*. Albuquerque: University of New Mexico Press.

Weber, John. 2015. *From South Texas to the Nation: The Exploitation of Mexican Labor in the Twentieth Century*. Chapel Hill: University of North Carolina Press.

Weinberger, Caspar, and Peter Schweizer. 1996. *The Next War*. Washington, DC: Regnery Publishing.

Wells-Barnett, Ida B. (1900) 2018. *Mob Rule in New Orleans*. Reprint, n.p.: CreateSpace Independent Publishing Platform. Citations refer to CreateSpace edition.

Wermund, Benjamin. 2019. "Rep. Joaquín Castro Calls for Resignation of 'White Nationalist' White House Adviser." *Houston Chronicle*, November 14, 2019. https://www.houstonchronicle.com/politics/texas/article/Rep-Joaquin -Castro-calls-for-resignation-of-14835086.php.

Wester, John C. 2020. "Path to Citizenship Needed Now More Than Ever." *Albuquerque Journal*, May 23, 2020. https://www.abqjournal.com/1458880/path-to-citizen ship-needed-now-more-than-ever.html.

Wilentz, Sean. 2019. "The Culmination of Republican Decay: Tim Alberta's 'American Carnage: On the Front Lines of the Republican Civil War and the Rise of President Trump.'" *New York Review of Books*, October 10, 2019. https:// www.nybooks.com/articles/2019/10/10/american-carnage-republican-decay/.

Williams, Pete, and Adam Edelman. 2020. "Supreme Court Upholds DACA, Says Trump Administration Cannot End Program." *NBC News*, June 18, 2020. https://www.nbcnews.com/video/supreme-court-upholds-daca-ruling-says -trump-administration-cannot-end-program-85364293991.

Wilson, Jason. 2019. "Leaked Emails Reveal Trump Aide Stephen Miller's White

Nationalist Views." *Guardian*, November 14, 2019. https://www.theguardian
.com/us-news/2019/nov/14/stephen-miller-leaked-emails-white-nationalism
-trump.

Wilson, Jill H. 2019. *Temporary Protected Status: Overview and Current Issues.* Homeland Security Digital Library. Washington, DC: Congressional Research
Service. March 22, 2019. https://www.hsdl.org/?abstract&did=823418.

———. 2020. *Temporary Protected Status: Overview and Current Issues.* Washington,
DC: Congressional Research Service. October, 26, 2020. https://fas.org/sgp
/crs/homesec/RS20844.pdf.

Wimmer, Andreas. 2002. *Nationalist Exclusion and Ethnic Conflict: Shadows of Modernity.* Cambridge, UK: Cambridge University Press

Wineapple, Brenda. 2020. "Dress Rehearsal for the Revolution." Review of *American
Demagogue: The Great Awakening and the Rise and Fall of Populism*, by J. D.
Dickey. *New York Review of Books*, March 12: 2020. https://www.nybooks.com
/articles/2020/03/12/american-demagogue-dress-rehearsal-for-revolution/.

Wing, Nick. 2010. "Tennessee GOPer Curry Todd: Illegal Immigrants Will Multiply
'Like Rats.'" *Huffington Post*, November 11, 2010. https://www.huffpost.com
/entry/curry-todd-illegal-immigrants_n_782102.

Wolff, Michael. 2018. *Fire and Fury: Inside the Trump White House.* New York: Henry
Holt & Company.

———. 2019. *Siege: Trump under Fire.* New York: Henry Holt and Company.

Wolgin, Phillip E., and Angela Maria Kelley. 2014. "5 Things You Need to Know about
Unaccompanied Children." Center for American Progress. June 18, 2014.
https://www.americanprogress.org/issues/immigration/news/2014/06
/18/92056/5-things-you-need-to-know-about-the-unaccompanied-minors
-crisis/.

Wood, Amy Louise. 2009. *Lynching and Spectacle: Witnessing Racial Violence in America, 1890–1940.* Chapel Hill: University of North Carolina Press.

Zamora, Emilio. 1993. *The World of the Mexican Worker in Texas.* The Centennial
Series of the Association of Former Students. College Station: Texas A&M
University Press.

———. 2009. *Claiming Rights and Righting Wrongs in Texas: Mexican Workers and Job
Politics during World War II.* College Station: Texas A&M University Press.

———. 2012. "Moving the Liberal-Minority Coalition up the Education Pipeline." In
The Struggle over Standards in Texas and the Nation, edited by E. Erekson,
89–100. New York: Palgrave Macmillan.

———. 2018. "The Fight for Mexican American Studies in Texas: The Biography of
a Cause." *Educational Equity, Politics & Policy* (blog). April 12, 2018. http://

texasedequity.blogspot.com/2017/04/the-mexican-fight-for-ethnic-studies
-in_12.html.

Zamora, Emilio, and Ángela Valenzuela. 2018. "Ethnic Studies and Community-
Engaged Scholarship in Texas: The Weaving of a Broader We." In *Rethinking
Ethnic Studies*, edited by R. Tolteka Cuauhtin, Miguel Zavala, Christine Sleet-
er, and Wayne Au, 328–44. Milwaukee, WI: Rethinking Schools Ltd..

Zengerle, Jason. 2019. "How America Got to 'Zero Tolerance' on Immigration: The
Inside Story." *New York Times Magazine*, July 16, 2019. https://www.nytimes.
com/2019/07/16/magazine/immigration-department-of-homeland-security.
html.

Zimmerman, Arely. 2012. "Documenting Dreams: New Media, Undocumented Youth
and the Immigrant Rights Movement." Media, Activism and Participatory
Politics Project. November 29, 2012. https://educatorinnovator.org/webinars
/arely-zimmerman-sangita-shresthova-documenting-dreams-new-media
-undocumented-youth-and-the-immigrant-rights-movement/.

———. 2018. "DREAMing Citizenship: Undocumented Youth, Coming Out and Pathways to Participation." In *By Any Media Necessary: The New Youth Activism*,
edited by Henry Jenkins, Sangita Shresthova, Liana Gamber-Thompson,
Neta Kligler-Vilenchik, and Arely Zimmerman, 186–218. New York: New
York University Press.

Zimmerman, Jonathan. 2005. *Whose America? Culture Wars in the Public Schools.*
Cambridge, MA: Harvard University Press.

Zoellner, Danielle. 2020. "American Children Are Using Trump's Words to Bully
Classmates, Report Finds." *Independent*, February 13, 2020. https://www
.independent.co.uk/news/world/americas/us-politics/trump-insults
-children-bully-us-school-racist-xenophobic-a9334911.html.

Zúñiga, Victor, and Rubén Hernández-León. 2005. *New Destinations of Mexican Immigration in the United States: Community Formation, Local Responses, and
Inter-Group Relations.* New York: Russell Sage Foundation.

CRISTINA BELTRÁN, Department of Social and Cultural Analysis, New York University

ALYSHIA GÁLVEZ, Department of Latin American and Latino Studies, Lehman College, CUNY

MICHELLE GARCÍA, journalist and filmmaker

PHILLIP (FELIPE) B. GONZALES, Department of Sociology (emeritus), University of New Mexico

Participants, "Taking Stock: The Shifting Terrain of Citizenship among People of Mexican Origin in the United States," School of Advanced Research Advanced Seminar, Santa Fe, New Mexico, March 10–14, 2019. Sitting left to right: coeditors Phillip (Felipe) B. Gonzales, Renato Rosaldo, Mary Louise Pratt. Invited participants standing left to right: Tomás Jiménez, Arely M. Zimmerman, Alyshia Gálvez, Ángela Valenzuela, Cristina Beltrán, Davíd Montejano, Michelle García, Matt Barreto. Absent: Ana Minian.

TOMÁS R. JIMÉNEZ, Department of Sociology and Center for Comparative Studies in Race and Ethnicity, Stanford University

DAVÍD MONTEJANO, Departments of Ethnic Studies and History (emeritus), University of California, Berkeley

MARY LOUISE PRATT, Departments of Social and Cultural Analysis and Latin American and Iberian Studies (emerita), New York University

RENATO ROSALDO, Department of Anthropology (emeritus), Stanford University and New York University

ÁNGELA VALENZUELA, Department of Educational Administration, University of Texas, Austin

ARELY M. ZIMMERMAN, Intercollegiate Chicana/o–Latina/o Studies, Pomona College

Native Americans: ambiguous status of, xi; assimilation and, 169; Bacon's Rebellion and, 35; colonialism and, 84, 108; disease and, 14, 182; education and, 168, 171; settler futurity and, 163

nativism: overview of, 7, 53n1; assimilation and, 72, 105; border wall and, 75; cruelty and, 40; demographics and, 31, 51, 71, 108; economics and, 70–71, 108; genealogy of, 107; language and, 66, 160; Obama and, 59; Republican Party and, 30. *See also* Herrenvolk democracy; white nationalism; white supremacy

naturalization, 61, 80, 88, 151

Navarrete, Rubén, 23

Navarro, Jose Antonio, 86

Nazi Germany, 14

Nelson, Michael, xvi

neo-Nazis, 2, 107

neoliberalism, 30

Nereyda, Dulce, 3, 4, 7, 23, 24

Never Trumpers, 24

New Mexico, xii–xiii, 156

New York State Youth Leadership Council, 113–14

Nicaragua, 130, 138n2, 139n11

Nicaragua and Cuban Adjustment and Relief Act, 131

Niezen, Ronald, 118

Nixon, Richard, 64

Nixon, Rob, 1

North American Free Trade Agreement (NAFTA), 62, 75

O'Daniel, Pappy Lee, 63–64

O'Reilly, Bill, 105

O'Rourke, Beto, 20, 81

O'Shea, Elena Zamora, 86

O'Sullivan, John L., 46

Obama, Barack: birtherism and, xix, 2, 60; child migrants and, xiv, 16, 115, 132, 133; deportations and, xv, 16, 109, 139n9, 149; nativism and, 59; reelection of, 67; temporary protected status and, 138n2; Trump and, xxii, 10

Oboler, Suzanne, xxvi–xxvii

Olson, Joel, 33, 43, 48

Operation Wetback, 61–62, 92

Oppenheimer, Andres, 105

Ortiz, Raúl, 83

Ortiz-Fonseca, Louie A., 123

Osnos, Evan, xxi

Our Boys (HBO series), 23

Palumbo-Liu, David, 105

pan-ethnic identity, 157

Paredes, Américo, 90

Patrick, Dan, 174

Pastor, Manuel, 94

Paxton, Ken, 80–81

Peck Virgil, 29

Peña, Devon, 173

Pérez, Georgina, 178n1

Perot, Ross, 65

Perry, Rick, 80

Phillips, Kevin, 64, 68

Pitts, Leonard, 5

pocketing, xx, xxiv, 5

Polk, James K., xii

Polletta, Francesca, 120

populism, 1, 2, 5, 53n1, 57, 67, 69

Portland, 52

postcolonial theory, x

poverty, 106, 154, 182

Presler, Scott, 22

propaganda, 14, 59, 103

Proposition 187, 65–67, 71, 79, 114

Proposition 209, 66

Proposition 227, 66

Protestantism, xx, 102, 106, 109

protests, vii, 20, 24–25, 52, 181–83

Puerto Rico, xxv–xxvi

raids, 133

Raspail, Jean, 6, 16

Reagan, Ronald, 53, 64, 79, 129

RealClearPolitics, 17

reconquest, 129

Reconstruction, 54–55n9

refugees, 137

CPSIA information can be obtained
at www.ICGtesting.com
Printed in the USA
LVHW092249270921
698884LV00005B/294